Nothing Is Impossible with God

Also by Shannon Bream

Finding the Bright Side

The Women of the Bible Speak

The Mothers and Daughters of the Bible Speak

The Love Stories of the Bible Speak

NOTHING IS IMPOSSIBLE WITH God

Eleven Heroes. One God.
Endless Lessons in
Overcoming.

SHANNON BREAM

Without limiting the exclusive rights of any author, contributor or the publisher of this publication, any unauthorized use of this publication to train generative artificial intelligence (AI) technologies is expressly prohibited. HarperCollins also exercise their rights under Article 4(3) of the Digital Single Market Directive 2019/790 and expressly reserve this publication from the text and data mining exception.

Unless otherwise noted, Scripture quotations are taken from The Holy Bible, New International Version®, NIV®. Copyright © 1973, 1978, 1984, 2011 by Biblica, Inc.® Used by permission of Zondervan. All rights reserved worldwide. www.Zondervan.com. The "NIV" and "New International Version" are trademarks registered in the United States Patent and Trademark Office by Biblica, Inc.®

Scripture quotations marked CSB® are taken from the Christian Standard Bible®, Copyright © 2017 by Holman Bible Publishers. Used by permission. Christian Standard Bible® and CSB® are federally registered trademarks of Holman Bible Publishers.

NOTHING IS IMPOSSIBLE WITH GOD. Copyright © 2026 by Fox News Network LLC. All rights reserved. No part of this book may be used or reproduced in any manner whatsoever without written permission except in the case of brief quotations embodied in critical articles and reviews. For information, address HarperCollins Publishers, 195 Broadway, New York, NY 10007. In Europe, HarperCollins Publishers, Macken House, 39/40 Mayor Street Upper, Dublin 1, D01 C9W8, Ireland.

HarperCollins books may be purchased for educational, business, or sales promotional use. For information, please email the Special Markets Department at SPsales@harpercollins.com.

hc.com

FIRST EDITION

Title page art © aura studio/stock.adobe.com; Folio art © artisttop/stock.adobe.com; Part opener art © TheMountBirdStudio/Adobe; ilonitta/stock.adobe.com; VECTOR ZONE/stock.adobe.com

Library of Congress Cataloging-in-Publication Data has been applied for.

ISBN 978-0-06-348765-9
ISBN 978-0-06-349713-9 (signed edition)
ISBN 978-0-06-351157-6 (Walmart exclusive edition)
ISBN 978-0-06-351656-4 (international edition)

Printed in the United States of America

26 27 28 29 30 LBC 6 5 4 3 2

For my momma, my first Bible teacher and lifelong model of what it means to overcome life's challenges by faithfully resting in our Savior Jesus Christ.

I have told you these things, so that in me you may have peace. In this world you will have trouble. But take heart! I have overcome the world.

—John 16:33

CONTENTS

Introduction...xiii

PART I
Overcoming When You Don't Understand God's Plan...1

Gideon's Imposter Syndrome:
Making a Choice When You Feel Overwhelmed...3

Moses's Social Anxiety:
Speaking Up When You're Alone...28

Peter's Fear:
When Our Tongues Are a Double-Edged Sword...52

PART II
Overcoming When It's Hard to Love Others...79

Joseph's Family Trauma:
What to Do When Every Institution Fails You...81

CONTENTS

Jonah's Anger:
Loving People When You Just
Don't Feel Like It...107

Daniel's Integrity:
Resisting the Culture When It
Conflicts with Your Convictions...132

Nehemiah's Wisdom:
Dreaming Big in the
Face of Opposition...158

PART III
Overcoming When God Feels Far Away...185

Noah's Patience:
Waiting on God in
Hard Times...187

Joshua's Obedience:
Staying an Optimist in a
Pessimist's World...211

Elijah's Discouragement:
How to Stop a Negative Spiral...235

Jesus:
God with Us Is the
Ultimate Overcomer...262

Acknowledgments...287

Index...289

Nothing Is Impossible with God

INTRODUCTION

Years ago, I suffered with a chronic illness that left me in enormous pain. I've shared publicly how I spent months (that bled into years) trying to find a doctor and a diagnosis, desperately searching for an end to the torment that had taken over my life. What I didn't know for the longest time was that I was suffering from a genetic condition known as map-dot-fingerprint dystrophy. Because of the disorder, the cells of my corneas don't properly attach to the underlying membrane. For years, I was tearing the surface of my corneas over and over again. Each tear was a 10 out of 10 on the pain scale, leaving me despondent and hopeless as my life turned into a blur of unending pain and depression.

I had nearly lost the will to go on when I finally found the doctor who was literally an answer to my prayers. I had asked the Lord, "If it's not Your will to heal me, will You please lead me to the right medical professional who can help me?" By the time I found Dr. Thomas Clinch, I was at the end of my rope. That very first visit to his office, he told me he knew what was going on *and* how to help me. It was as if I'd won the Powerball and MegaMillions all at the same time. I'd forgotten what it felt like to have the tiniest glimmer of hope after such a long season of suffering. But as I prepared to leave his office, he said the words I'll never forget: "There's no cure."

It felt like the cruelest trick, to finally have a diagnosis and then to be struck with a gut punch: my nightmare would never come to an end. This was my face-to-face realization that in my own strength, I was up against insurmountable odds.

What I would eventually come to learn is that there are concrete ways to manage the disease in a way that makes life worth living again! But as I got out of that office as quickly as possible that day, I just wanted to hide in my car and unleash the sobs I could barely hide from the receptionist.

As I got into the car, knowing my husband Sheldon was waiting for my call, I just lost it. I wept until I almost couldn't breathe. I hadn't thought I could get any lower, and yet there I was in my car entertaining the thought of just driving it off a bridge. I cried out to the Lord, begging for some comfort. I heard His voice, not aloud, but in my spirit. It was unmistakable. He said the same words that He said to Gideon in Judges 6:16, "I will be with you." He didn't tell me I'd be healed or that all would suddenly be right in my world. Instead, the promise was that He would walk with me *in* it—as flawed and painful as it was. And that has been enough, as I navigated the medications and surgery that eventually put an end to nearly all of the physical (and emotional) pain the disease had unleashed on me.

If we know God has already won the battle, why do we still struggle? The Christian life often doesn't feel like the stained-glass images we may remember from childhood—happy, holy, hopeful. What do we do when we feel stuck in a spiritual rut?

The reality is, people in the Bible often felt the exact way we do. And by spending time in their stories, we can find the truths and tools we need to find victory over our challenges, just like they did long ago.

PART I
Overcoming When You Don't Understand God's Plan

When I was younger, I thought being a Christian meant that nothing bad could ever happen to me as long as I "followed the rules." So when real life kicked in, I had to ask some hard questions. If God promises to "always" be with us, why is life still so hard sometimes?

Our worldly instinct is that success looks like strength, control, and comfort. But the Bible's idea of strength is so different from ours because it's more like a child relying on a parent than a bodybuilder relying on his training. We all start as spiritual bodybuilders, assuming that God's blessing will look like winning the physical and social lottery and coasting to victory on a wave of cheers. Yet maturing as a Christian means becoming more childlike in a certain sense—more dependent, more vulnerable, and at the same time, strangely—less afraid. Think about how perplexing it is that the Son of God would tell His disciples—big musclebound fishermen—to become like little children.

The next three chapters follow characters who had to learn the counterintuitive lesson that God is our strength. Gideon seemed to have been chosen because he appeared weak—his obedience was fragile, but that's all God needed. Moses has plenty of bravado, but he had to learn a totally different sort of courage. Peter wore his heart on his sleeve from the beginning, but his brashness concealed a hidden insecurity. Still, when he finally did understand, his faith was tremendous.

Corrie Ten Boom once said, "When a train goes through a tunnel and it gets dark, you don't throw away your ticket and jump off. You sit still and trust the engineer." What's heartening about Gideon, Moses, and (eventually) Peter is that they had faith even when they didn't understand God's plan or purpose.

GIDEON'S IMPOSTER SYNDROME

Making a Choice When You Feel Overwhelmed

Judges 6–8

Have you ever felt called to something, yet completely ill-equipped to actually do it? If so, you'll likely love the story of Gideon as much as I do. While many secular advice books will tell you the answer to this state of self-doubt is to cultivate a deeper belief in yourself, the Bible has an answer that's quite different. The story of Gideon reveals that the secret to self-doubt is not more self, but more God.

Since my Sunday school days years ago, it's a tale that's captured my imagination. The words of Judges 6–8 feel especially descriptive to me, taking readers along on a roller coaster of competing emotions, tough choices, and—ultimately—a resounding victory. By the time Gideon got to the win the Lord had promised, neither his position nor his resources had changed. What *had* changed was his ability to depend on God and trust that it is His power and promises that make overcoming any odds possible.

But before we get to that, let's look at where this all started. It's a common theme: Israel was in trouble. Just one chapter earlier, in Judges 5, Israel was celebrating a forty-year period of peace brought on by the victory only God could have delivered through His faithful servant, Deborah. Her story had started the same way as Gideon's: "Israel did evil in the eyes of the LORD" (Judges 4:1), yet despite the peace that her faithfulness brought about, Israel had relapsed into rebellion.

"Prone to Wander"

The book of Judges is full of this repeated rhythm: Israel did evil, fell under judgment, and was eventually rescued by a God-appointed judge. But this salvation never lasted very long before Israel strayed again. Ultimately, the cycle would shift when the people of Israel decided they wanted to be more like their pagan neighbors and asked the Lord for a king. But in Gideon's day, that was far in the future. At the beginning of his story, Israel was at the low ebb of the sin-redemption cycle, having turned its back on the God who had delivered His people so many times.

Israel! What are you doing?! Though our heavenly Father consistently pursued His people with His unending love, the Israelites were often distracted and downright disobedient. They spent years chasing lifeless idols, the sort of deceptive false gods whom the prophets denounced as faithless lovers and dangerous dead ends. Before I start to sound too judgy here, I confess that I see myself in all these stories of people whose wandering hearts routinely got them into trouble.

The lyrics of one of my favorite hymns, "Come Thou Fount of Every Blessing," capture it succinctly:

Prone to wander, Lord, I feel it,
prone to leave the God I love;

here's my heart; O take and seal it;
seal it for thy courts above.

Why is it always easier to see the foolishness of others, to smugly tell ourselves we'd never be so careless and sinful? I picture myself trying to flag down the engineers of a train, "Stop! The tracks are completely washed out just ahead!" Then I sigh in knowing exasperation as they fail to slam on the brakes and meet the tragedy waiting around the corner.

But am I really more often the one warning or the one driving the train? How many people have tried to flag *me* down over the years? How many times did *I* fail to listen and instead go full steam ahead? With that in mind, I try to give Israel of old some grace.

When we catch up with it in Judges 6, the Lord had given Israel over into the hands of the Midianites because its people had left Him, His laws, and His protection. Many years before this, Israel defeated the Midianites, almost wiping them out. Though the defeat was devastating, the Midianites had regrouped and were now a persistent thorn in Israel's side, raiding and pillaging freshly grown crops.

By Gideon's time, the Midianite raiders had become so numerous that they were analogized to a plague of insects, devouring the flourishing places of Israel:

> Because the power of Midian was so oppressive, the Israelites prepared shelters for themselves in mountain clefts, caves and strongholds. Whenever the Israelites planted their crops, the Midianites, Amalekites and other eastern peoples invaded the country. They camped on the land and ruined the crops all the way to Gaza and did not spare a living thing for Israel, neither sheep nor cattle nor donkeys. They came up with their

livestock and their tents like swarms of locusts. It was impossible to count them or their camels; they invaded the land to ravage it. Midian so impoverished the Israelites that they cried out to the LORD for help.

Judges 6:2–6

Decades of peace weren't enough to keep Israel on track. It wasn't until the people were once again completely demoralized and overrun that they decided they needed to check in with their Maker, crying out for deliverance from their oppressors. They were living in caves as hideouts. Seven cycles of attempting to raise crops, only to have them completely wiped out. Sin always starts out as an alluring option, but living under oppression and despair is not where any of us wants to end up.

It would be easy to gloss over how they had arrived at this moment, a time when hordes of invaders easily and thoroughly decimated Israel's crops. Their intent was to "ravage" the land, and that's exactly what happened. But when the people of Israel called to Him, God didn't respond with immediate deliverance. He wanted them to remember what had led to their utter calamity, so:

> He sent them a prophet, who said, "This is what the LORD, the God of Israel, says: I brought you up out of Egypt, out of the land of slavery. I rescued you from the hand of the Egyptians. And I delivered you from the hand of all your oppressors; I drove them out before you and gave you their land. I said to you, 'I am the LORD your God; do not worship the gods of the Amorites, in whose land you live.' But you have not listened to me."

Judges 6:8–10

I rescued you. I delivered you from every adversary. I gave you their very land! I told you exactly what not to do. You didn't listen. Yes, the truth hurts. But before we can move forward into healing, it's important to acknowledge it if our sin is what led us to a place of broken fellowship with our heavenly Father. He gives us free will, just as He did His chosen people. But free will doesn't mean a free pass, and there are always consequences for sin. Instead of feeling crushed by guilt, we should recognize that this discomfort is meant to drive us to a God who's eager to forgive and restore us.

Israel was constantly slogging through this cycle: time of peace and blessing, straying, oppression, cries for help, redemption, straying. It happened on repeat, as it often does with us. Centuries later, we see the same conversation when Hosea urges the people:

> "Come, let us return to the LORD.
> He has torn us to pieces
> but he will heal us;
> he has injured us
> but he will bind up our wounds."
>
> Hosea 6:1

The Lord did allow His people to be injured. He will permit circumstances that turn our hearts back to Him, if that's what it takes.

Threshing in a Winepress

The first person in Israel to understand this should have been Gideon. We first meet him in the midst of this crisis. It's important to note something that immediately would have stuck out to an ancient reader: Gideon is no king or chieftain. He's the everyday son of a farmer and descendant of a patriarch, Manasseh, who was most famous for being passed over by the Lord in favor of his brother (for that story, check out Genesis 48).

When we're introduced to him, Gideon is hard at work, but in secret. Because of the oppression of the Midianites, Gideon was threshing wheat in a winepress. At that time, threshing would normally be done out in the open. The wind would help in the refining process, separating the wheat (the heavier material) from the chaff, which was lighter and could be blown away. By contrast, a winepress was often carved into rock, fully enclosed and damp. It's unlikely there was any breeze, making it a tough place to thresh wheat. And yet that's where Gideon was laboring—in a hidden spot, less than ideal for the physical work he was doing.

This is where "the angel of the Lord" met him and proclaimed, "The Lord is with you, mighty warrior" (Judges 6:12). Mighty warrior?! This was a man essentially hiding from the enemy, trying to pull together a crop in what was probably a most inconvenient way. I can't imagine he was feeling very mighty at the time. In fact, Gideon's first words in response were, "Pardon me, my lord" (Judges 6:13), a polite beginning to a series of questions that demonstrate how deeply he'd missed the angel's point.

While the angel spoke to him in particular—as a specific individual—Gideon's response rephrased the promise to make it about Israel, not himself. Rather than celebrate the arrival of this divine message—and Messenger—Gideon launched into a cross-examination about why Israel was suffering.

. . . if the Lord is with us, why has all this happened to us? Where are all his wonders that our ancestors told us about when they said, 'Did not the Lord bring us up out of Egypt?'

But now the LORD has abandoned us and given us into the hand of Midian."

Judges 6:13

Um, what? God comes to visit you, and instead of immediately celebrating His majesty in deepest reverence and gratitude, you start blaming Him? Oh wait . . . I've done that, too. Finding myself in need of rescue, I've asked God how and why He's allowed me to wind up in a jam, too blinded by my dullness to my own sin to acknowledge how I got there. As we'll see, Gideon also struggled to imagine himself as someone the Lord could raise up. He couldn't believe that he truly did have the ability to overcome—as long as the Lord was with him. His imagination was limited by focusing only on himself and not on God.

The Lord was not there to debate Gideon; He was calling him to action:

> The LORD turned to him and said, "Go in the strength you have and save Israel out of Midian's hand. Am I not sending you?"

Judges 6:14

The Christian Standard Bible says it this way:

> I am sending you!

God didn't take Gideon's bait, trying to shift the call away from being a personal one to arguing about Israel more broadly.

God referenced the strength Gideon already had, suggesting it was enough for what the Lord was telling him to do. What you have—plus what the Lord brings to the battle—will always be enough. Ultimately, your inadequacies (perceived or real) are never a limit on God's ability to equip you for the task He's assigned you to.

But not yet ready (willing?) to take on what must have felt like a nearly insurmountable task, Gideon answered:

> "Pardon me, my lord," Gideon replied, "but how can I save Israel? My clan is the weakest in Manasseh, and I am the least in my family."
>
> Judges 6:15

Gideon quickly pointed out all the reasons he didn't think he was the man for the job. *My clan is the weakest one, and I'm the very lowest in my own family. I'm not set up for success!* Gideon understood more this time, but he was still not hearing what God was saying. The Lord's point was that true strength comes from being called by God, not from surface-level qualities like earthly status or physical might.

This is why the Lord often chooses the most unlikely vessel: a scrawny shepherd boy, a stutterer, a slave. In the New Testament, Christ went to not only the least likely but often the *least liked:* prostitutes, tax collectors, lowly fishermen. What matters is not how the world views us, or even how we see ourselves, but the truth that our heavenly Father *knows* about us.

> The LORD answered, "I will be with you, and you will strike down all the Midianites, leaving none alive."
>
> Judges 6:16

GIDEON'S IMPOSTER SYNDROME

"I will be with you." It's a phrase that stops me in my tracks whenever I read it. Those very words were a heavenly gift to me at one of the darkest moments of my life, as I recounted in the introduction. Like me, Gideon couldn't know the good that was coming when God first made that pledge to him. He definitely wanted some assurance that this too-good-to-be-true offer from the Lord was legit.

> Gideon replied, "If now I have found favor in your eyes, give me a sign that it is really you talking to me. Please do not go away until I come back and bring my offering and set it before you."
> And the LORD said, "I will wait until you return."
> Gideon went inside, prepared a young goat, and from an ephah of flour he made bread without yeast. Putting the meat in a basket and its broth in a pot, he brought them out and offered them to him under the oak.
>
> Judges 6:17–19

Revival Requires Trusting the Creator, Not Created Things

At the time, the people of Israel often combined devotion for Yahweh with worship of pagan idols, like Asherah poles, which were symbols or carvings that represented a Canaanite fertility goddess. Asherah poles were made of wood and often associated with natural settings, like hills and trees (1 Kings 14:23). If Gideon grew up in a culture that blurred the lines between pagan gods and Yahweh, he might have instinctively made a sacrifice under a tree instead of in a temple. But something is about to happen that no false God could ever do.

The angel of God said to him, "Take the meat and the unleavened bread, place them on this rock, and pour out the broth." And Gideon did so. Then the angel of the LORD touched the meat and the unleavened bread with the tip of the staff that was in his hand. Fire flared from the rock, consuming the meat and the bread. And the angel of the LORD disappeared.

Judges 6:20–21

Whoa! Gideon asked for a sign, and he got it. And then it hit him: he wasn't just talking to a man, or a prophet, or even an ordinary angel, but someone even higher. If his idea of God had been blurred with Asherah, it wasn't any longer!

When Gideon realized that it was the angel of the LORD, he exclaimed, "Alas, Sovereign LORD! I have seen the angel of the LORD face to face!"

But the LORD said to him, "Peace! Do not be afraid. You are not going to die."

Judges 6:22–23

Have you ever had that moment? Knowing that you've heard from Him? Knowing that you've been in His presence? I'm not sure we ever get more than the tiniest glimpse of the true glory and majesty of our God. He knows we could only take so much. Gideon was moved! He had a holy fear of God, and he built an altar to the Lord on that very spot.

Having gotten through to His humble servant, the Lord asked Gideon to take some real steps of faith. They would require courage.

That same night the LORD said to him, "Take the second bull from your father's herd, the one seven years old. Tear down your father's altar to Baal and cut down the Asherah pole beside it. Then build a proper kind of altar to the LORD your God on the top of this height. Using the wood of the Asherah pole that you cut down, offer the second bull as a burnt offering."

Judges 6:25–26

Why was this such a big ask? God was asking Gideon to tackle the symbol of his people's sin, the god they prayed to for protection. Even though God's purpose was to remove the false protection and replace it with true security, Gideon's actions would be seen as treasonous and reckless.

Idolatry had taken firm root in the Israelites' culture and in Gideon's own family. Things like the Asherah pole had become firmly embedded in their religious and social norms. Keep in mind, God had repeatedly and concretely told the Israelites not to have Asherah poles around.

Break down their altars, smash their sacred stones and cut down their Asherah poles.

Exodus 34:13

... cut down their Asherah poles and burn their idols in the fire.

Deuteronomy 7:5

> . . . burn their Asherah poles,
>
> Deuteronomy 12:3

> Do not set up any wooden Asherah pole beside the altar you build to the LORD your God . . . for these the LORD your God hates.
>
> Deuteronomy 16:21–22

To anyone observing the law and following the Lord, the Asherah poles were absolutely a no-no. There was no nuance in what He said. There was no argument or room for misunderstanding. And yet idols were so fully and comfortably integrated into the Israelites' lives that a command to destroy them literally equated to giving Gideon a life-threatening assignment.

Is there anything in this world that has slowly found its way into your heart and life—something the Lord has been clear doesn't belong? When the entire world around us is embracing the unholy, it can seem radical to say it has to go. It requires some level of bravery on our part, depending on the issue. Years ago, I got caught up in a super popular Netflix series that was downright addicting. It was also full of very adult themes and scenes, and the conviction in my heart really started to blossom. Everyone was talking about it, including me! Yet I came to know it was time to make a clean break. One of my coworkers could not fathom what was so objectionable about a TV show that I had drawn a line in the sand. He must have said "but why?" at least a dozen times. I tried to articulate that—for me—it had become an Asherah pole. Not the easiest explanation, but one that was spot-on!

Idols are things we rely on in the place of God. Often, like that TV show, they have that "addictive" quality. Whether or not they're actually bad things, they take up an inappropriate amount of attention and value. If we can't walk away from a created thing, are we really trusting that God is our ultimate refuge, or are we relying on something else? That was the question Gideon faced.

I might have suffered a little bit of workplace awkwardness, but that's nothing compared to what was coming for Gideon. He was well aware of the danger.

> So Gideon took ten of his servants and did as the LORD told him. But because he was afraid of his family and the townspeople, he did it at night rather than in the daytime.
>
> In the morning when the people of the town got up, there was Baal's altar, demolished, with the Asherah pole beside it cut down and the second bull sacrificed on the newly built altar!
>
> They asked each other, "Who did this?"
>
> When they carefully investigated, they were told, "Gideon son of Joash did it."
>
> The people of the town demanded of Joash, "Bring out your son. He must die, because he has broken down Baal's altar and cut down the Asherah pole beside it."
>
> Judges 6:27–30

We can only assume these are people of Israel who are so incensed that Gideon had struck down *something God had forbidden them to have* that they were looking to kill him. The Israelites had embraced the idols and false gods of their neighbors, directly in conflict with what God had clearly commanded them to do. Even though the Asherah poles were clearly not protecting them from their enemies, they had so internalized their enemy's logic that they saw an attack on the idols as an attack on national security.

To his credit, Gideon's father answered the demands on his son's life with wit and wisdom. He turned the townspeople's logic on its head. He said:

> "If Baal really is a god, he can defend himself when someone breaks down his altar."
>
> Judges 6:31b

This, coming from a man who had an altar to Baal and an Asherah pole that had just been destroyed. We can't know from the passage why Joash pivoted so quickly on the issue. Was it because of his love for his son, or did the Lord already know that something within Joash's heart was aware that the idols he was worshiping had always been worthless?

It was not just Joash who had a change of heart, but all of Israel. Suddenly, they discovered the courage that was nowhere to be found before. At this same time, the enemies of Israel were gathering and joining forces. Led by the Spirit, Gideon began to call together his own army—by the tens of thousands. By his own assessment, he was the lowest of the low. Just a few verses back, the people were ready to kill Gideon. Fast-forward to 32,000 men heeding his call to go into battle.

There was no sign in the story that Gideon had changed in a dramatic way, though his confidence must have been bolstered by the incident with the Asherah poles. He even got an iconic nickname. His father's phrase, "let Baal contend," became Gideon's new name. But it seems clear that what actually drew people to Gideon was the power of the Spirit within him. It's a good reminder for when you're feeling overwhelmed: what actually animates your success isn't your own strength or charisma, but the very breath of the living God. It's not your own skill or knowledge, but He who is with you.

Obedience Comes Before Understanding

When He called to Gideon hiding out in the winepress, the Lord didn't spell out the future for him, and He probably won't for you either. Instead, with each step of faith that Gideon took, God was upending Gideon's assessment of his own abilities and worthiness—and equipping him for the task.

Yet even as those forces showed up to follow Gideon into the fight, he hesitated to follow through. He stopped to ask God for a confirmation of his call—not once, but twice.

> Gideon said to God, "If you will save Israel by my hand as you have promised—look, I will place a wool fleece on the threshing floor. If there is dew only on the fleece and all the ground is dry, then I will know that you will save Israel by my hand, as you said." And that is what happened. Gideon rose early the next day; he squeezed the fleece and wrung out the dew—a bowlful of water.
>
> Then Gideon said to God, "Do not be angry with me. Let me make just one more request. Allow me one more test with the fleece, but this time make the fleece dry and let the ground be covered with dew." That night God did so. Only the fleece was dry; all the ground was covered with dew.
>
> Judges 6:36–40

Gideon had already had the awe-inspiring experience of coming face-to-face with God. He admitted at the beginning of this passage that the Lord had "promised" to save Israel by Gideon's hand. He acknowledged that continuing to press the Lord may stir up His wrath. Yet he asked for more. God met Gideon where he was at—in his apprehension—providing the assurance that the mission at hand was divine and guaranteed. That didn't mean Gideon would be done with doubt . . . but this was enough to persuade him to gather up the forces that responded to his call and move toward taking on the Midianites.

Biblical scholars debate what we should take from these verses. Are we wrong to ask God for His clearest guidance . . . repeatedly? Are we out of line to ask Him to confirm what we believe He's already called us to do? There are times the Lord gave assurances and signs to those who asked. Hezekiah (2 Kings 20:8–11) and Moses (Exodus 4:1–9) come to mind. When another Israelite king, Ahaz, refused to ask for a sign that God offered him, he was even rebuked by the prophet Isaiah for testing God's patience (Isaiah 7). But in other cases, Jesus disapproves of looking for a sign or needing proof (John 20:29: "Blessed are those who have not seen and yet have believed.")

The distinction seems to be between people looking for information with expectation vs. looking with doubt. Just like Gideon, Hezekiah and Moses were seeking confirmation, not pressing God for a magic trick or trying to entrap Him. Treating the Holy Spirit like a Magic-8 ball is something we see from hypocritical religious (Matthew 16:1–4) and political leaders (Luke 23:8) in the New Testament, even the enemy himself as he tried to entangle Christ during His time of fasting in the desert by demanding evidence of his deity (Matthew 4:1–11; Luke 4:1–13).

Often, the Lord responds in different ways to people's expressions of uncertainty, even if those expressions seem on the surface very similar. We can assume that variations in His response are due to His own discernment of the questioner's motivations. Romans 8 teaches us that God searches our hearts, looking for "the mind of the Spirit."

Because God can discern our motives, He knows whether we are weak and in need of assurance or arrogant and petulant when we ask for a sign. Psalm 78 recounts His frustration with the Israelites.

> They willfully put God to the test
> by demanding the food they craved.
> They spoke against God;
> they said, "Can God really
> spread a table in the wilderness?
> True, he struck the rock,
> and water gushed out,
> streams flowed abundantly,
> but can he also give us bread?
> Can he supply meat for his people?"
> When the LORD heard them, he was furious;
> his fire broke out against Jacob,
> and his wrath rose against Israel,
> for they did not believe in God
> or trust in his deliverance.
>
> Psalm 78:18–22

When we cross the line into rebellion and attempt to test the God of the universe, we are no longer humble servants seeking His seal of blessing and direction. I believe the Lord has compassion when we are both genuinely fearful *and* also willing to move forward.

Glory in Jars of Clay

Often, the first step of faith we take is followed by an even more nerve-racking ask. I believe that if we knew just how far we were going to be coaxed outside of our comfort zone in the end, most of us would never take that first leap. Gideon was about to get stretched even further.

> The LORD said to Gideon, "You have too many men. I cannot deliver Midian into their hands, or Israel would boast against me, 'My own strength has saved me.'"
>
> Judges 7:2

How well our Heavenly Father knows us! Again and again, He leads us into situations we could never resolve on our own. The victory must come from Him alone. It not only builds our own spiritual muscles, but it also sends a message to the world: *God did this.* He knew His people intimately, their propensity to disregard His clear work on their behalf. That meant Gideon would have to trust. The Lord goes on:

> "Now announce to the army, 'Anyone who trembles with fear may turn back and leave Mount Gilead.'" So twenty-two thousand men left, while ten thousand remained.
> But the LORD said to Gideon, "There are still too many men. Take them down to the water, and I will thin them out for you there. If I say, 'This one shall go with you,' he shall go; but if I say, 'This one shall not go with you,' he shall not go."
> So Gideon took the men down to the water. There the LORD told him, "Separate those who lap the water with their tongues

as a dog laps from those who kneel down to drink." Three hundred of them drank from cupped hands, lapping like dogs. All the rest got down on their knees to drink.

The LORD said to Gideon, "With the three hundred men that lapped I will save you and give the Midianites into your hands. Let all the others go home." So Gideon sent the rest of the Israelites home but kept the three hundred, who took over the provisions and trumpets of the others.

Judges 7:3–8

Three . . . hundred? Remember back in Judges 6, we're told Israel's enemies came like "a great swarm of locusts." They couldn't be numbered. And now Gideon had gone from tens of thousands at his side to just three hundred. There's nothing like being stripped of our self-reliance and pushed out of our comfort zone to illustrate just how dependent our entire existence is on our Creator.

As the Midianites gathered below him in a valley, the Lord told Gideon it was time for action.

During that night the LORD said to Gideon, "Get up, go down against the camp, because I am going to give it into your hands. If you are afraid to attack, go down to the camp with your servant Purah and listen to what they are saying. Afterward, you will be encouraged to attack the camp."

Judges 7:9–11a

This verse makes me chuckle just a little. The Lord knew Gideon's heart and how far he'd already come. He built in the provision: *I know you may still be afraid, but I've got something for you.*

So he and Purah his servant went down to the outposts of the camp. The Midianites, the Amalekites and all the other eastern peoples had settled in the valley, thick as locusts. Their camels could no more be counted than the sand on the seashore.

Gideon arrived just as a man was telling a friend his dream. "I had a dream," he was saying. "A round loaf of barley bread came tumbling into the Midianite camp. It struck the tent with such force that the tent overturned and collapsed."

His friend responded, "This can be nothing other than the sword of Gideon son of Joash, the Israelite. God has given the Midianites and the whole camp into his hands."

When Gideon heard the dream and its interpretation, he bowed down and worshiped. He returned to the camp of Israel and called out, "Get up! The LORD has given the Midianite camp into your hands."

Judges 7:11b–15

Doesn't our Father know we can be faint of heart? Over and over, He nudged Gideon on the path He had already mapped out for him. He can use us even when we doubt, even when we hesitate. Gideon's story makes that clear. Yet each step he took forward was one more step toward *overcoming*—both his fear and the odds against him.

Dividing the three hundred men into three companies, he placed trumpets and empty jars in the hands of all of them, with torches inside.

"Watch me," he told them. "Follow my lead. When I get to the edge of the camp, do exactly as I do. When I and all who are with me blow our trumpets, then from all around the camp blow yours and shout, 'For the Lord and for Gideon.'"

Gideon and the hundred men with him reached the edge of the camp at the beginning of the middle watch, just after they had changed the guard. They blew their trumpets and broke the jars that were in their hands. The three companies blew the trumpets and smashed the jars. Grasping the torches in their left hands and holding in their right hands the trumpets they were to blow, they shouted, "A sword for the Lord and for Gideon!" While each man held his position around the camp, all the Midianites ran, crying out as they fled.

When the three hundred trumpets sounded, the Lord caused the men throughout the camp to turn on each other with their swords. The army fled to Beth Shittah toward Zererah as far as the border of Abel Meholah near Tabbath. Israelites from Naphtali, Asher and all Manasseh were called out, and they pursued the Midianites. Gideon sent messengers throughout the hill country of Ephraim, saying, "Come down against the Midianites and seize the waters of the Jordan ahead of them as far as Beth Barah."

So all the men of Ephraim were called out and they seized the waters of the Jordan as far as Beth Barah.

Judges 7:16–24

The trumpets used in this battle were more specifically shofars, or ram's horns. They were powerfully loud instruments that could call the Israelites to repentance, celebrate a religious ceremony, or function as a prompt to military action. Imagine the sound of three hundred of them being blown at once, above a valley of unsuspecting Midianites sleeping soundly below. The trumpets had been taken from the entire army, including those who'd already left. So what the Midianites thought they were hearing was the attack of a much larger force. Those blasts were followed by the crash of three hundred clay jars being shattered, followed by three hundred blazing torches illuminating the skies.

One pastor, Geoff Ziegler, puts it this way:

> In a sense, the tools Gideon's army carries are symbolic of what they are. These 300 are only jars of clay; but they carry the light, the glory of God.

I love that thought, which reminds me of Paul's admonition in the New Testament:

> But we have this treasure in jars of clay to show that this all-surpassing power is from God and not from us.
>
> 2 Corinthians 4:7

Just like in Gideon's case, God works through imperfect vessels even now. The glory is all His, but what a gift that we get to partner with Him here on earth. Truly, the pressure is off when God invites us to attempt the impossible, because only He can achieve it.

When the dust settled and the people of Israel realized they had been rescued yet again, did they turn all their praise and worship to the Lord? Nope. Much like when they would demand that God give them a king at the end of the book of Judges, they turned their adoration on a human source—Gideon—and not on God Himself.

> The Israelites said to Gideon, "Rule over us—you, your son and your grandson—because you have saved us from the hand of Midian."
>
> But Gideon told them, "I will not rule over you, nor will my son rule over you. The LORD will rule over you."
>
> Judges 8:22–23

This was the very reason the Lord told Gideon he couldn't let him take the thousands who had answered the call to arms into battle: *Israel won't give Me the credit.* But Gideon was wise enough to do so when the moment came.

Judges 8 goes on to tell us that Midian was subdued "and did not raise its head again" against the Israelites (v. 28). For the remainder of Gideon's life, there was peace. He returned home, raised a family, and "died at a good old age" (v. 32). And then this happened:

> No sooner had Gideon died than the Israelites again prostituted themselves to the Baals. They set up Baal-Berith as their god and did not remember the LORD their God, who had rescued them from the hands of all their enemies on every side. They also failed to show any loyalty to the family of Jerub-Baal (that is, Gideon) in spite of all the good things he had done for them.
>
> Judges 8:33–35

The solution to imposter syndrome is not to lean into self-belief, like the Israelites who worshiped created things. It's also not to disregard our virtues entirely, like the Israelites who disrespected Gideon's heroism. Instead, it's to see ourselves as we actually are—imperfect creatures in need of the God who saves. With that truth in mind, we aren't crushed every time we remember our weaknesses—we remember that God loves us anyway. And we won't be puffed up by our strengths—we'll know they're a gift from God. Gideon's story is an authentic illustration for us of how relying on God can give us true freedom from fear.

That's the answer to Gideon's question, too. He had asked, "If God is with us, why has all this happened to us? Where are all his wonders that our ancestors told us about when they said, 'Did not the LORD bring us up out of Egypt?'" God's intimacy with Israel had been interrupted by the people's sin. The nation's misfortunes had happened because it was necessary to wean them away from their useless idols and back to worshiping the One they had abandoned. God doesn't ask much—even the obedience of a chronic doubter like Gideon is enough for Him to work. But He cannot, by His nature, be "with" a sinful people who insist on leaving Him.

Israel wasn't there yet. Instead, we see another chapter in Israel's history ending as it began, with God's people rejecting Him and chasing after worldly pleasures that would never satisfy. He never gave up on them, though, repeatedly raising up godly men and women to serve as the vehicles for His rescue and redemption. There would be still more to *overcome*.

Study Questions

1. What is the reason—or reasons—you think God chose Gideon to take on this task?
2. Where should we find the balance between being self-sufficient and responsible vs. depending on God for outcomes?

3. How is it biblically unsound to follow the philosophy that you don't need anything or anyone but yourself to navigate through life?
4. Has there been a time when God accomplished something in your life that was "immeasurably more than all we ask or imagine" (Ephesians 3:20)? Where do you need to ask Him to do that in your circumstances right now?
5. What does it mean that God will "be with" us?

MOSES'S SOCIAL ANXIETY

Speaking Up When You're Alone

Exodus 1–14

I have a test for most audiences when I show up to speak. I've got a couple of self-deprecating jokes right off the top. If I don't get even a polite chuckle, I know it's going to be a rough thirty minutes and I better cut the corny stuff and stick to more serious content.

But because I know what it's like to be up front, I am careful to be a good audience member! When I'm on the other side of the equation, sitting in the audience, I probably look a little wacky because I'm smiling and nodding and cheering on that speaker like nobody's business! Finding just one friendly face can feel like a lifeline. If we can find the mental or emotional assurance that our message isn't bombing, we will discover that the physical reaction to the anxiety is much more manageable.

What strikes fear in your heart? Makes you go weak in the knees or even feel faint? What keeps you up at night and distracts you from the joy in life? There are endless surveys about what truly scares Americans—from terror attacks to economic collapse. Some of these issues shift and cycle over time, but you know what remains consistently on the list? Public speaking. Research shows a literal physical manifestation of panic for most people when they think about walking into the spotlight on stage or in a boardroom: excess sweating, shaking, elevated heart rate, or nausea. Maybe you've had a combo!

The reason for this is more than just a fear of speaking poorly. It has to do with the anxiety over how you're being perceived, of being vulnerable and exposed to a crowd. It has everything to do with our social confidence.

So imagine starting from that place of sheer terror of public speaking, then having one of the most epic showdowns with one of the most powerful men in the world, and winding up as the spokesman for a nation of millions. It happened to Moses. You might think God would pick a man who'd eagerly jump at the chance to be one of the greatest communicators of all time, who had no fear of social rejection at all. But Moses was just the opposite. The first thing he did in the book of Exodus was resolve an argument with deadly violence. How could this man possibly become the great lawgiver and mediator?

Slave to Prince

His story starts with a bold, brave mother—who defied the law of the day that required all Hebrew male babies to be thrown into the Nile River—a certain death. It was a horrific scheme cooked up by Pharaoh, who had become alarmed at the rate of growth of the Hebrew people in Egypt. Centuries before, Joseph had been divinely positioned to save his people when famine drove them to Egypt looking for help. Had Joseph's jealous, scheming brothers not sold him into slavery, he would never have risen to the highest echelons of power in Egypt and been in a position to help them, after years of unjust punishment and suffering. (There's much more on Joseph's story in the pages ahead.) It's hard to imagine a more perfect illustration of Romans 8:28 than Joseph's roller coaster of a life's journey:

> And we know that in all things God works for the good of those who love him, who have been called according to his purpose.

Joseph was a man of integrity, a faithful servant to a different Pharaoh hundreds of years before Moses arrived on the scene. During those intervening centuries, the people of Israel had flourished, despite their oppression—and Egyptian leaders had become concerned. That led to the barbaric plan to wipe out their future generations by murdering defenseless infants.

If you were an impartial observer who dropped into Joseph's or Moses's stories in their early phases, you likely would not have believed what they would eventually become. Joseph had to become a slave to become a prince. Moses started as a prince but became a political refugee on the run. At first blush, their stories might seem full of unnecessary suffering, but in fact, God often forges strength in His servants by putting them through the crucible of weakness. That's exactly what would happen with Moses, whose life in many ways paralleled that of Joseph, but not in the way he might have expected.

By the time Moses showed up, the centuries had eroded the respect and admiration the Egyptians once had for Joseph, his extended family—and their God. The Israelites had multiplied to such an extent that Pharaoh no longer saw them as a blessing but as a threat.

Neither the Hebrew midwives nor Moses's own mother, Jochebed, complied with the edict to kill the male babies. Instead, Jochebed hid baby Moses for three months, and then she crafted a small, waterproof basket, put Moses in it, and placed it among the reeds in the Nile under the careful watch of his older sister, Miriam (Exodus 2:2–4). Miriam watched as Pharaoh's daughter found the basket and had compassion on her brother; then Miriam offered to "get one of the Hebrew women to nurse the baby" (Exodus 2:7). Miriam went straight back to her mom, who happily nursed her own baby Moses for a time and then had him delivered to the palace to become the Pharaoh's daughter's son.

If you know his story, you know that Moses still very much had a connection to the enslaved Hebrew people in Egypt, despite his royal upbringing. It was when he witnessed one of them being abused that Moses made a decision that changed everything.

> One day, after Moses had grown up, he went out to where his own people were and watched them at their hard labor. He saw an Egyptian beating a Hebrew, one of his own people. Looking this way and that and seeing no one, he killed the Egyptian and hid him in the sand.
>
> Exodus 2:11–12

One of his own people. Moses never lost that link, and in his mind, his kinship meant he should fight on behalf of his people. Moses clearly wanted his deed to remain a secret, but the rumor spread about what he had done.

> The next day he went out and saw two Hebrews fighting. He asked the one in the wrong, "Why are you hitting your fellow Hebrew?"
>
> The man said, "Who made you ruler and judge over us? Are you thinking of killing me as you killed the Egyptian?" Then

Moses was afraid and thought, "What I did must have become known."

When Pharaoh heard of this, he tried to kill Moses, but Moses fled from Pharaoh . . .

Exodus 2:13–15

Moses spent decades running from the fallout of this event. Long before the Israelites spent forty years lost and wandering in the wilderness, Moses had his own period of isolation and drifting.

Prince to Fugitive

Happily for Moses, his efforts to defend others from injustice weren't rejected by everyone. After he saved a group of women from rival shepherds in the desert, Moses settled among the women's people, the Midianites. They did share some heritage as fellow descendants of Abraham, but they were not from the line of Sarah and Abraham. The Midianites came through Abraham's wife, Keturah, after the death of Sarah (Genesis 25:1–2). Moses married the daughter of Jethro, a Midianite priest. Far from the comforts of the Egyptian palace, he tended to flocks and built a family in the desert.

This seems to be Moses's first step in fully identifying with the Hebrew people, who were, traditionally, shepherds. When he arrived in Midian, the women he rescued identified him as an "Egyptian" (Exodus 2:19). But he began to reject the habits of Egypt, even as he had already rejected Pharaoh's unjust rule. If the customs in Egypt were still the same as they were in Joseph's day, shepherding was seen as a "detestable" occupation (Genesis 46:34), so it would have been doubly humbling for Moses to accept such a job. All the while, the Israelites continued to suffer in bondage in Egypt. But God was listening and positioning His servant, Moses, to act.

> During that long period, the king of Egypt died. The Israelites groaned in their slavery and cried out, and their cry for help because of their slavery went up to God. God heard their groaning and he remembered his covenant with Abraham, with Isaac and with Jacob. So God looked on the Israelites and was concerned about them.
>
> Exodus 2:23–25

All throughout the Bible, we watch as God sends "saviors" to His people. They were all temporary victors; none of them was able to deliver full redemption—until the arrival of Jesus Christ, His Son. In many of these stories in the Old Testament, we see an infinite God calling on the flawed and frightened to partner with Him to accomplish the (humanly) impossible. Sometimes they were intimidated by people and circumstances beyond their control. Sometimes it was the person in the mirror who presented the biggest challenge. I don't know any adult who hasn't struggled with self-doubt at some point. The question is how we deal with it in light of a call from our heavenly Father.

The Burning Bush

When the Lord showed up unexpectedly one day, Moses was doing what he'd done for decades. God's appearance in the mundane demonstrates there is meaning in the work we do every day, whether at home or out in the workforce. Moses was faithful, working for his father-in-law as a shepherd. We see no grumbling about how great life used to be at the palace, no daydreaming about going back to the life of a prince—just the methodical work of a dutiful man. God can and will show up wherever you are laboring, whether or not you think anyone else is aware of your diligence.

> Now Moses was tending the flock of Jethro his father-in-law, the priest of Midian, and he led the flock to the far side of the wilderness and came to Horeb, the mountain of God. There the angel of the LORD appeared to him in flames of fire from within a bush. Moses saw that though the bush was on fire it did not burn up. So Moses thought, "I will go over and see this strange sight—why the bush does not burn up."
>
> When the LORD saw that he had gone over to look, God called to him from within the bush, "Moses! Moses!"
>
> And Moses said, "Here I am."
>
> Exodus 3:1–4

I am nearly 100 percent certain I would not have had such a calm reaction. Had Moses heard from the Lord before, maybe during those lonely days and nights of tending to the flocks? Was he so humble and attuned to the Lord that His showing up in the burning bush didn't faze Moses? Whatever their past relationship had been, Moses knew enough to have a reverent, holy fear.

> "Do not come any closer," God said. "Take off your sandals, for the place where you are standing is holy ground." Then he said, "I am the God of your father, the God of Abraham, the

God of Isaac and the God of Jacob." At this, Moses hid his face, because he was afraid to look at God.

> Exodus 3:5–6

This same God had made a covenant with Abraham long before, and He was now making a personal visit to Moses, a man who had killed a man and then fled Egypt in fear for his own life. God knew and saw His people's suffering; He heard their cries for help. He had a plan to rescue them and to send them into a land "flowing with milk and honey" (Exodus 3:8). Moses undoubtedly knew of the Israelites' continued suffering, but he had probably never imagined how the Lord planned to resolve it. When his earlier attempt to save his kinsmen was rejected, he must have been crushingly discouraged. If the Hebrew slaves weren't willing to join a rebellion to overthrow their captors, what hope was there?

But the Lord had a plan that wouldn't look like any other rebellion in history. It would start with what any strategist would tell you is a terrible mistake—letting your enemy know you're coming. God told Moses:

> "So now, go. I am sending you to Pharaoh to bring my people the Israelites out of Egypt."
>
> Exodus 3:10

Say what? The last time we saw anything about a pharaoh and Moses, it was because Egypt's top leader wanted to kill him. And though the pharaoh God was calling Moses to confront was not the same man as the one who had ordered the death of the Hebrew male babies, Moses had to wonder whether the story of his killing of the Egyptian (Exodus 2:11–12) still lingered in Egyptian memory. Imagine being the adopted son of Egyptian royalty (a Hebrew male born under a death sentence) who had so betrayed the Egyptian people that he had blood on his hands and a price on his head—and being asked to go back and face off against someone with the power to execute you. Moses's reply to the Lord makes perfect sense by our human standards—at least by mine!

> But Moses said to God, "Who am I that I should go to Pharaoh and bring the Israelites out of Egypt?"
>
> Exodus 3:11

Probably the same question I would have asked. Lord, are you kidding me? I'm a shepherd, gone from that life for decades. And my life may be over if I go back!

> And God said, "I will be with you. And this will be the sign to you that it is I who have sent you: When you have brought the people out of Egypt, you will worship God on this mountain."
>
> Exodus 3:12

I will be with you. Those words are so personal to me, as I discuss elsewhere in the book. They were really the only words Moses needed in that moment, but he was far from done arguing about his assignment. Bookmark that promise that the people would return to Horeb (also called Mount Sinai). It's a place of great significance for the Israelites, both collectively and for key individuals throughout the Old Testament.

Fugitive to Prophet

It is a glorious thing to see all the ways God was weaving Moses's story together so that he was equipped and positioned at just the right place and time to lead the Israelites to the promised land. His mother, Jochebed, was brave and bold—along with his sister, Miriam. They defied Pharaoh's orders, just as the Hebrew midwives did. It's no coincidence that Moses was given life by being set adrift into the Nile, the very river where he should have been sent to die. It was Pharaoh's daughter who gave him the name Moses, which means "drawn from the water" (Exodus 2:10). His earliest years were spent being raised by his own mother, who undoubtedly prayed over him and taught him the ways of his people. Moses then grew up in Pharaoh's palace, where he got the best education academically, culturally, and politically. "Moses was educated in all the wisdom of the Egyptians," the deacon Stephen would later say (Acts 7:22). One church father would argue that in the same way that the Hebrews despoiled the Egyptians of gold and silver, Moses took pagan learning and turned it to God's purposes, and that we should, too.

Moses was uniquely prepared to understand how Egypt's most elite leaders and society functioned. He spoke their language, literally and figuratively. Even after his fatal choice made him a man on the run, Moses was still being prepared for the critical assignment the Lord had already scripted for him. He became immersed in the ways of the desert, the realities of a non-royal life. At the ripe old age of eighty—as a refugee who felt unworthy and unable to do what God was calling him to—Moses was already more of an expert for the tasks ahead than he could humanly perceive.

When we are confronted with a challenge that seems beyond our abilities (or let's be honest, contrary to our desires), we're often more eloquent than an expert defense attorney, making the case for why we're all wrong for the job. Moses was ready with his list of excuses as to why he couldn't possibly do what God was asking.

In Exodus 3:12, the Lord told Moses he would be the one to lead the people out of slavery. God is timeless; He has already been in the future we may be fearful about. He knows what's coming. He's plotted out our path, every step. He is never surprised by anything. And in this case, He had already guaranteed victory. While Moses had been so in awe of the Lord that He knew better than to look in His direction, his timid human heart didn't seem to believe God could achieve the unthinkable—especially through him. Moses could only perceive the here and now. It's easy to feel like God is all-powerful in moments of spiritual ecstasy, but do we really think God is at work when we're out in the real world of traffic jams and bus stops and shabby funeral homes?

Where have I been guilty of the same in my own heart? I can sing all the worship songs, memorize the verses, pray without ceasing. But there are times when I've also drawn a line as to how far I believe God's power and promises extend. Would I ever verbalize that? No. But have I *acted* as if there is a limit to God's omnipotence? I have. Thankfully, just as He did with Moses, God knows our hearts and when we need some divine reassurance for the work ahead.

> Moses said to God, "Suppose I go to the Israelites and say to them, 'The God of your fathers has sent me to you,' and they ask me, 'What is his name?' Then what shall I tell them?"
>
> God said to Moses, "I AM WHO I AM. This is what you are to say to the Israelites: 'I AM has sent me to you.'"
>
> God also said to Moses, "Say to the Israelites, 'The LORD,

the God of your fathers—the God of Abraham, the God of Isaac and the God of Jacob—has sent me to you.'
"This is my name forever,
the name you shall call me
from generation to generation."

Exodus 3:13–15

I AM. Period. God instructed Moses to gather the elders of Israel and tell them who'd sent him. "The elders of Israel will listen to you," God promised, seemingly intuiting that this was the main thing Moses was worried about (Exodus 3:18). Moses and the elders were directed to go to Pharaoh, but the Lord acknowledged that the current leader of Egypt would not let them go—at least not without some divine intervention.

"So I will stretch out my hand and strike the Egyptians with all the wonders that I will perform among them. After that, he will let you go.

"And I will make the Egyptians favorably disposed toward this people, so that when you leave you will not go empty-handed. Every woman is to ask her neighbor and any woman living in her house for articles of silver and gold and for clothing, which you will put on your sons and daughters. And so you will plunder the Egyptians."

Exodus 3:20–22

Once again, God outlined the triumphs that were to come. The victory was locked in, a sure thing. And it's not just that Egypt would eventually release millions of enslaved people at the core of their (conscripted) labor force, but they would also send them off with added wealth in their pockets.

Moses remained unconvinced. *What if it doesn't work?* Even though God had already assured Moses that it would, he wanted reassurance—and the Lord was about to provide it.

God had Moses drop his staff, and it turned into a snake, then back into a staff when Moses picked it up. Then He had Moses put his hand into his cloak, only to pull it out covered in disease. Another tuck back into the cloak, and his hand was healed. If those two miracles didn't work to convince Pharaoh, then God told Moses to throw water from the Nile (the river where he had been sentenced to death) onto the ground and watch it turn to blood.

> Moses said to the Lord, "Pardon your servant, Lord. I have never been eloquent, neither in the past nor since you have spoken to your servant. I am slow of speech and tongue."
>
> The Lord said to him, "Who gave human beings their mouths? Who makes them deaf or mute? Who gives them sight or makes them blind? Is it not I, the Lord? Now go; I will help you speak and will teach you what to say."
>
> But Moses said, "Pardon your servant, Lord. Please send someone else."
>
> Exodus 4:10–13

Have you ever argued with God? Have you ever told Him He's wrong about you? How our distrust and frail hearts must sometimes frustrate Him. Exodus 4:14 tells us "the Lord's anger burned against Moses," but He didn't give up on him. Thank goodness He *never* gives up on us.

I get it; public speaking can feel like an especially vulnerable proposition. Standing in front of a crowd you hope to inform and entertain, while fearing the audience won't engage at all, is nerve-racking. It can trigger the fight-or-flight response that makes your mind and body think you're actually facing an existential threat. I have had all kinds of experiences with public speaking. One memorable one involved a man who seemed very uninterested, and he spent part of my presentation picking his nose and then fell asleep. It's true.

My first year of law school, I was terrified to learn that my final grade in our Research & Writing class would include arguing our case in front of a "jury"—including our professor. I went to her office in tears. I felt paralyzed by the level of fear this assignment provoked. Certainly there had to be a way I could salvage my grade even if I skipped that part of the semester? Not a chance. And my professor had zero empathy for my mini breakdown. I suspect she'd had many teary-eyed, hysterical first-year law students sit and give her the same speech I'd unloaded. She reminded me that she'd spent the year equipping all of us for this very eventuality *and* that she had complete and total confidence in my ability to do it. And that was that—*get to work!*

You would think that Moses had much bigger fears, like winding up dead for standing up to Pharaoh. But as we've seen, Moses had physical courage to spare—he killed an abusive Egyptian, and he drove off the attackers in Midian. In order to defend his sheep, he likely had to face wild animals. But this challenge required a different sort of bravery—the courage to take a social risk, to be vulnerable as a thinker and communicator. Moses, despite his training in the Egyptian language and customs, didn't feel equipped for that sort of job.

God agreed to bring Moses's brother Aaron onto the team.

Moses was instructed to give Aaron the words to say, and the Lord would speak through them. Moses went to get Jethro's blessing to go after his people, and he eventually met up with Aaron. Together, they gathered the elders of the Israelites and did as God had commanded them, telling them what the Lord had said and performing the signs He'd enabled them to do. The elders were so grateful God had considered their suffering that they bowed down and worshiped.

Obedience Can Make Things Worse Before It Makes Them Better

Just as God had warned, Pharaoh did not take kindly to their request that he allow the Israelites to leave and worship the Lord. In his day, the Egyptian leader was likely considered a god himself.

> Pharaoh said, "Who is the Lord, that I should obey him and let Israel go? I do not know the Lord and I will not let Israel go."
> Then they said, "The God of the Hebrews has met with us. Now let us take a three-day journey into the wilderness to offer sacrifices to the Lord our God, or he may strike us with plagues or with the sword."
> But the king of Egypt said, "Moses and Aaron, why are you taking the people away from their labor? Get back to your work!" Then Pharaoh said, "Look, the people of the land are now numerous, and you are stopping them from working."
> That same day Pharaoh gave this order to the slave drivers and overseers in charge of the people: "You are no longer to supply the people with straw for making bricks; let them go and gather their own straw. But require them to make the

same number of bricks as before; don't reduce the quota. They are lazy; that is why they are crying out, 'Let us go and sacrifice to our God.' Make the work harder for the people so that they keep working and pay no attention to lies."

Exodus 5:2–9

Not only did Pharaoh say no, but he also told the slave drivers to take away the straw the Israelites had been using to make bricks without changing the quota they were expected to produce. Life lesson: When God asks you to do something, things will often get worse before they get better. The Israelites went to Pharaoh, hoping to find some relief, only to be threatened. Moses and Aaron, God's messengers, were about to get an earful:

> ... they said, "May the LORD look on you and judge you! You have made us obnoxious to Pharaoh and his officials and have put a sword in their hand to kill us."

Exodus 5:21

Moses immediately ran back to the Lord to ask why—when he did as directed—it brought nothing but trouble. "[Y]ou have not rescued your people at all," he complained to God (Exodus 5:23).

The Lord was blunt with Moses: *Watch me.* It could only be God who would deliver His people under these circumstances, so He sent Moses back to the people with a message.

> "Therefore, say to the Israelites: 'I am the LORD, and I will bring you out from under the yoke of the Egyptians. I will free you from being slaves to them, and I will redeem you with an

outstretched arm and with mighty acts of judgment. I will take you as my own people, and I will be your God. Then you will know that I am the LORD your God, who brought you out from under the yoke of the Egyptians. And I will bring you to the land I swore with uplifted hand to give to Abraham, to Isaac and to Jacob. I will give it to you as a possession. I am the LORD."

Exodus 6:6–8

But the Israelites didn't want to hear it. "[T]hey did not listen to him because of their discouragement and harsh labor" (Exodus 6:9). I wonder who Moses was more afraid of speaking to at this point: the Israelites or Pharaoh?

The Lord told Moses to go back to Pharaoh and command that he let the Israelites go. Moses protested, "If the Israelites will not listen to me, why would Pharaoh listen to me?" (Exodus 6:12).

But Moses and Aaron were faithful. At the ripe old ages of eighty and eighty-three, the brothers went back into the fight. And what an epic showdown it was. Time and again, Pharaoh refused and then promised to relent and allow the people to go. Each time he refused to keep his promise, another devastating plague was unleashed by God.

Here are the ten plagues in order:

1. Water turned to blood
2. Infestations of frogs
3. Infestations of gnats
4. Infestations of flies
5. Death of livestock
6. Painful boils
7. Hail

8. Swarms of locusts
9. Suffocating darkness
10. Death of all firstborn

It was that last, catastrophic blow that finally loosened Pharaoh's grip.

A Sacrificial Lamb

In the midst of that sweep of death, the Passover came to life. God provided a way for His people to be shielded against that final, fatal judgment on Egypt. By spreading the blood of a sacrificed spotless lamb over their doorframes, the Israelites would be saved. Just as the ultimate sacrificial lamb would come in the form of Jesus Christ one day, the lamb of Passover illustrated the salvation to come. It was a ceremony the Lord asked His people to commemorate for all generations, so that descendants of those slaves would remember the freedom and rescue He provided when they were deep in despair and bondage.

At last, Pharaoh had had enough. He just wanted the Hebrews gone at that point, but remember God's vow to Moses that they wouldn't leave Egypt empty-handed?

> The Israelites did as Moses instructed and asked the Egyptians for articles of silver and gold and for clothing. The LORD had made the Egyptians favorably disposed toward the people, and they gave them what they asked for; so they plundered the Egyptians.
>
> Exodus 12:35–36

Finally free to journey to the promised land, the Israelites were on their way. But I love the detail noted in Exodus 13:17 that the Lord sent them on a longer route than necessary. He didn't want them to have to face the Philistines, lest they face war and "change their minds and return to Egypt." As I said earlier, He's already been in our future, and He knew the Israelites—despite being freed from oppressive slavery—would eventually grow weary of traveling in the desert and romanticize their time in Egypt. So the Lord gave them a miraculous, visible sign of His presence to reassure and guide them: a cloud by day and a pillar of fire by night (Exodus 13:21).

But just when the freed Israelites began to breathe a sigh of relief, Pharaoh changed his mind (again). Despite the absolute devastation of the ten plagues, the loss of so many members of his workforce was a jolt to Pharaoh and the Egyptian economy. As the Israelites camped by the Red Sea, Pharaoh and his army showed up in force. Gripped with fear, the Israelites re-upped their complaints to Moses. *Why did you bring us out here to die? Why didn't you just let us stay and serve the Egyptians?*

Perfect Love Casts Out Fear

It's at this point that we see how much Moses has changed since his early years in the desert. Once consumed by self-doubt and terror, he boldly stood and spoke.

> Moses answered the people, "Do not be afraid. Stand firm and you will see the deliverance the LORD will bring you today. The Egyptians you see today you will never see again. The LORD will fight for you; you need only to be still."
>
> Exodus 14:13–14

The man who once tried to talk God out of using him now refused to cower before a swarm of Egyptian chariots and soldiers headed right at him. Just as the Lord had told him, the people would be delivered and free, and Moses was boldly guaranteeing them the same. He had overcome the self-doubt that seemed entirely justifiable to his human mind. But the people he was leading were just at the beginning of that journey. Moses had learned that in his weakness was God's strength (2 Corinthians 12:10). Though he hadn't doubted his physical ability to get things done, Moses's fears when God approached him were tied more to his feelings of inadequacy and perceived inability to persuade.

Moses's main fear had been rejection by his own people. Standing up to the chariots of the Egyptians while rallying his own disbelieving people showed how fully he had mastered his social anxiety, combining his trust in God with concrete communication and action.

How can we learn the same lessons that Moses did? Let's consider his speech in Exodus 14:13–14 phrase by phrase.

Don't be afraid. Moses was saying don't focus on your own emotions, but on anticipating that what God has promised you is true. He has no doubts about your future.

Stand firm. That anticipation of deliverance should keep us from reacting in knee-jerk fear. In moments of trepidation—and they will come—don't waver. Remember, the enemy is constantly seeking to intimidate you out of believing what you know to be truth.

See His deliverance. Open your eyes. Don't miss it. Sometimes God chooses a different path than the one we would prefer. The more we resist or drop to the ground in a tantrum, the more we delay His perfect plan. What the Israelites were about to witness would blow their minds, but they had to be watching.

He will fight for you. So many powerful verses come to mind:

> The LORD is with me; I will not be afraid.
> What can mere mortals do to me?
>
> Psalm 118:6

> If God is for us, who can be against us?
>
> Romans 8:31

Be still. Okay, this might be the hardest one for me. I am a problem solver, an action taker. I say it often, my husband claims I have two speeds: 100 mph and asleep. Bottom line, I generally need to be in REM to be still. Don't you know those Israelites wanted to panic, to gather their little ones, and try to make a run for it? They could see nothing but a watery grave in front of them and sure death behind them. Moses, the onetime stuttering coward, confidently told them everything was going to be okay.

The Word of God Is a Sword

God directed Moses to raise his staff, stretch out his hands, and watch the miracle unfold. This miracle took place not only for the salvation of the Israelites, but also to spread the word of God's authority far beyond the Red Sea.

> I will harden the hearts of the Egyptians so that they will go in after them. And I will gain glory through Pharaoh and all

his army, through his chariots and his horsemen. The Egyptians will know that I am the Lord when I gain glory through Pharaoh, his chariots and his horsemen."

Exodus 14:17–18

And just a few verses later, that's exactly what happened. All night long, the Lord sent a strong wind to blast back the waters and allow the Israelites to travel to safety on dry land. The Egyptians chased after them and instantly regretted it.

> During the last watch of the night the Lord looked down from the pillar of fire and cloud at the Egyptian army and threw it into confusion. He jammed the wheels of their chariots so that they had difficulty driving. And the Egyptians said, "Let's get away from the Israelites! The Lord is fighting for them against Egypt."
> . . . the Lord swept them into the sea. The water flowed back and covered the chariots and horsemen—the entire army of Pharaoh that had followed the Israelites into the sea. Not one of them survived. . . .
> And when the Israelites saw the mighty hand of the Lord displayed against the Egyptians, the people feared the Lord and put their trust in him and in Moses his servant.

Exodus 14:24–25, 27–28, 31

The people *trusted* Moses—a man who trusted neither himself nor the Lord when he was sent on this momentous assignment. It's neat to remember that Moses is the one who wrote this account of what happened. He repeatedly tells on himself, transparently sharing the doubt and defiance he had when talking with the very God of the universe. After 430 years of captivity, the people of Israel were delivered under the leadership of a man who would rather have hidden out with the sheep.

Moses—a man who claimed he wasn't a good communicator—authored the foundations of the Bible. That includes the book of Deuteronomy, which many in the Jewish faith refer to as *Devarim*. That translates as "words." It begins, "These are the words Moses spoke to all Israel . . ." (Deuteronomy 1:1). It is the same Hebrew word Moses used in Exodus 4:10 to say he was not eloquent. In Hebrew, he had literally said, "I am not a man of words." Now, he's not just become a man of words; he's become the man who delivers *the* words of the Lord. He found his voice with God's help. Here's how he's described in Acts:

> Moses was educated in all the wisdom of the Egyptians and was powerful in speech and action.
>
> Acts 7:22

But he was just the first part of God's glorious plans for us.

> For the law was given through Moses; grace and truth came through Jesus Christ.
>
> John 1:17

In fact, Jesus harkened back to Moses when the people He'd come to save (once and for all) couldn't recognize the Messiah standing in front of them.

> If you believed Moses, you would believe me, for he wrote about me. But since you do not believe what he wrote, how are you going to believe what I say?
>
> John 5:46–47

Moses began the story of God's journey to rescue and redeem us—he prophesied the importance of the sacrificial lamb and gave us the "words" that revealed God's plan of salvation. Jesus will write the final chapter, be the final Lamb, and be the final "Word" that "became flesh" (John 1:14).

Study Questions

1. Has there been a time when God called you to act, and you tried to talk Him out of it? What was behind your hesitance? How did you eventually make peace with the assignment?
2. Moses wasn't afraid of a physical challenge, but he worried about one that involved persuasion and confrontation—some social anxiety. Why is the latter often the tougher hurdle?
3. It's unlikely you've seen a burning bush inhabited by God Himself, but where and how does He show up in your life? How can you be more attuned to His prompting?
4. How does it impact your thinking when you acknowledge that God has already seen every bit of your future and that nothing surprises Him?
5. How did God work through Moses's weakness to transform him from meek to mighty? What is God working on in your life right now?

PETER'S FEAR

When Our Tongues Are a Double-Edged Sword

Primarily the Gospels and Acts

Bold and brash, fiery and unbridled—if you know much about Peter, that's probably your first impression of him. And you're not wrong. He spoke his mind, felt deeply, and acted quickly. But everything that made Peter passionate was also a defining strength of his. Like each of us as believers, he was a work in progress. His impulsiveness meant he bravely followed Christ without hesitation and stood firm in the face of the church's early persecution. It also meant the Savior who Peter cherished had to right some of his wrongs and even put him in his place on occasion.

I can see many of Peter's qualities in my late father, Ed. I chuckle when I think about how his overconfidence and competitive nature led to one of our favorite family stories. He was attending a special Parents' Weekend with me at Liberty University during my senior year there. During a special luncheon for some of the seniors, the question was asked, "Who came from the farthest to be here today?" Tallahassee, my hometown, was a few states away, but I knew there were students from all over the globe, so I did not expect us to win that contest. One gentleman called out, "Panama City!" My father, assuming the man was referring to the city in the Florida Panhandle, quietly mumbled to me, "That's only a couple of hours from us." He then proudly yelled out for the entire crowd, "Tallahassee, Florida!" To which the other father replied, "Panama City . . . Panama." Cringe! We laughed about that for years, about how my father should have known better than to blurt out a claim when—viewed logically—he had very little chance of being the actual winner. But he was excited, lost in the moment, and quick to take action—just like Peter.

When the authorities showed up to arrest Jesus in the hours before he was brutally beaten and crucified, it was Peter who stepped in to defend Christ. He sliced off the ear of the high priest's servant, which Jesus quickly restored.

At first blush, that impetuous move by Peter makes him appear gutsy. But often those who are most demonstrative operate from a place of fear. Jesus reprimanded Peter in that moment. He had repeatedly told His closest confidants of what was coming, and just before Peter struck that servant, Jesus had already consented to go with his captors. Peter's violence and his betrayal came from the same place. He was the living embodiment of one proverb: "The words of the reckless pierce like swords."

But the beauty in Peter's story, and ours, is that none of this ever meant he couldn't be redeemed and used by the Lord. In fact, Jesus reached into the places where Peter had failed the most to call him to greatness. Peter clearly learned the lesson well—so well that he went on to become a mighty preacher and a martyr for the faith. What a turnaround! In fact, the rest of that proverb could outline Peter's journey from recklessness to wisdom:

> The words of the reckless pierce like swords, but the tongue of the wise brings healing.
>
> Proverbs 12:18

So how did he get there?

An Unstable Rock: Peter's Call (John 1:35-42, Matthew 4:18-22, Mark 1:16-20, Luke 5:1-11)

Peter's brother, Andrew, was already a follower of John the Baptist when he first heard of Jesus. He overheard John refer to his cousin, Jesus, as "the Lamb of God" (John 1:36). Andrew and another follower of John the Baptist both approached Jesus, and they spent the rest of the afternoon with Him (John 1:37-39).

> Andrew, Simon Peter's brother, was one of the two who heard what John had said and who had followed Jesus. The first thing Andrew did was to find his brother Simon and tell him, "We have found the Messiah" (that is, the Christ). And he brought him to Jesus.
> Jesus looked at him and said, "You are Simon son of John. You will be called Cephas" (which, when translated, is Peter).
>
> John 1:40-42

In Aramaic, Cephas means rock. That's also what Peter translates to in Greek. A quick sneak peek ahead shows us just how intentional Christ's renaming was. Later, when Peter made his first confession of Jesus's true identity as "the Messiah, the Son of the Living God" (Matthew 16:16), Jesus identified this faith as a rock. Recognizing the moment, Jesus said:

you are Peter, and on this rock I will build my church, and the gates of Hades will not overcome it.

> Matthew 16:18

But much would transpire before Peter got to that defining moment with Jesus. There would be tests of Peter's faith; some he'd pass—others he would fail. The underlying truth never changed, though. The Lord can transform our failures into opportunities for His grace.

Jesus formally called Andrew and Peter while they were working as fishermen at the Sea of Galilee. As they cast their nets, He said simply, "Come, follow me and I will send you out to fish for people" (Matthew 4:19; Mark 1:17). In Luke 5:6-7, Jesus performed a miracle, filling their nets with a huge catch of fish. In all the passages, the fishermen's response was the same.

At once they left their nets and followed Him.

From that day forward, the men were part of Jesus's inner circle, traveling along with Him on His journey of miracles, compassion, teaching, redemption, devastating death, and glorious resurrection. It strikes me that along the way, Peter experienced some of the highest highs and lowest lows of those accompanying Christ. As bold as he was in standing up to Jesus's enemies, Peter was also undergoing a transformation of his own—many times not yet fully comprehending that he was walking with the Son of God or what Christ would have to suffer so that all could be saved.

A Ghost on the Sea (Matthew 14:13-31)

Because his brother had already introduced him to Jesus, Peter had some knowledge of Christ when He called him into ministry at the Sea of Galilee. But in many ways, Peter wouldn't *truly* understand who Jesus was for much of their friendship. He loved the part of his Master that proclaimed kingdoms and victory—but he was baffled and alarmed by Jesus's call to servanthood and suffering. Until Peter understood that true kingship was the way of the cross, he would not really know Jesus.

Peter was front and center for things in Jesus's ministry that could only be described as supernatural, but there were indications along the way that he was still in the process of fully grasping Jesus's role as humanity's true Savior. We shouldn't feel like failures as believers when we experience our own doubts and questions. If those who walked with Jesus Himself stumbled along their faith journeys, it's only logical that we would deal with uncertainty, too. I've always been struck by the line often quoted from a 1787 letter written by Thomas Jefferson:

"Question with boldness even the existence of a God; because, if there be one, he must more approve of the homage of reason, than that of blindfolded fear."

God can handle our questions, but would prefer that we wholeheartedly choose Him with our minds, hearts, and souls. When I've wrestled with uncertainty, I've simply asked God to meet me exactly where I am, to show me who He is, to reveal Himself. That's just what Jesus did for Peter.

One of Peter's biggest moments put all those human qualities on display—as in his decision to walk on water to Jesus in the midst of a stormy sea (Matthew 14:28-29). It came at a deeply difficult time for Christ and His disciples. John the Baptist had been beheaded by Herod. Jesus must have been grieved by the loss of His cousin, but since Peter's brother Andrew—and probably another one of the Twelve—had been John the Baptist's disciples first, they must have felt heartbroken, too.

In the wake of the devastating news, Jesus retreated to a "solitary place" by boat (Matthew 14:13). But that didn't stop the people who were increasingly in awe of Him. They gathered from towns all over, and though He must have been grieving, Jesus had compassion on the people and "healed their sick" (Matthew 14:14).

It was getting late, and the disciples worried about the people and what they would eat. They asked Jesus to send the crowds away so they could go to nearby villages and find food.

> Jesus replied, "They do not need to go away. You give them something to eat."
>
> Matthew 14:16

To me, this seems like a foreshadowing that went beyond physical hunger. When Christ urged His disciples to feed the people, that would eventually encompass their spiritual needs as well. The disciples argued they had just five loaves of bread and two fish. But after Jesus blessed those meager offerings and sent them out through the crowds, five thousand men (aside from the additional women and children) ate until they were full, and twelve baskets were left over.

It's a beautiful picture of what happens when we share God's Word and truth. It will always multiply exponentially. It's not a zero-sum game. The gospel replicates, it grows and expands—reaching every heart that will listen. There is no limit to how many people it can transform.

It was in the wake of the loss of John the Baptist and the exhaustion of ministering to the five thousand that Jesus directed the disciples to get in a boat and go ahead of Him on their next journey while He dismissed the crowd. As the disciples crossed the Sea of Galilee (also referred to as the Lake of Gennesaret), Scripture says their boat was buffeted by the wind and waves, already far from land. Then, something unexpected happened: "Shortly before dawn, Jesus went out to them, walking on the lake" (Matthew 14:25). He didn't have a boat, but as the Creator of the elements, He could simply take to the water and stride through the storm.

> When the disciples saw him walking on the lake, they were terrified. "It's a ghost," they said, and cried out in fear.
>
> But Jesus immediately said to them: "Take courage! It is I. Don't be afraid."
>
> "Lord, if it's you," Peter replied, "tell me to come to you on the water."
>
> "Come," he said.
>
> Then Peter got down out of the boat, walked on the water and came toward Jesus. But when he saw the wind, he was afraid and, beginning to sink, cried out, "Lord, save me!"
>
> Immediately Jesus reached out his hand and caught him. "You of little faith," he said, "why did you doubt?"
>
> And when they climbed into the boat, the wind died down. Then those who were in the boat worshiped him, saying, "Truly you are the Son of God."
>
> Matthew 14:26–32

This is the perfect picture of what is a constant struggle for many believers: fear versus faith. Right away, Jesus greeted the disciples with the admonition, "Don't be afraid." Peter could have simply waited for Christ to reach the boat. Instead, as impetuous as ever, he wanted to do what he often did—take action. Peter is often criticized for sinking into the water in fear, but let's give the man credit for stepping out of that boat! He's the only one who did.

The incident also underscores how far Peter had to go in his faith. If he had fully grasped Christ's divinity, he wouldn't have feared what the rough seas could do to him. No doubt this event nudged Peter ever closer to the unshakable faith that equipped him to build the early church, even at the cost of his own life.

The Transfiguration and Confession (Mark 9:2-10, Matthew 16:13-23)

By this time, Peter wasn't just one of the twelve disciples accompanying Christ during His relatively brief earthly ministry. Scripture reveals Peter was a member of the trio that Jesus kept closest to Him, along with James and John. They were there when Christ raised the young daughter of a religious leader from the dead (Mark 5:37-42). They were also together at the Transfiguration.

> ... Jesus took Peter, James and John with him and led them up a high mountain, where they were all alone. There he was transfigured before them. His clothes became dazzling white, whiter than anyone in the world could bleach them. And there appeared before them Elijah and Moses, who were talking with Jesus.
>
> Peter said to Jesus, "Rabbi, it is good for us to be here. Let us put up three shelters—one for you, one for Moses and one for Elijah." (He did not know what to say, they were so frightened.)

> Then a cloud appeared and covered them, and a voice came from the cloud: "This is my Son, whom I love. Listen to him!"
>
> Suddenly, when they looked around, they no longer saw anyone with them except Jesus.
>
> As they were coming down the mountain, Jesus gave them orders not to tell anyone what they had seen until the Son of Man had risen from the dead. They kept the matter to themselves, discussing what "rising from the dead" meant.
>
> Mark 9:2–10

We see here again this mixture of awe, fear, and confusion. The disciples knew that Jesus was the Son of God, but they simply couldn't fully understand what that meant. This wasn't the first time Jesus had predicted His death. Peter had already discussed the possibility of Jesus's death, and it didn't end well. It came on the heels of Peter's clear acknowledgment of who Christ was.

> When Jesus came to the region of Caesarea Philippi, he asked his disciples, "Who do people say the Son of Man is?"
>
> They replied, "Some say John the Baptist; others say Elijah; and still others, Jeremiah or one of the prophets."
>
> "But what about you?" he asked. "Who do you say I am?"
>
> Simon Peter answered, "You are the Messiah, the Son of the living God."
>
> Jesus replied, "Blessed are you, Simon son of Jonah, for this was not revealed to you by flesh and blood, but by my Father in heaven."
>
> Matthew 16:13–17

What a great moment! This was a momentous breakthrough in the disciples' understanding of who Jesus was. But it seems Peter only partially got it. Though Peter proclaimed Jesus as the Messiah, he still thought it appropriate to argue with Him!

> From that time on Jesus began to explain to his disciples that he must go to Jerusalem and suffer many things at the hands of the elders, the chief priests and the teachers of the law, and that he must be killed and on the third day be raised to life.
>
> Peter took him aside and began to rebuke him. "Never, Lord!" he said. "This shall never happen to you!"
>
> Jesus turned and said to Peter, "Get behind me, Satan! You are a stumbling block to me; you do not have in mind the concerns of God, but merely human concerns."
>
> Matthew 16:21–23

At this point, there was still a gap between Peter's declaration that Jesus was the Son of God and his understanding of what Jesus would have to suffer in order to accomplish our salvation.

If you'll notice, Peter often used absolutes like "never" and "always." A marriage counselor once cautioned my husband and me against using them too often. It doesn't leave much room for discussion or compromise. "You never do the dishes!" "You never come home when you say you will!" It locks the speaker into a position with very little room to maneuver, and it often got Peter into a pinch. It earned him a quick rebuke when he tried to challenge the truth of what Jesus was telling him. Jesus was trying to prepare Peter for all that was coming, but his human mind couldn't comprehend it. I'm not above arguing with God either, and I cringe when I think about my feeble attempts to "outwit" Him.

The Triumphal Entry and Last Supper
(Matthew 21:1–11, John 13:1–17,
Matthew 26:31–35, Luke 22:31–32)

Jesus knew that His crucifixion was coming, but it's understandable that Peter would adamantly resist anything viewed as a threat to the One he understood to be the Messiah. It must have been difficult to fathom that the people would so quickly turn on the Man who had entered Jerusalem to shouts of praise and adulation. Jesus's arrival in Jerusalem had electrified the whole city:

> "Hosanna to the Son of David!"
> "Blessed is he who comes in the name of the Lord!"
> "Hosanna in the highest heaven!"
>
> Matthew 21:9

Immediately, Jesus set about speaking truth, stirring up His critics, and refusing to bend under growing pressure. The religious leaders schemed and plotted, hoping to entangle Him in a religious riddle He couldn't solve. Time and again, He turned their baited questions back onto them. They only grew in frustration and determination to find a way to silence Him. Jesus repeatedly told the Twelve that His death was coming, even specifying that He would be crucified (Matthew 20:19). Events were in motion.

Soon, Jesus knew it was time for His betrayal. The disciples prepared for a meal they didn't realize would become what we now celebrate as the Last Supper. I love this beautiful verse that sets up what was about to unfold:

It was just before the Passover Festival. Jesus knew that the hour had come for him to leave this world and go to the Father. Having loved his own who were in the world, he loved them to the end.

John 13:1

He loved them to the end. And He was about to give them a physical manifestation of that. Jesus wrapped a towel around His waist and began to do what would have been unthinkable at that time. Washing the feet of those who traveled the dusty roads in their sandals was the work of the servants or slaves in a household. A revered rabbi would never have been the one to stoop to that task. But Jesus was no ordinary spiritual teacher.

[H]e poured water into a basin and began to wash his disciples' feet, drying them with the towel that was wrapped around him.
He came to Simon Peter, who said to him, "Lord, are you going to wash my feet?"
Jesus replied, "You do not realize now what I am doing, but later you will understand."
"No," said Peter, "you shall never wash my feet."
Jesus answered, "Unless I wash you, you have no part with me."
"Then, Lord," Simon Peter replied, "not just my feet but my hands and my head as well!"

John 13:5–9

Right on cue, Peter's passion drove his extreme responses. *No way are You washing my feet—never! It's the only way to be united with You? Okay, then wash all of me!* Despite not understanding, Peter leaped ahead anyway. But Christ wanted His disciples to get the lesson far beyond a footbath. Only by the Greatest lowering Himself to be the Least could He show them what they must do once He was gone.

> "You call me 'Teacher' and 'Lord' and rightly so, for that is what I am. Now that I, your Lord and Teacher, have washed your feet, you also should wash one another's feet. I have set you an example that you should do as I have done for you. Very truly I tell you, no servant is greater than his master, nor is a messenger greater than the one who sent him. Now that you know these things, you will be blessed if you do them."
>
> John 13:13–17

Was Peter truly getting it? It was at that same dinner that Jesus did something His devoted, intense follower found even more shocking than the foot washing: He predicted Peter's denial.

> Peter replied, "Even if all fall away on account of you, I never will."
>
> "Truly I tell you," Jesus answered, "this very night, before the rooster crows, you will disown me three times."
>
> But Peter declared, "Even if I have to die with you, I will never disown you."
>
> Matthew 26:33–35

Never. There it is again. Peter made another definitive promise he wouldn't keep. Jesus already knew how Peter would continue to fall short, but notice He didn't tell him that it would end their relationship. In my heart, I believe Jesus had compassion for Peter in this moment. In the account of this story in Luke, Jesus told Peter that He had already been interceding for him.

"... I have prayed for you, Simon, that your faith may not fail. And when you have turned back, strengthen your brothers."

Luke 22:32

He already knew what was coming, and He also knew how it would break Peter's heart. He knows exactly how each of us will fail, and yet He doesn't simply close the page on us as if we're irredeemable. He stands by, ready to envelop us in His loving arms when we return.

Gethsemane (Matthew 26:36–46, Mark 14:66–72)

Before Peter would deny his connection to Christ, he would first fail to be the faithful friend the Messiah needed in the gut-wrenching hours leading up to His torture and death. Following their momentous dinner and Jesus's disturbing predictions, He took the trio (Peter, James, and John) with Him as He went to pray in the garden of Gethsemane. He was "sorrowful and troubled" and He told them, "My soul is overwhelmed with sorrow to the point of death. Stay here and keep watch with me" (Matthew 26:38). It was during this time that Jesus asked His Father to take the brutal assignment from Him if it was possible, but He clearly deferred to God's will. He was in agony.

Then he returned to his disciples and found them sleeping. "Couldn't you men keep watch with me for one hour?" he asked Peter. "Watch and pray so that you will not fall into temptation. The spirit is willing, but the flesh is weak."

Matthew 26:40–41

Peter, the one who vowed to lay down his life for Jesus, couldn't even keep his eyes open to pray for Him in a time of great emotional crisis. Three times Christ returned to find that His inner circle had failed Him. They were about to find out just why He so wanted their support.

Judas, who had arranged to betray Jesus, showed up with soldiers and religious leaders carrying torches and weapons. In response, Jesus didn't fight back or call down angels from heaven as He could easily have done, but He willingly submitted to those who had shown up to take Him prisoner. But not everyone was on the same page . . .

Then Simon Peter, who had a sword, drew it and struck the high priest's servant, cutting off his right ear. (The servant's name was Malchus.)

John 18:10

But Jesus answered, "No more of this!" And he touched the man's ear and healed him.

Luke 22:51

Peter must have been shocked, once again, to find his Master acting in such a seemingly self-defeating way. Jesus had already told the disciples that following Him meant taking up a cross (Matthew

16:24), but apparently none of them really believed that. Perhaps that's why, seeing what was happening, "all the disciples deserted him and fled" (Matthew 26:56). Jesus was then taken away, and He went willingly.

Peter then turned around and "followed him at a distance" (Matthew 26:58, Mark 14:54, Luke 22:54). He watched as his Lord was dragged to a sham trial involving the men who had long salivated at the prospect of silencing Him once and for all.

In all four of the Gospels, we witness Peter doing the very thing he passionately vowed he would not. Rather than readily allowing himself to be linked to Jesus, Peter went into self-protection mode.

> While Peter was below in the courtyard, one of the servant girls of the high priest came by. When she saw Peter warming himself, she looked closely at him.
>
> "You also were with that Nazarene, Jesus," she said.
>
> But he denied it. "I don't know or understand what you're talking about," he said, and went out into the entryway.
>
> When the servant girl saw him there, she said again to those standing around, "This fellow is one of them." Again he denied it.
>
> After a little while, those standing near said to Peter, "Surely you are one of them, for you are a Galilean."
>
> He began to call down curses, and he swore to them, "I don't know this man you're talking about."
>
> Immediately the rooster crowed the second time. Then Peter remembered the word Jesus had spoken to him: "Before the rooster crows twice you will disown me three times." And he broke down and wept.
>
> Mark 14:66–72

Luke 22:61 says that "The Lord turned and looked straight at Peter." How utterly crushing. We all hope that, faced with a life-or-death decision to confirm or deny our allegiance to Christ, we would stand bravely and without hesitation. I will never forget the story we covered back in 2015 of twenty-one Christians captured by ISIS and taken to a beach to be executed. The terrorists produced a video so the world could witness the horror. They offered the twenty Egyptians and one Ghanaian man the chance to renounce Jesus and be spared from death. Not a single one of them did. I cried over the courage and sacrifice of those men. They reportedly repeated the words "Lord Jesus Christ" as they were killed.

Prior to Jesus's arrest, I'm sure fiery Peter believed he would do the same. When he failed to be courageous enough to acknowledge his connection to Christ, his soul bore the heavy weight of regret and shame. He would face the choice again, many times, and Peter's response in those future tests would be wholly different. So what changed?

The Way of the Cross (John 20:1–22)

He would become a pillar of the early church, but first Peter would have to walk through the utter devastation of Jesus's death and come to truly understand the purpose of Jesus's mission on earth. Even after all the times Jesus had told them He would rise from the dead, in the days after the crucifixion a grieving Peter still didn't understand. On Easter, after the women who first saw Jesus conveyed the news to Peter, he ran to the tomb with John, but found it baffling.

> So Peter and the other disciple started for the tomb. Both were running, but the other disciple outran Peter and reached

the tomb first. He bent over and looked in at the strips of linen lying there but did not go in. Then Simon Peter came along behind him and went straight into the tomb. He saw the strips of linen lying there, as well as the cloth that had been wrapped around Jesus' head. The cloth was still lying in its place, separate from the linen. Finally the other disciple, who had reached the tomb first, also went inside. He saw and believed. (They still did not understand from Scripture that Jesus had to rise from the dead.)

John 20:3–9

Luke 24:12 summarizes Peter's visit to the empty tomb this way:

Peter, however, got up and ran to the tomb. Bending over, he saw the strips of linen lying by themselves, and he went away, wondering to himself what had happened.

I imagine Peter and John were in a state of physical and emotional exhaustion and confusion. Did they replay their conversations with Jesus, trying to make sense of what they'd all just lived through? When did they begin to consider the possibility that He was indeed alive—just as He had told them He would be?

In the days that followed, to the amazement and great joy of His disciples, Jesus appeared to many of them. He showed them the scars on His hands and feet, and demonstrated that He was not a "ghost" or apparition. He asked for food to eat! During this time, there must have been a focus on restoration and forgiveness. After all, these frightened men had rushed into hiding rather than rushing to His defense. Whatever those conversations, Jesus also had plenty to say about the future. It was at one of these meetings that Jesus officially deputized and equipped the disciples.

> And with that he breathed on them and said, "Receive the Holy Spirit. If you forgive anyone's sins, their sins are forgiven; if you do not forgive them, they are not forgiven."
>
> John 20:22–23

The Second Calling of Peter (John 21:1–17)

When Jesus appeared again later, Peter had a starring role. He'd clearly require a more specific approach than this general gifting of the Spirit. Just like when they were first called, Peter and some others had decided to fish but weren't having much luck. The resurrected Jesus, unrecognized by the men, was on shore and called out to them.

> He said, "Throw your net on the right side of the boat and you will find some." When they did, they were unable to haul the net in because of the large number of fish.
>
> John 21:6

As soon as one of the disciples cried out, "It is the Lord!" Peter reacted with his characteristic zeal—jumping into the water to get to shore as quickly as he could (John 21:7). As Jesus sat beside a fire where fish and bread were being warmed, He asked the men to bring some of the fish they'd miraculously caught. Again, Peter leaped into action.

> So Simon Peter climbed back into the boat and dragged the net ashore. It was full of large fish, 153, but even with so many the net was not torn.
>
> John 21:11

It seems Jesus was giving Peter yet another hint about what was to come. You may not be able to catch fish (convert men) without Me, but with Me, your nets will overflow.

While Peter and Jesus must have talked many times in the days after His resurrection, I wonder if Peter had made any overt attempt to seek forgiveness and reconciliation over his very public failure in denying Christ three times. Peter's guilt must have felt like a constant, open wound. After they'd shared a meal, Jesus set about restoring and clarifying Peter's calling.

> When they had finished eating, Jesus said to Simon Peter, "Simon son of John, do you love me more than these?"
>
> "Yes, Lord," he said, "you know that I love you."
>
> Jesus said, "Feed my lambs."
>
> Again Jesus said, "Simon son of John, do you love me?"
>
> He answered, "Yes, Lord, you know that I love you."
>
> Jesus said, "Take care of my sheep."
>
> The third time he said to him, "Simon son of John, do you love me?"
>
> Peter was hurt because Jesus asked him the third time, "Do you love me?" He said, "Lord, you know all things; you know that I love you."
>
> Jesus said, "Feed my sheep."
>
> John 21:15–17

Having denied Jesus three times, Peter got three chances to pledge his commitment to the Lord. Having prompted Peter to affirm his love for God, Jesus gave him a new mission. He predicted the martyr's death that His disciple would suffer, and made Peter a shepherd. What would that job entail? Jesus told us, earlier in the Gospel of John:

> "The good shepherd lays down his life for the sheep. The hired hand is not the shepherd and does not own the sheep. So when he sees the wolf coming, he abandons the sheep and runs away. Then the wolf attacks the flock and scatters it. The man runs away because he is a hired hand and cares nothing for the sheep."
>
> John 10:11–13

Peter wouldn't run away again, but he would instead become a good shepherd. He would take the admonition and run with it. Not only did Peter no longer hesitate to align with Christ, but he also channeled the intense devotion with which he'd always acted into risking everything to build the early church. He had finally found the true purpose for his boldness, now that he had shed fear for love. He would no longer live by the sword.

Jesus had given the disciples an initial gifting of the Holy Spirit and returned to heaven. His ascension is recorded in Luke 24 and Acts 1.

> Then they worshiped him and returned to Jerusalem with great joy. And they stayed continually at the temple, praising God.
>
> Luke 24:52–53

Peter Becomes a Good Shepherd
(Acts 2, 12:1–18)

The disciples had swung from the depths of despair to the greatest joy; their mission was just beginning. Peter was front and center, boldly living out the instructions Jesus had given him.

Days later, Pentecost arrived.

> Suddenly a sound like the blowing of a violent wind came from heaven and filled the whole house where they were sitting. They saw what seemed to be tongues of fire that separated and came to rest on each of them. All of them were filled with the Holy Spirit and began to speak in other tongues (languages) as the Spirit enabled them.
>
> Now there were staying in Jerusalem God-fearing Jews from every nation under heaven. When they heard this sound, a crowd came together in bewilderment, because each one heard their own language being spoken.
>
> Acts 2:2–6

Imagine the scene. The roaring sound of something like a tornado, small flames dancing through the building and stopping on each disciple. And suddenly, each of them could speak a language he had never spoken before. It was mind-blowing! And only possible because of the Holy Spirit's empowering. Because people were gathered in Jerusalem from many nations, they would hear the message and carry it home with them.

Peter stepped up and delivered a sermon for the ages. He walked the people through the law and writings they knew—words they understood and respected. Peter showed them how Jesus had fulfilled the prophecies of old and was their Messiah.

> "Therefore let all Israel be assured of this: God has made this Jesus, whom you crucified, both Lord and Messiah."
>
> When the people heard this, they were cut to the heart and said to Peter and the other apostles, "Brothers, what shall we do?"
>
> Peter replied, "Repent and be baptized, every one of you, in the name of Jesus Christ for the forgiveness of your sins. And you will receive the gift of the Holy Spirit. The promise is for you and your children and for all who are far off—for all whom the Lord our God will call."
>
> With many other words he warned them; and he pleaded with them, "Save yourselves from this corrupt generation." Those who accepted his message were baptized, and about three thousand were added to their number that day.
>
> Acts 2:36–41

Peter, a man who had been shattered by his denial of Christ, delivered the first evangelical sermon to a massive crowd and witnessed three thousand people come to know the Messiah.

It was *after* his failures that Peter became an even more powerful advocate for the gospel. Not that Peter took his failures in stride—no, he was deeply grieved by the ways he'd betrayed his Savior. If you ever run into a Christian leader who almost seems proud of moral failure because it gives them "authenticity" or "credibility," they've not learned Peter's lesson. That lesson is that any reliance on our own strength will end in failure.

It reminds me of the ancient Japanese art of kintsugi, which the modern world has come to celebrate more widely in recent years. Kintsugi—which means "golden joinery"—illustrates a breathtakingly beautiful picture of restoration. Rather than discarding broken pottery, Japanese artisans would meticulously reassemble objects by using a special mixture based in tree sap and dusted with precious metals. An art historian named Kelly Richman-Abdou explains it for *My Modern Met*:

> Once completed, beautiful seams of gold glint in the conspicuous cracks of ceramic wares, giving a one-of-a-kind appearance to each "repaired" piece.
>
> This unique method celebrates each artifact's unique history by emphasizing its fractures and breaks instead of hiding or disguising them. In fact, kintsugi often makes the repaired piece even more beautiful than the original, revitalizing it with a new look and giving it a second life.

When the Lord redeems us, our cracks and imperfections aren't hidden—they're often highlighted, not because our brokenness is beautiful, but because His grace is. His golden touch on our lives, as with Peter's, produces something much more lovely than where we began—stronger and truly exquisite.

Peter had a new boldness—grounded in love, not in fear or recklessness. With God's anointing, Peter went on to perform many miracles—healing the infirm and raising a woman from the dead (Acts 9:40). He also received a supernatural intervention so powerful that even the believers who'd gathered to pray for it had a hard time believing when it came to fruition. Peter had been jailed by Herod, who already had multiple Christ-followers killed. The church "was earnestly praying to God for [Peter]" (Acts 12:5). The night before he was set to go to trial, Peter was sleeping between two soldiers and wrapped in chains. An angel showed up in that cell and the chains fell away. The angel safely guided Peter past multiple security guards and an iron gate until he was free on the streets.

That's when Peter decided to go see the folks who were interceding for him:

> Peter knocked at the outer entrance, and a servant named Rhoda came to answer the door. When she recognized Peter's voice, she was so overjoyed she ran back without opening it and exclaimed, "Peter is at the door!"
>
> "You're out of your mind," they told her. When she kept insisting that it was so, they said, "It must be his angel."
>
> But Peter kept on knocking, and when they opened the door and saw him, they were astonished. Peter motioned with his hand for them to be quiet and described how the Lord had brought him out of prison.
>
> Acts 12:13–17

Years later, it was Peter who advocated for Gentiles before the Jerusalem Council. He knew God had extended the gift of salvation beyond just His chosen Jewish people. Peter proclaimed that it was not necessary for non-Jewish believers to observe the old Jewish law and its requirements, like circumcision.

> "Brothers, you know that some time ago God made a choice among you that the Gentiles might hear from my lips the message of the gospel and believe. God, who knows the heart, showed that he accepted them by giving the Holy Spirit to them, just as he did to us. He did not discriminate between us

and them, for he purified their hearts by faith. Now then, why do you try to test God by putting on the necks of Gentiles a yoke that neither we nor our ancestors have been able to bear? No! We believe it is through the grace of our Lord Jesus that we are saved, just as they are."

Acts 15:7–11

Indeed, the same grace that covered and restored Peter is available today to all who will believe in Christ and His sacrifice. Despite Peter's impulsive, reckless decisions and failures, he was always part of God's bigger plan. No matter how much you and I may feel like we have failed, God is waiting to renew and rescue us. He promises to meet us there and ultimately turn it to His glory.

As Paul wrote to the Philippians:

But one thing I do: Forgetting what is behind and straining toward what is ahead, I press on toward the goal to win the prize for which God has called me heavenward in Christ Jesus.

Philippians 3:13–14

Study Questions

1. The Scripture says that John saw and believed, but also that he didn't understand that Jesus had to be raised from the dead. What do you think it means to believe without fully understanding?
2. When Jesus approaches on the stormy waters, are you willing to get out of the boat? What keeps you from leaving a

place that may seem secure (and isn't) instead of stepping out into the unknown (but secure) path with Christ?

3. What do you think Peter's main motivations were for denying Jesus? Was it about protecting himself, or something else?
4. Peter shares a lot in common with Moses, who also had to go from being an impulsive rebel to a shepherd of God's people. As critically important preachers, how did they each go from using their tongues as weapons to instruments of healing?
5. What about Peter's transformation most inspires you, and where would you say you currently are on your own journey?

PART II
Overcoming When It's Hard to Love Others

If God is "with" us, then why are my enemies thriving? Part of the scandal of the Gospel is not that God loves "us," but that He can love our enemies, too.

That's easy to believe on paper, but what about in reality? Sometimes it's easier to forgive hypothetical enemies than the steady "drip drip drip" of an annoying coworker or relative. What about when family doesn't love you like you think they should? What about when God nudges you to reach out to the people you like least? What about when you feel abandoned or surrounded by naysayers?

Joseph, Jonah, Daniel, and Nehemiah faced all sorts of different challenges. Joseph exhibited an astonishing ability to overcome betrayal from people who should have cared for him. Jonah was the opposite case! He was tasked to preach God's compassion, but he clearly didn't understand it himself. Daniel dealt with faithfulness in exile, and Nehemiah with the challenge of leading in a hostile environment.

All of these figures realized in one way or another that loving others starts with loving God, but also that loving God must be accompanied by loving others.

JOSEPH'S FAMILY TRAUMA

What to Do When Every Institution Fails You

Genesis 37–50

We have all walked through seasons that are confusing, trying, even infuriating. Each time we manage to pull ourselves back together, another unexpected (and unwelcome) wave comes crashing over our lives—washing away the progress we've made at building stability, joy, or meaning. I've had times when I was grasping for peace or safety, only to be thrown off balance yet again. We wouldn't be human if we didn't wonder what God was up to. It's an eye-opening experience to see in hindsight how circumstances were being woven together in a way that eventually makes sense. But some of those answers won't come this side of heaven. Whether we get the "why" during this lifetime or not, the Old Testament gives us a model of how to walk faithfully through the storms of life: Joseph.

One of the most well-known verses associated with this humble, faithful man is one that believers often cling to when injustice rears its ugly head.

> You intended to harm me, but God intended it for good . . .
>
> Genesis 50:20

Joseph had an incredible response to suffering, born from a soul full of forgiveness and graciousness. Joseph's words in Genesis 50:20 followed years of unjust punishment and false accusations, and they were spoken to the very men who nearly cost Joseph his life—his own brothers. Time and again, the institutions—family, friends, the law—that should have protected Joseph . . . didn't. One by one they failed him. Is God sovereign over all things? Yes, but He was already miles ahead of Joseph on his journey and *intended it all for good*.

If you've been betrayed in any way, you've gotten a taste of Joseph's early life. If that came at the hands of your own family or people you trusted, it cuts straight to your soul in a different way. So what happens when you're repeatedly asked to turn the other cheek? The truly miraculous part of Joseph's story is not that he survived betrayal and suffering but that he didn't let it poison his faith in God and honorable view of authority. Instead of becoming bitter, Joseph trusted God and overcame the unfaithfulness of others—modeling what true fatherhood, brotherhood, and leadership look like.

Sins of the Father

Where young Joseph started and where he ended up are beautiful bookends, but the tragedy and pain in between those mountaintops is a valley of gut punches that must have seemed unfair—even cruel—at the time they landed. Keep in mind, he was born into a dysfunctional family. Don't you love how the Bible doesn't sugarcoat some of its most famous families? Joseph's father was Jacob. He's known for a lot of things, including teaming up with his mother to deceive his dying father, Isaac, into giving him the birthright that belonged to his older twin brother, Esau. Jacob got a taste of his own medicine when his future father-in-law gave him not the bride he'd been so enamored of that he worked for seven years to earn her hand—but her older sister, whom Jacob had shown zero interest in. Once again, Jacob had tried to upend the rightful order of things, breaching custom by asking to marry the younger sister while the older remained single. Having been tricked into marrying Leah, Jacob then had to commit to another seven years of labor in order to marry her younger sister, Rachel. My heart breaks wondering if Leah constantly felt like a second-class citizen. Yet her grief at being unloved by her husband was tempered by the fact that God had given her the most socially important thing for a woman in her era—the ability to have children. Leah bore many sons for Jacob, while Rachel despaired about having none. The two sisters had a war of wills, pushing Jacob even to sleep with their servant girls so they could have proxy children in their quest to become top mother. Eventually, Rachel had a child of her own, Joseph; then she died in childbirth with her second son, Benjamin.

The fallout of this tangle of relationships, lies, and bitterness landed on the children. Joseph was the golden boy, the first son of the favorite wife. It was no secret that Joseph was the preferred son of Jacob, whose name had been changed to Israel following a divine wrestling match (Genesis 32:28).

> Now Israel loved Joseph more than any of his other sons, because he had been born to him in his old age; and he made an ornate robe for him. When his brothers saw that their father loved him more than any of them, they hated him and could not speak a kind word to him.
>
> Genesis 37:3–4

Hated him. Their father even had a special garment made for Joseph, often referred to as a coat of many colors. What was Jacob thinking? Did he think his affection for Joseph, as proclaimed by this costly garment, would spill over into the hearts of the rest of his family? Did he think they'd be impressed by how handsome Joseph looked in a princely garment? All Joseph's older half-brothers were not only unimpressed, but downright hostile. After all, who wouldn't be? Joseph was their younger brother, but he was being treated with all the honor of a firstborn. And it appears Joseph also couldn't read the room.

> Joseph had a dream, and when he told it to his brothers, they hated him all the more. He said to them, "Listen to this dream I had: We were binding sheaves of grain out in the field when suddenly my sheaf rose and stood upright, while your sheaves gathered around mine and bowed down to it."
>
> His brothers said to him, "Do you intend to reign over us? Will you actually rule us?" And they hated him all the more because of his dream and what he had said.
>
> Then he had another dream, and he told it to his brothers. "Listen," he said, "I had another dream, and this time the sun and moon and eleven stars were bowing down to me."
>
> When he told his father as well as his brothers, his father rebuked him and said, "What is this dream you had? Will your mother and I and your brothers actually come and bow down to the ground before you?" His brothers were jealous of him, but his father kept the matter in mind.
>
> Genesis 37:5–11

I have always struggled to understand why Joseph would share these dreams with his jealous siblings. Was he so unaware of their disdain for him? Did the security of his father's favoritism blind him to his brothers' anger? I picture him as sort of an Old Testament Elle Woods in *Legally Blonde*, showing up perky and positive—expecting everyone to be happy to see him and hear about his dreams. Spoiler alert: They weren't.

Am I My Brother's Keeper?

As you'll see later in Joseph's story, he had a God-given gift for interpreting dreams. Yet we don't see him deciphering what these dreams he shared with his family meant—it's not clear that he understood they were predictions not just of an overturned family hierarchy but of his family's eventual salvation. Did he somehow know and yet keep it close to the vest? Scripture does not indicate that he did. It seems he'd be eager to share the knowledge. Could he have possibly imagined all the suffering and struggle that would come into his life before those dreams ever came to fruition?

In any case, his older half-brothers were fed up. One day, while the older brothers were off tending their father's flocks, Jacob decided to send Joseph to go to them and then bring back a report. Scholars say the journey was likely more than sixty miles each way, and Joseph was just a teenager at the time. Once before, Joseph had taken a bad report about some of his older brothers back to his father (Genesis 37:2). After that, I imagine his brothers felt every visit from Joseph was like having a hall monitor come see what they were doing, so he could go back to rat them out. It was much more than sibling irritation at that point.

> But they saw him in the distance, and before he reached them, they plotted to kill him.

> "Here comes that dreamer!" they said to each other. "Come now, let's kill him and throw him into one of these cisterns and say that a ferocious animal devoured him. Then we'll see what comes of his dreams."
>
> Genesis 37:18–20

His oldest brother, Reuben—unlike the others—seemed to have a conscience. But his intervention still left plenty of room for Joseph to be in danger. Reuben cooked up a plan to let his brothers throw Joseph into a pit, then Reuben would return later and get the favored son home safely. It's as if Reuben was taking on his father's habit of lying. He was willing to misdirect his brothers but not fully mislead them. (We see elsewhere in the story, in Genesis 35, that Reuben destroyed his standing as the firstborn by having an affair with his father's concubine, Bilhah, who was the mother of two of his brothers. No wonder he didn't feel popular enough to challenge the others!)

Still, Reuben deserves credit for planning to save the brother who'd supplanted him as the favored son. But before he could rescue Joseph, his brothers had sold the teenage boy into slavery to a traveling caravan (Genesis 37:28). They willingly handed their brother over to the Ishmaelites, the descendants of Ishmael, the son of Abraham and Hagar (see Genesis 16:15), and the Midianites, the descendants of Midian, the son of Abraham and Keturah (Genesis 25:2). Joseph was triply betrayed! His middle brothers threw him into a pit. His oldest brother failed to lead the others. And his distant cousins willingly accepted payment to take Joseph to slavery in Egypt.

What a shock this must have been to Joseph's system. He was dutifully on the assignment his father had given him, wearing his special coat, and living as the favored son—secure and confident.

Suddenly, this teenager was betrayed by his own family and dragged off to a foreign land as a captive.

Reuben was outraged when he returned and realized Joseph was gone. But he was still willing to join his brothers' wicked plot when his younger brother, Judah, cooked up a lie that would crush their father's heart. They took Joseph's special robe, dipped it in the blood of a goat they'd slaughtered, then took it home to let Jacob's mind run wild. He was inconsolable, devastated. These men were so jealous and evil that they made a decision they knew would wreck their father's life. At what point did any of them begin to feel the weight of guilt from what they'd done? Even if any of them wavered, he could hardly confess that Joseph was now in a far-off land in bondage. In their mind, being a slave in Egypt was practically the same thing as being dead. What good would it do Jacob to know the truth?

But they were wrong. Even though the circumstances of his exile were difficult, it didn't take Joseph long to flourish in Egypt.

An Orphan in Egypt

Joseph was sold as a slave to Potiphar, an officer of Pharaoh and captain of the guards.

> The LORD was with Joseph so that he prospered, and he lived in the house of his Egyptian master. When his master saw that the LORD was with him and that the LORD gave him success in everything he did, Joseph found favor in his eyes and became his attendant. Potiphar put him in charge of his household, and he entrusted to his care everything he owned. From the time he put him in charge of his household and of all that he owned, the LORD blessed the household of the Egyp-

tian because of Joseph. The blessing of the LORD was on everything Potiphar had, both in the house and in the field. So Potiphar left everything he had in Joseph's care; with Joseph in charge, he did not concern himself with anything except the food he ate.

Genesis 39:2–6

Scripture never mentions Joseph attempting to escape or trying to make his case about how unjust his situation was. Instead, we see a young man so committed to living with integrity that his master trusted him implicitly. God was with him, and others could see it. The Lord was glorified by Joseph's humility and virtue. Joseph was an example of Paul's later command:

> Do everything without grumbling or arguing, so that you may become blameless and pure, "children of God without fault in a warped and crooked generation." Then you will shine among them like stars in the sky as you hold firmly to the word of life.

Philippians 2:14–16

Time and again, despite his circumstances, Joseph did shine like a star. Even as he traveled a road of hardship and mistreatment, he was witnessing God's goodness. The people around him in Egypt who didn't share his beliefs were still moved by his character. No doubt the Lord allowed them to see His favor on Joseph.

I'm human; when I'm stuck in a situation far from the path I'd imagined for myself, it's easy to slip into a critical, ungrateful posture. We'll all walk through those valleys. Struggling with infertility while attending your third baby shower of the summer? Forced to watch the promotion you worked for go to a backstabbing coworker? Discouraged because the healing you've prayed for—for yourself or someone you love—isn't happening? What the enemy means for evil, God means for good. Your loving heavenly Father is absolutely aware of every single thing you have—and will—walk through.

I would never have chosen to struggle through years of excruciating pain, but boy, did that experience make me more empathetic! It also opened so many doors for me to share my faith and a testimony of God's goodness. The enemy definitely used my health issues to drive me to despair, but surprising silver linings still materialize from that dark season. Just this week, I got an email from a woman who is struggling with the same physical issue, and it truly blessed me to pray for and encourage her and to talk through treatment options. I desperately needed a lifeline during that time in my life, and I'm grateful God now allows me to be that to others.

Joseph made the best of each situation he was dragged into. It was through his faithfulness that Potiphar's life was blessed. But Potiphar wasn't the only one who admired Joseph; his wife also did—but for very different reasons. Scripture tells us that Joseph was "well built and handsome" (Genesis 39:6), and his master's wife noticed. She repeatedly tried to seduce him, and each time Joseph refused her advances.

> "With me in charge," he told her, "my master does not concern himself with anything in the house; everything he owns he has entrusted to my care. No one is greater in this house than I am. My master has withheld nothing from me except

you, because you are his wife. How then could I do such a wicked thing and sin against God?"

Genesis 39:8–9

Joseph was committed to honoring not only his earthly master but also his heavenly One. Even though he'd been despised by his brothers and sold into a life of slavery in a foreign land, Joseph remained steadfast in his faithfulness to the Lord. Unlike his older brother Reuben, he didn't jump at a chance to subvert authority and have an affair.

Despite Joseph's repeated refusals of her advances, Potiphar's wife didn't give up. One day after she'd grabbed his garment, Joseph literally ran from her—leaving his cloak behind (Genesis 39:12). Note: This is how we should respond to any temptation that threatens to make us cave. Don't stay and argue; don't try to use logic—get away.

Potiphar's wife didn't take the rejection well. Instead, she tried to act as if Joseph was the one who'd attacked her. Once again, Joseph had been serving with humility and integrity—favored by the head of the household—when someone else abused their power in order to betray him. He was about to be thrown in jail for a crime he didn't commit.

It's interesting to note that Joseph likely could have been executed based on the false accusations. Did Potiphar, knowing the man of integrity that Joseph was, have some doubts about his wife's version of events? Whatever the reality, Joseph was sent to a prison specifically for Pharaoh's prisoners (Genesis 39:20). Even there, God was still directing Joseph's steps. And even when everything in his life was sending him the message that obedience and righteousness would do him no good, Joseph showed great character, because the Lord had chosen him.

> ... the LORD was with him; he showed him kindness and granted him favor in the eyes of the prison warden. So the warden put Joseph in charge of all those held in the prison, and he was made responsible for all that was done there. The warden paid no attention to anything under Joseph's care, because the LORD was with Joseph and gave him success in whatever he did.
>
> Genesis 39:21–23

Light in the Dark; Wisdom in a Prison

Joseph had been knocked down, yet he was still so trustworthy that he was put in charge of the prison holding him captive. Joseph showed up with excellence, dedicated to honoring God regardless of the unfair circumstances that had stolen years of his young life.

He was eventually joined in that prison by Pharaoh's chief cupbearer and top baker. We don't know the circumstances of how those two men wound up there, but we know they were in custody "for some time" (Genesis 40:4)—and also that Joseph had been assigned to attend to them. Yet another puzzle piece fell into place, something that wouldn't have seemed significant at the time, but it was critical to saving God's chosen people—and eventually the world.

One night, both the cupbearer and baker had dreams that troubled them. Joseph saw their distress the next day and asked about their sadness. That's something he could have easily ignored. *I shouldn't even be here; who cares about why someone else is having a rough day?* But Joseph was a Colossians 3 kind of guy:

> Whatever you do, work at it with all your heart, as working for the Lord, not for human masters, since you know that you will receive an inheritance from the Lord as a reward. It is the Lord Christ you are serving.
>
> Colossians 3:23–24

Joseph offered to interpret their dreams, all the while pointing to God as the source of the information. He had good news for the cupbearer; the man would be restored to his position.

> But when all goes well with you, remember me and show me kindness; mention me to Pharaoh and get me out of this prison.
>
> Genesis 40:14

Look back just a bit to that earlier passage, when the Scripture said the Lord showed "kindness" to Joseph (Genesis 39:21): the Hebrew word is *hesed*, a common term that is better translated as lovingkindness, steadfast love, or a covenantal obligation. Bible teacher Michael Card translates *hesed* to mean "When the person from whom I have a right to expect nothing gives me everything." It's almost always about God's steadfast love, but Joseph uses the same word to ask the cupbearer to return his kindness.

Joseph's interpretation of the cupbearer's dream was spot-on, yet when that man was returned to his position and welcomed back into the palace, he did nothing to plead Joseph's case. "He forgot him" (Genesis 40:23), neglecting to show Joseph *hesed* in response to his good deed. By the way, the baker's dream had a totally different outcome. Just as Joseph predicted, he died just days later (Genesis 40:22).

Two years went by, and Joseph remained stuck in prison. Did he pray that God would explain why—despite his fidelity—he was an innocent prisoner held in a foreign dungeon far from his adoring father and previously comfortable life? It would have been human to feel frustration, even abandonment. The Bible is full of people who cried out, sometimes in anger, when they couldn't see God's hand working through their circumstances. He can take our questions, our grief, our anger. Ultimately, though, faith is about accepting that there is always more happening than we can discern in the moment.

> "Whom did the LORD consult to enlighten him,
> and who taught him the right way?
> Who was it that taught him knowledge,
> or showed him the path of understanding?"
>
> Isaiah 40:14

> "Who has known the mind of the Lord?
> Or who has been his counselor?"
>
> Romans 11:34

> "God is exalted in his power.
> Who is a teacher like him?
> Who has prescribed his ways for him,
> or said to him, 'You have done wrong'?"
>
> Job 36:22–23

The threads of Joseph's story were weaving together in God's perfect tapestry. He was never forgotten. The Lord was always aware and in control. The years the locusts had stolen would be restored (Joel 2:25). When people fail us, over and over again, it can be difficult to keep trusting that goodness is possible. But Joseph understood that even when human beings' steadfast love runs dry, God's love never will. This understanding was undergirded by his habit of gratitude, consistently crediting the Lord when others praised him. It's easier to resist our tendency to take God's goodness for granted when we make a habit of thanking Him.

From a Cell to a Palace

Joseph's gift from God, the ability to interpret dreams, was about to get him called up to the big leagues. Pharaoh had a pair of dreams so troubling that he called in every magician and wise man in Egypt. Not a single one could figure out what the king's dreams, filled with cows and grain, could possibly mean. Finally, the cupbearer who had been in prison with Joseph remembered the young Hebrew's divine gifts. Pharaoh immediately sent for Joseph, who cleaned up and rushed to be of service.

> Pharaoh said to Joseph, "I had a dream, and no one can interpret it. But I have heard it said of you that when you hear a dream you can interpret it."
> "I cannot do it," Joseph replied to Pharaoh, "but God will give Pharaoh the answer he desires."
>
> Genesis 41:15–16

Could this finally be Joseph's ticket to freedom? Following years of injustice, instead of blurting out his case, Joseph humbly pointed the glory to God.

Pharaoh related the dreams to Joseph in great detail. As he began to interpret them, Joseph was deeply respectful, but repeatedly said it was God who was revealing the truth. Not only was Joseph able to tell Pharaoh that Egypt would have a time of plenty followed by seven years of famine, but he also instructed Pharaoh on how to make sure that the Egyptian people would be sustained during that difficult season. We're so used to picturing teenage Joseph that it can be easy to forget that by this time, he was a thirty-year-old man (Genesis 41:46), scrubbed up but still calloused by years of prison. Between his handsome face, calm demeanor, and supernatural insight, he must have seemed like an irresistible charismatic authority to a privileged Egyptian king who'd never faced such hardship.

> So Pharaoh asked them, "Can we find anyone like this man, one in whom is the spirit of God?"
>
> Then Pharaoh said to Joseph, "Since God has made all this known to you, there is no one so discerning and wise as you. You shall be in charge of my palace, and all my people are to submit to your orders. Only with respect to the throne will I be greater than you."
>
> So Pharaoh said to Joseph, "I hereby put you in charge of the whole land of Egypt." Then Pharaoh took his signet ring from his finger and put it on Joseph's finger. He dressed him in robes of fine linen and put a gold chain around his neck. He had him ride in a chariot as his second-in-command, and people shouted before him, "Make way!" Thus he put him in charge of the whole land of Egypt.

> Then Pharaoh said to Joseph, "I am Pharaoh, but without your word no one will lift hand or foot in all Egypt."
>
> Genesis 41:38–44

Hold the phone! Joseph went from the prison to the palace in a matter of hours. He wasn't just freed from captivity, he was exalted to the highest echelons of Egyptian society and power after spending years behind bars, falsely accused of attempted sexual assault. This man, who never stopped serving in quiet humility, had basically been given the keys to the kingdom in one fell swoop. Later, Joseph described his elevated position as his becoming "a father to Pharaoh" (Genesis 45:8). Throughout his story, we see Joseph becoming the patriarch his brothers couldn't be. And here, in advising the king, Joseph became a more righteous father than he himself had known.

But as glorious as this turn of events is, in many ways it's just the beginning of Joseph's story. Not only had Joseph been vindicated, but God was also positioning him (as He had all along) to be right where He needed Joseph to be to save His people.

Would the True Firstborn Stand Up?

Joseph's interpretations of the king's dreams came true. He wisely stewarded the abundance during the seven good years and made sure Egypt was fully prepared for the seven years of famine that followed.

> When all Egypt began to feel the famine, the people cried to Pharaoh for food. Then Pharaoh told all the Egyptians, "Go to Joseph and do what he tells you."

> When the famine had spread over the whole country, Joseph opened all the storehouses and sold grain to the Egyptians, for the famine was severe throughout Egypt.
>
> Genesis 41:55–56

The very next verse signals to us just how interesting this story is about to get. It wasn't just the Egyptian people coming to Joseph for help, but people of "all the world" (Genesis 41:57). So the very sons of Jacob who once plotted to kill their brother Joseph were about to need him to save their lives.

Joseph was thirty years old when he went into service for Pharaoh, so he was at least thirty-nine at this point—meaning he hadn't seen his brothers for twenty-two years. Like everyone else in the surrounding areas, Jacob and his household were beginning to suffer from the famine. When Jacob heard there was grain in Egypt, he sent his sons to get some for their families. He sent the ten older sons, but he kept his youngest son, Benjamin, at home. Remember, Benjamin was the only remaining son of Jacob's beloved late wife, Rachel. Off to Egypt the other brothers went.

> Now Joseph was the governor of the land, the person who sold grain to all its people. So when Joseph's brothers arrived, they bowed down to him with their faces to the ground.
>
> Genesis 42:6

Joseph must have been stunned to see his brothers. As his brothers bowed to him, the dreams that nearly got Joseph killed decades earlier were finally coming true. Remember their sneering: *Do you intend to reign over us? Will you actually rule us?* His jealous, scheming brothers were now at his mercy. They didn't recognize the teenager they'd mocked and sold into slavery as the wise, respected, powerful ruler who held their lives in his hands. But Joseph most certainly recognized them.

It's in these interactions we begin to see a different side to Joseph—one who suffered years of heartbreak. His anger was justified. Who *would* trust this pack of scoundrels? He didn't let them off easily. Instead, he accused his brothers of being spies and asked about their family. He learned his father Jacob was alive, along with his younger brother, Benjamin.

Joseph had his brothers imprisoned for three days, then he made a deal. He kept Simeon and said he'd only be released if the brothers went back home and returned to Egypt with Benjamin. Joseph's plan was purportedly about the brother disproving the claim that they'd only come as spies.

And this was when Joseph first heard part of the *other* side of the story. For all he knew up until this point, his brothers were comfortable with what they'd done to him all those years ago. But then he overheard them speaking in Hebrew, wondering whether this calamity was happening to them because of their cruelty to Joseph. They spoke of how "distressed" Joseph had been, and how their current "distress" must be God's divine karma, repaying to them what they deserved (Genesis 42:21).

Reuben, who'd tried to save Joseph from that pit his brothers had thrown him into, spoke up.

> "Didn't I tell you not to sin against the boy? But you wouldn't listen! Now we must give an accounting for his blood."
>
> Genesis 42:22

Such an amazing nugget in the very next verse: "They did not realize Joseph could understand them, since he was using an interpreter" (Genesis 42:23). We're told Joseph turned away from them to weep, and then he had Simeon essentially taken hostage, in a sense "kidnapping" one of the brothers who had kidnapped him.

The brothers left in great dismay. What a disaster! But a strange one—for once on the road, they discovered their silver was in their bags. Joseph had sent them away with plenty of grain—and secretly had the silver they'd brought as payment returned to their bags. He also gave them provisions for their journey. Despite Joseph's mistrust and hurt, he still treated them with *hesed*. But their own guilty consciences made Joseph's kindness seem sinister to them.

> Their hearts sank and they turned to each other trembling and said, "What is this that God has done to us?"
>
> Genesis 42:28

Guilt is a powerful and oppressive thing. It can poison our instincts as much as betrayal does and make us view everyone as untrustworthy. I wonder if the brothers had spoken of Joseph over the years, or if they'd buried any acknowledgment of their horrible sin after seeing how the loss of Joseph had nearly destroyed Jacob? They were in a world of trouble (or so they thought), and they knew asking Jacob to let them take Benjamin back to Egypt was not going to go over well.

The brothers returned home and told their father about the silver that had somehow found its way back into their bags, and that made Jacob afraid, too. As they argued over taking Benjamin back, Jacob reminded them he'd already lost Joseph, and Simeon was being held captive, too. Despite Reuben's offer of his son's lives as a pledge for Benjamin's safety, Jacob wouldn't trust his firstborn to complete the task.

This created a stalemate. The brothers didn't immediately head back to Egypt. They first used up the grain they'd bought on that initial trip. During that time, did Simeon, who'd been in on the plot against Joseph, fear he'd never leave the Egyptian prison? Was Joseph keeping tabs on him while he languished there?

Judah's Redemption

When they finally ran out of food, Judah stepped up to the plate with a different sort of promise. He made a vow to his father to be *personally* responsible for Benjamin—believing the only way he'd be able to get grain for all of them was to have their youngest brother with them when they approached Joseph again. Jacob made sure they didn't go empty-handed. He sent them with all the best items from their land and twice the silver they'd taken the first time around.

When Joseph saw that his brothers had returned with Benjamin, he ordered a great feast for all of them at his home. But the brothers were skeptical, still unaware that Joseph was their brother and worried that the silver planted in their bags for their first trip home was a cover to now have them overpowered and forced into slavery. How ironic! The very thing they'd done to Joseph had become their own worst fear. But again, they were not repaid in kind. What they got instead of revenge was the return of Simeon and a lavish banquet. Twice more during this interaction, the brothers bowed to Joseph, as he had dreamed (Genesis 43:26, 28). But none of that mattered to Joseph; it was when he saw his beloved younger brother, Benjamin, that he was "deeply moved" and left them so his tears wouldn't give him away (Genesis 43:30).

After their feast, Joseph once again instructed his staff to send his brothers away with all the food they could take—along with the double portion of silver they'd brought. But that wasn't all. Joseph also had them tuck his silver goblet into Benjamin's bag. Once they left, he sent his steward after them to confront them about "stealing" the valuable cup. They immediately denied they would ever repay Joseph's kindness with disrespect and theft. Obviously, Joseph knew the truth—but he was also testing his brothers to see if they were changed men. After all, they *had* once repaid kindness with cruelty. Now it was time to see if they'd do the same again.

The stage was set for the final test. As the brothers begged for mercy, Joseph offered a deal. He told them they could all leave—as long as they left Benjamin behind. Would they save themselves by tossing off their youngest brother, as they had so easily done to Joseph decades before? Once again, as in the initial cover-up of Joseph's kidnapping, it was Judah who spoke up. But this time, his actions were very different. Judah tried to make their case, explaining how much Jacob loved Benjamin.

> "So now, if the boy is not with us when I go back to your servant my father, and if my father, whose life is closely bound up with the boy's life, sees that the boy isn't there, he will die. . . .
>
> "Now then, please let your servant remain here as my lord's slave in place of the boy, and let the boy return with his brothers. How can I go back to my father if the boy is not with me? No! Do not let me see the misery that would come on my father."
>
> Genesis 44:30–31, 33–34

How indeed? Judah knew *exactly* how devastated his father would be, because he'd witnessed that very thing twenty years earlier. At the hands of his own deception, Judah had ripped out Jacob's heart—watching as he fell apart, believing that Joseph was dead. Now, he advocated for his father and for his innocent young brother. He did what he should have done in the first place.

Joseph could see that the brothers had no intention of letting that scene repeat with Benjamin. Judah himself offered to stay instead—giving up his own life. That was the final straw. Joseph finally broke down, sending away his household staff and dropping the biggest reveal of all time.

> Joseph said to his brothers, "I am Joseph! Is my father still living?" But his brothers were not able to answer him, because they were terrified at his presence.
>
> Genesis 45:3

I'll bet!

> Then Joseph said to his brothers, "Come close to me." When they had done so, he said, "I am your brother Joseph, the one you sold into Egypt! And now, do not be distressed and do not be angry with yourselves for selling me here, because it was to save lives that God sent me ahead of you. For two years now there has been famine in the land, and for the next five years there will be no plowing and reaping. But God sent me ahead of you to preserve for you a remnant on earth and to save your lives by a great deliverance.

"So then, it was not you who sent me here, but God. He made me father to Pharaoh, lord of his entire household and ruler of all Egypt."

Genesis 45:4–8

Did their knees buckle? Did anyone faint? I hope when we get to heaven, the Lord will show this scene on movie night! *What you meant for evil, God meant for good! It isn't your fault; God sent me here.*

Rather than blast them with the revenge they deserved, Joseph rejoiced that the horrible thing they had done to him had put him in a position to save their entire family, which would flourish into the nation of Israel. No executing or jailing them. No speech exposing their evil and drenching them in shame. Just celebration—joy that he was perfectly situated to save them all. The years of slavery and jail and false accusations were all wiped away with the realization that his father was alive and he had the God-given power to save them all. He even included, *Don't beat yourselves up.*

Joseph urged his brothers to go back home and then return to Egypt with the whole family, giving them the land of Goshen in which to settle and multiply.

Then he threw his arms around his brother Benjamin and wept, and Benjamin embraced him, weeping. And he kissed all his brothers and wept over them. Afterward his brothers talked with him.

Genesis 45:14–15

That Pharaoh was apparently overjoyed for Joseph's family shows the bond of affection that had grown between the two leaders, based in large part on Joseph's continued integrity despite the many betrayals he'd suffered. An Egyptian moving company was sent to go get everyone. The caravan included animals, gifts, food, and provisions. Joseph watched as they left.

> Then he sent his brothers away, and as they were leaving he said to them, "Don't quarrel on the way!"
>
> Genesis 45:24

That verse makes me chuckle. But what a conversation they probably had on the way back. Not only would they be able to return with Benjamin and Simeon safe, but they also had fantastic provisions and the promise of a valuable piece of land where they could resettle and thrive. There was a problem, though . . . how were they going to explain to Jacob how Joseph ended up as the number two in command of Egypt? Did they ever confess to Jacob what they'd done, or did he simply believe Joseph had been kidnapped while on his way to see his brothers in the fields? It's one of the mysteries Scripture doesn't explicitly resolve for us.

It does give us a beautiful glimpse into Joseph and Jacob's reunion, though.

> As soon as Joseph appeared before him, he threw his arms around his father and wept for a long time.
>
> Israel said to Joseph, "Now I am ready to die, since I have seen for myself that you are still alive."
>
> Genesis 46:29–30

Jacob spent seventeen more years in Egypt, reunited with Joseph and continuing to watch his family grow. And when his life came to an end, he made Joseph promise to carry his bones to be buried where his "fathers" were—not in Egypt. Joseph made good on that vow, and later asked that, following his own death, his bones would eventually wind up in the promised land (Genesis 50:25).

What a life of honor Joseph led. Despite losing his freedom, a false attack on his character, and being tossed aside by someone with the power to advocate for his release, he continued to exalt and trust his heavenly Father. He also broke the cycle of betrayal in his family. Every time an authority failed him, Joseph continued to trust that the ultimate Authority would not. Every time his integrity was repaid with cruelty, he continued to serve others, drawing from what God had given him. Even in the final test of Joseph's trust, he unconditionally forgave the ones who had betrayed him, and in the process, became the faithful, loving brother that he'd never experienced.

Joseph's story is a powerful picture of Jesus, the ultimate Savior to come. They both served their fathers faithfully, watching over their sheep. They were both subjected to false accusations and condemned as criminals. After a time of suffering, each was exalted. And that resulted in them being in a position to save others. What misguided, mortal men did to them, God used to bring about salvation. In preserving the nation of Israel through Joseph, the Lord made sure that Jesus the Messiah would one day arrive to offer salvation to every precious soul God will ever create—to those who will accept.

God isn't ever the source of evil, but He can use it. So the next time you're caught in the trap of injustice, don't be afraid to ask Him what He's up to. He knows we need His help to keep going when the path ahead is shrouded in uncertainty. He may not immediately shine a spotlight onto all that lies ahead, but we can trust that He is working all things for good to those who love Him and are called according to His purpose (Romans 8:28).

Study Questions

1. Have trusted relationships or institutions failed you? How did that impact your ability to love, trust, and serve others?
2. How do you tend to react when undermined or abandoned by someone you trusted to have your back? Has that experience ever prompted you to lean even more deeply into your heavenly Father's unconditional love?
3. What principles can you take from Joseph's consistent willingness to serve faithfully in an unjust or unpleasant situation?
4. Have you ever wondered what God is up to when your life seems to be much more different than you planned? Were you able to see in hindsight how He was working at the time?
5. Where have you seen *hesed* in action in your life? How can you practice it with others?

JONAH'S ANGER

Loving People When You Just Don't Feel Like It

Jonah 1–4

Jonah is one of the myriad stories in the Bible that we—in modern times—are able to look at with the benefit of thousands of years of hindsight. Frankly, I can catch myself being pretty darn judgy toward the prophet Jonah. God gave him a clear directive, but instead of obeying, Jonah turned and ran in the opposite direction—away from what God had called him to. *How dare he!?* But the truth is, there's plenty in Jonah's story that applies to me—and may apply to you, too. And there's so much more to it!

Running from God

Like many other key stories in Scripture, Jonah's isn't a perfect fairy tale. It's full of disobedience, whining, and ultimately—redemption. But this prophet sure took the long way around to getting there. This is a man who said he worshiped God, and that may have been true—but he certainly wasn't *following* Him. Was he motivated by fear for his own life, or was Jonah driven more by his own prejudice that made him unwilling to go and extend the message of God's mercy to people he believed were less deserving than he himself was? Let's unpack it.

> The word of the LORD came to Jonah son of Amittai: "Go to the great city of Nineveh and preach against it, because its wickedness has come up before me."
>
> Jonah 1:1–2

God's command was pretty straightforward: *Nineveh is evil; go share My message with them.* The Bible doesn't record any type of answer from Jonah, no arguing or attempts at persuasion. Instead, he bolted.

> But Jonah ran away from the LORD and headed for Tarshish. He went down to Joppa, where he found a ship bound for that port. After paying the fare, he went aboard and sailed for Tarshish to flee from the LORD.
>
> Jonah 1:3–4

Heading in that direction would have sent Jonah traveling east, probably around 500 miles or so. Where did he go instead of Nineveh? If you believe, as most scholars do, that Tarshish was in modern-day Spain—Jonah was headed roughly 2,500 miles to the west. It's probably about as far as he could have planned to go at that time—the end of the known world.

He wasn't just putting distance between himself and God's mission. He was also figuring out an elaborate way to procrastinate. The ships that carried trading goods to and from Tarshish were renowned as long-distance vessels, sailing for years at a time. They were so famous that in those days any big, long-distance ship was often called a "ship of Tarshish." It was a specific brand! Jonah probably thought he'd placed his bet on a sure thing, moving himself in time *and* space away from God's intention.

But why was he betting against God in the first place? There were likely many reasons Jonah decided not only to disobey the Lord's order but also to defy it in every way possible. Nineveh was a major city in the Assyrian Empire, and the Assyrians were brutal people. I almost hesitate to include the accounts of what the Assyrians did to those they conquered, but it's important context for understanding how Jonah felt about them. Warning, it's not for the squeamish.

According to historical records and images of artwork reviewed by the Center for Online Judaic Studies, here's a bit of what the Assyrians celebrated:

- Cutting off the limbs, noses, and ears of troops that had been captured
- Gouging out their eyes
- Hanging decapitated heads on trees around a defeated city
- Impaling captives, ripping out their tongues or skinning them alive

It's grisly, wicked stuff. And maybe we can better comprehend why Jonah wanted nothing to do with going to preach to Nineveh. A generation before Jonah, one such brutal Assyrian king had attacked Israel during the days of King Ahab, according to a recording of the battle on an Assyrian monolith. While the Assyrians didn't conquer the country, the Israelites would have remembered and resented their brutality. Given this context, who wouldn't *want* to run away from what these barbarous people were capable of?

Jonah's actions demonstrate how easy it is to fall into disobedience. If you are intent on shunning God and fleeing from His directions, the enemy will make it as easy as possible for you. How he delights in seeing the faithful lose their nerve, even openly defy God. But the flip side of that is true as well. Our Father specializes in giving us divine assistance in our struggle.

> And God is faithful; he will not let you be tempted beyond what you can bear. But when you are tempted, he will also provide a way out so that you can endure it.
>
> 1 Corinthians 10:13

Jonah caught a ride with the enemy instead. But, as we'll see later, it may not have been fear of what the Assyrians could do to him—but fear that they would actually repent and share in God's mercy—that may have motivated Jonah.

Here's the thing: God didn't ask Jonah's opinion. He desires that *all* be redeemed, including those we can easily identify as evil. It's likely Jonah saw himself as superior to the people he'd been called to minister to. But we all have an equal need for God's mercy. Just a single sin separates us from His holiness, which Jonah knew, but he hadn't connected the dots to realize that humanity's shared status of separation means each one of us needs saving. And God doesn't hang out a "do not enter" sign for the worst of the worst.

> The Lord is gracious and compassionate,
> slow to anger and rich in love.
> The Lord is good to all;
> he has compassion on all he has made.
>
> Psalm 145:8–9

JONAH'S ANGER

Like others before him, Jonah had made the fatal mistake of replacing God with a false image of his own imagination—an abstract idol who lacked the compassion that is deep in the Lord's heart. He should have considered the words of the prophet Ezekiel, who had said:

> "Say to them, 'As surely as I live, declares the Sovereign LORD, I take no pleasure in the death of the wicked, but rather that they turn from their ways and live.'"
>
> Ezekiel 33:11

On the other hand, as we'll see later, the problem might not be that Jonah had mistaken the Lord as dispassionate, but that he was worried God *was* compassionate toward the "wrong" people. Let's read on.

The Lord had plans, and he wasn't going to let Jonah simply slink off into the setting sun.

> Then the LORD sent a great wind on the sea, and such a violent storm arose that the ship threatened to break up. All the sailors were afraid and each cried out to his own god. And they threw the cargo into the sea to lighten the ship.
> But Jonah had gone below deck, where he lay down and fell into a deep sleep. The captain went to him and said, "How can you sleep? Get up and call on your god! Maybe he will take notice of us so that we will not perish."
>
> Jonah 1:4–6

A Storm of Judgment

Several things are going on in this passage. A massive storm erupts and rattles (almost) everyone to their core. These pagan sailors were terrified and began praying to the gods they believed in. Jonah wasn't part of the prayer meeting; he was snoozing.

Was Jonah so comfortable in his disobedience and sin, actively running away from God, that he was able to casually fall "into a deep sleep"? Are there sins in our lives that have become so commonplace that we, too, are able to go on about our routines, not stopping to acknowledge that we are defying a holy God? Do we, like Jonah, think our plans are better? Do we openly rebel and wrongly assume that the path we choose for our lives will lead us to peace—even when we're opposing what our heavenly Father is telling us to do? Are we even so callous that, having secured our own eternal destiny, we're indifferent (or worse!) about the fate of others?

Interestingly, there's an echo between Jonah and Jesus—both feature in stories of being asleep in a boat, only to be woken by frightened sailors (for Jesus's version, see Matthew 8). While Jonah would need to sacrifice himself to quiet the sea, Jesus did not—He is master of the waves Himself. In both stories, God proves He is fully in control.

It wouldn't take long for his fellow passengers to find out just what Jonah was up to. Like many pagans, they were polytheists, which meant they didn't believe there was just one God, but many. You could invoke a god for every problem you might have, from the god of the sea to the god of the mountains. So naturally, the pagan sailors thought the way to handle the situation was to figure out which god was angry and how to appease him or her.

Then the sailors said to each other, "Come, let us cast lots to find out who is responsible for this calamity." They cast lots and the lot fell on Jonah. So they asked him, "Tell us, who is responsible for making all this trouble for us? What kind of work do you do? Where do you come from? What is your country? From what people are you?"

He answered, "I am a Hebrew and I worship the LORD, the God of heaven, who made the sea and the dry land."

This terrified them and they asked, "What have you done?" (They knew he was running away from the LORD, because he had already told them so.)

Jonah 1:7-10

You can see here the sailors trying to triangulate the type of being that Jonah worships by identifying his work, nationality, country, and people. But with his answer, Jonah reveals God isn't just a regional deity, but Lord of the whole earth.

There's something strange about Jonah's claim, however, that as a Hebrew, he worships "the LORD, the God of heaven, who made the sea and dry land." He's not been worshiping! Disobedience is the opposite of worship. And how can he actually believe God is omnipresent? If you believe God is really the Lord of all of heaven and earth, what would make you think you could run and hide from Him anywhere on the planet? Remember Jonah headed to Tarshish "to flee from the LORD" (Jonah 1:3). Was God not going to be with him on that trip and present in that foreign land when Jonah arrived?

Perhaps, despite his words, Jonah still thinks—or at least wants—God to be just the God of the Hebrews, and thus just the God of the land of Israel. But God makes clear throughout Scripture that He is indeed the God of the whole earth.

> For the eyes of the LORD range throughout the earth to strengthen those whose hearts are fully committed to him.
>
> 2 Chronicles 16:9

> Where can I go from your Spirit?
> Where can I flee from your presence?
> If I go up to the heavens, you are there;
> if I make my bed in the depths, you are there.
> If I rise on the wings of the dawn,
> if I settle on the far side of the sea,
> even there your hand will guide me,
> your right hand will hold me fast.
>
> Psalm 139:7–10

> [God] says, "It is too small a thing for you to be my servant to restore the tribes of Jacob and bring back those of Israel I have kept. I will also make you a light for the Gentiles, that my salvation may reach to the ends of the earth."
>
> Isaiah 49:6

Despite Jonah's defiance, God's mercy is evident throughout his journey. Even when Jonah attempted to outrun God, the pagan sailors Jonah took along for the ride came to know the Lord.

The sea was getting rougher and rougher. So they asked him, "What should we do to you to make the sea calm down for us?"

"Pick me up and throw me into the sea," he replied, "and it will become calm. I know that it is my fault that this great storm has come upon you."

Instead, the men did their best to row back to land. But they could not, for the sea grew even wilder than before. Then they cried out to the LORD, "Please, LORD, do not let us die for taking this man's life. Do not hold us accountable for killing an innocent man, for you, LORD, have done as you pleased." Then they took Jonah and threw him overboard, and the raging sea grew calm. At this the men greatly feared the LORD, and they offered a sacrifice to the LORD and made vows to him.

Jonah 1:11–16

A Human Sacrifice Averted

Even though Jonah's actions had put all their lives in danger, I love the little nugget tucked into this story that the sailors tried to get back to dry land in the midst of this raging storm so they could drop him off. Here, they were breaking from pagan habits. They rejected human sacrifice. In Romans 2:12–14, Paul says that even though pagans don't have God's law, they show that the law is written on every human heart when they follow it by instinct or feel guilty after breaking it. Here, these men were trying to obey the law of God by trying their hardest to avoid murder.

What do you make of the fact that when they tried to save Jonah, the "seas grew even wilder than before"? Jonah insisted he go overboard, but the sailors didn't toss him before begging the Lord (not their gods) not to punish them for doing it. In an instant, the storm was over, and we see those pagan sailors quickly embraced the God of Jonah—even though the prophet himself was doing the opposite! You know what happened next.

> Now the LORD provided a huge fish to swallow Jonah, and Jonah was in the belly of the fish three days and three nights.
>
> Jonah 1:17

As is so often the case in the Old Testament, the main character's story gives us a picture of Christ and the lasting rescue that would eventually come through His death and resurrection. An ancient Hebrew reader would have been struck by how Jonah was asking the sailors to act out a human sacrifice, which was a pagan ritual God commanded His people to reject. But just like God asking Abraham to sacrifice his son Isaac, this seemingly pagan ritual would ultimately be transformed by God's miraculous intervention.

That's because those stories, foreshadowing Christ, have a twist averting the human sacrifice: salvation from death. Isaac was saved when God provided a ram. Jonah will be saved when God provides a "huge fish." Which is why the final and most significant parallel of the story of Jonah with the story of Jesus is what happens once Jonah descends into the depths of the sea.

In Matthew 12, Jesus Himself outlined the parallel.

> For as Jonah was three days and three nights in the belly of the great fish, so will the Son of Man be three days and three nights in the heart of the earth. The men of Nineveh will rise

up in the judgment with this generation and condemn it, because they repented at the preaching of Jonah, and now something greater than Jonah is here.

> Matthew 12:40–41

And for good measure, He let the Pharisees that He was speaking to know that He was even more of a Savior than Jonah ever could be. Christ's admonition appears in Luke 11 as well.

> For as Jonah was a sign to the Ninevites, so also will the Son of Man be to this generation.
>
> Luke 11:30

It's because of Christ's sacrifice and payment for our debt that we can all share in the mercy that the sailors enjoyed and that God was calling Jonah to share with the Ninevites as well.

> Therefore, since we have a great high priest who has ascended into heaven, Jesus the Son of God, let us hold firmly to the faith we profess. For we do not have a high priest who is unable to empathize with our weaknesses, but we have one who has been tempted in every way, just as we are—yet he did not sin. Let us then approach God's throne of grace with confidence, so that we may receive mercy and find grace to help us in our time of need.
>
> Hebrews 4:14–16

When You're in the Fish

Even in the belly of that giant fish, Jonah was getting mercy, too. God could have easily let him perish in the violent storm. Instead, He gave the prophet some time to think.

It's amazing how quickly things can crystallize when you have nothing to do but sit and ponder what you've done wrong. This practice was definitely in my mom's playbook when I was a rambunctious kid. She believed in spankings, and I earned a few over the years. But far worse than the momentary sting on my hind end was the piercing of my heart when I knew I'd disappointed her. "Go into your room and think about what you've done. I'll be in later," she'd say. Who knows if I waited for five minutes or an hour? It felt like an eternity! Whatever foolish choice I'd made suddenly felt completely unworthy of the agony I suffered sitting in my quiet Holly Hobbie bedroom, waiting for Mom to show up. I prayed for the whole process to fast-forward so I could quickly be back in her good graces. Jonah prayed, too.

> From inside the fish Jonah prayed to the Lord his God. He said:
> "In my distress I called to the Lord,
> and he answered me.
> From deep in the realm of the dead I called for help,
> and you listened to my cry.
> You hurled me into the depths,
> into the very heart of the seas,
> and the currents swirled about me;
> all your waves and breakers
> swept over me.
> I said, 'I have been banished

from your sight;
yet I will look again
toward your holy temple.'
The engulfing waters threatened me,
the deep surrounded me;
seaweed was wrapped around my head.
To the roots of the mountains I sank down;
the earth beneath barred me in forever.
But you, LORD my God,
brought my life up from the pit.

"When my life was ebbing away,
I remembered you, LORD,
and my prayer rose to you,
to your holy temple.

"Those who cling to worthless idols
turn away from God's love for them.
But I, with shouts of grateful praise,
will sacrifice to you.
What I have vowed I will make good.
I will say, 'Salvation comes from the LORD.'"

Jonah 2:1–9

Talk about a turnaround. Jonah knew he was a goner without the Lord's intervention, and he cried out for His help. In God's mercy, He let Jonah sit safely inside that fish. What about you? What "fish" has the Lord allowed you to sit in, rather than allowing you to head down the path you were stubbornly marching toward?

I had a very difficult breakup shortly before I met my husband.

My heart felt like it had been ripped out of my chest and driven over by a monster truck—multiple times. I was crazy about the guy, but I knew I had to end it. I didn't want to. I ignored the red flags. I dug in my heels. And then a couple of things happened that were so painful I felt like God was allowing me to be completely miserable so that I would walk away, and by His strength I did. As Jonah prayed, "[t]hose who cling to worthless idols turn away from God's love for them" (Jonah 2:8). People we love can become idols, and I knew it. That breakup didn't feel like God's mercy at the time, but in retrospect, there's no doubt it was.

I also didn't enjoy getting fired from my very first television job after I'd left my legal career behind and begun pursuing journalism. "You're the worst person I've ever seen on TV, and you'll never make it," my new boss told me two weeks after he joined the station where I started. Did I have room for improvement? Heck yeah, always will. But was I also crushed by the harshness of his words? You bet. It felt horrible, but absent that firing, I would have been completely content to stay there in Tampa and build my media career on the local level in a wonderful market. Think of all the things I would have missed had that boss not kicked me out of the nest: lunches at the White House with multiple presidents, interviewing world leaders and traveling the globe, being the first to break news on the steps of the Supreme Court when history was made. Getting fired was a mercy. It taught me the importance of humility, hard work, and dreaming big. I had months of "sitting in the fish" (unemployment) to think about how God was calling me to live my life.

Those cauldrons are often where our truest prayers are uttered. They can be a quiet "Lord, help me" or a loud outpouring of our grief. Either way, He will always be listening. Jonah's prayer was wrapped with shouts of praise and a vow to share the message of

God's salvation. He has a key insight about his mistakes thus far. He prays,

> "Those who cling to worthless idols
> turn away from God's love for them."
>
> Jonah 2:8

With that:

> And the LORD commanded the fish, and it vomited Jonah onto dry land.
>
> Jonah 2:10

The Reluctant Prophet

Wherever Jonah had been floating around in that fish, the journey was over. Now he had vows to keep and a trip to make. It was time to extend God's grace to a people he more likely wished the Lord would wipe from the face of the earth. Luckily for Jonah, and for all of us, God is all about second chances.

> Then the word of the LORD came to Jonah a second time: "Go to the great city of Nineveh and proclaim to it the message I give you."
> Jonah obeyed the word of the LORD and went to Nineveh. Now Nineveh was a very large city; it took three days to go through it. Jonah began by going a day's journey into the city, proclaiming, "Forty more days and Nineveh will be

overthrown." The Ninevites believed God. A fast was proclaimed, and all of them, from the greatest to the least, put on sackcloth.

Jonah 3:1–5

This was no Billy Graham multiday crusade, no eloquent sermon or multiverse altar call. Yes, Jonah obeyed—but I'm always a bit baffled by his message. *Hey, you've got forty days and then you're done.* That's it?! But it turns out this was enough. It's notable that after a long period of conquering, the Assyrians had fallen on hard times, with central authority splintered among regional governors, and their war efforts had ground to a halt along with plagues and rebellions. Around this time, there was even a solar eclipse (763 BC) that would have been seen as an omen. Perhaps this made the people of one Assyrian city particularly eager for redemption.

We must always remember the Holy Spirit can—and does—work in situations long before we arrive. Had He primed their hearts, and Jonah missed the original time on closing the deal? These folks were ready for repentance. We're told every one of the Ninevites—*every one*—went into mourning. What a contrast their immediate action is to the foot-dragging of God's prophet. And it wasn't over yet.

When Jonah's warning reached the king of Nineveh, he rose from his throne, took off his royal robes, covered himself with sackcloth and sat down in the dust. This is the proclamation he issued in Nineveh:

"By the decree of the king and his nobles:

Do not let people or animals, herds or flocks, taste anything; do not let them eat or drink. But let people and animals be covered with sackcloth. Let everyone call urgently on God. Let them give up their evil ways and their violence. Who knows? God may yet relent and with compassion turn from his fierce anger so that we will not perish."

When God saw what they did and how they turned from their evil ways, he relented and did not bring on them the destruction he had threatened.

Jonah 3:6–10

The king of Nineveh went further in his repentance than anyone else. *Don't even let your cows snag a bite of grass!* The king acknowledged that there were no promises in Jonah's message; there was no deal-making. But he held out hope that God would show compassion. He also recognized that the Lord was capable of wiping them out. Perhaps he intuited that God was, like himself, a king, and if a king wants an enemy's total destruction, he doesn't announce his attack in advance—but if he wishes for reconciliation or surrender to his terms, he gives his opponent warning. Still, it was quite an imaginative leap for an Assyrian ruler to suppose that the God of Jonah was a God of compassion.

Like the pagan sailors, the king of Ninevah's instinct about God was more accurate than Jonah's. God was moved by the repentance of the Ninevites and had mercy on them.

If you think your obedience and your prayers cannot sway the heart of God, mark Jonah 3:10 in your Bible. All throughout Scripture, we see God moved by prayer, grief, or pleading. And what encouragement to see that this most evil group of people could have their slates wiped clean! Rejoice! Right? *Jonah, look at what God accomplished through you, even though you ran from Him in disobedience. You've been redeemed, too!*

But to Jonah this seemed very wrong, and he became angry. He prayed to the LORD, "Isn't this what I said, LORD, when I was still at home? That is what I tried to forestall by fleeing to Tarshish. I knew that you are a gracious and compassionate God, slow to anger and abounding in love, a God who relents from sending calamity. Now, LORD, take away my life, for it is better for me to die than to live."

But the LORD replied, "Is it right for you to be angry?"

Jonah 4:1–4

Another translation says Jonah was "greatly displeased and became furious" (CSB). We tread into dangerous territory when we substitute our reasoning (or emotions) for God's judgment. What right did Jonah have to be angry about God saving anyone and everyone? He even throws it back at the Lord. *I told You this would happen—that You'd give these awful people a chance! That's why I didn't want to come!* So, Jonah's resistance to going to Nineveh wasn't about fearing for his life after all. What Jonah actually feared most was that God *would* have mercy on Nineveh. He was ticked . . . and dramatic: *just kill me!*

Jonah's Lament

Instead of engaging with his theatrics, the Lord asked Jonah a searing question: Is it right for you to feel the way you do?

Jonah's answer was the one we sometimes give if we're being honest—we pout.

> Jonah had gone out and sat down at a place east of the city. There he made himself a shelter, sat in its shade and waited to see what would happen to the city.
>
> Jonah 4:5

I may be wrong, but I don't think Jonah went and camped out outside the city so he could cheer on the people's revival and rescue. I don't think we'd be wrong to interpret this passage as Jonah pulling up a chair so he could see if the city returned to its wicked ways and melted down instead.

In His tender mercy (now for the sailors, Jonah, *and* the people of Nineveh), God met Jonah where he was—literally and figuratively. We may have bad attitudes and feel that our joy has been stolen when "the wicked prosper." But that doesn't give us license to assume they are wholly evil and beyond God's merciful redemption.

I think of a story I covered that grabbed headlines for years—the rise and fall of Bernie Madoff. For decades, he lured investors into a web of lies, a Ponzi scheme that would eventually crumble, costing his clients tens of billions of dollars. But even when others raised red flags about the unbelievable returns he was able to provide (for a while), he continued to be celebrated and lauded as a financial genius. Alarm bells were ringing. And yet the awards kept coming. I can only imagine the frustration of the few who were yelling at the top of their lungs that it was all a scam. They watched as Madoff sat on high-profile boards, was the subject of glowing media profiles, and was celebrated for his supposed generosity. All of it was built on the backs of people and organizations who lost nearly everything when his deception was ultimately exposed.

There were rare clients who chose not to sue when it all came crashing down, or actually offered words highlighting the good things Madoff had done over the years. I wonder how those words landed with the individuals, families, and charities who were devastated by his decades-long scam. *How could you possibly find anything good in this man?* And yet isn't that what God does with us? And He does it without a false idea of our virtues. He's not fooled by the façade we put up for our friends. God is like the victim of a scam who forgives the conman with no illusions whatsoever, because He has paid the cost Himself. If we come to Him in repentance and humility, He covers us with the righteousness of Christ—viewing us with the righteousness of His Son, not our record of sin.

Jonah was still unable to view his enemies in that light, somehow blinded to the very forgiveness God had meted out to him.

> Then the LORD God provided a leafy plant and made it grow up over Jonah to give shade for his head to ease his discomfort, and Jonah was very happy about the plant. But at dawn the next day God provided a worm, which chewed the plant so that it withered. When the sun rose, God provided a scorching east wind, and the sun blazed on Jonah's head so that he grew faint. He wanted to die, and said, "It would be better for me to die than to live."
>
> But God said to Jonah, "Is it right for you to be angry about the plant?"
>
> "It is," he said. "And I'm so angry I wish I were dead."
>
> Jonah 4:6–9

Not to make light of this situation, but it feels like Jonah has gone full-on hangry. He's this upset about a vine? Side note: he'd never make it at my house. It's incredibly thoughtful when someone sends over flowers or a treat when I'm recovering or grieving, but if you send an actual plant to my house, it has entered what I refer to as Foliage Death Row. My sweet friend, Eun, brought me a stunning orchid when I was recovering from surgery a while back. My first thought as I hugged her and welcomed her in for a chat was *This poor thing will never survive here.* And it did not.

Back to Jonah. It's enough that he tells God: *yes, I'm justified in being this mad!* But also: *I'm so furious about this plant dying that I wish I was dead, too.* He's upset, he's uncomfortable, and he's questioning God's plan. It's a stew of ungratefulness and self-pity that will end up tasting very bitter to the person eating it. All along, God was illustrating a point.

> But the LORD said, "You have been concerned about this plant, though you did not tend it or make it grow. It sprang up overnight and died overnight. And should I not have concern for the great city of Nineveh, in which there are more than a hundred and twenty thousand people who cannot tell their right hand from their left—and also many animals?"
>
> Jonah 4:10–11

A prophet, a man of God, a messenger from the Lord Himself—upset that his message of warning was heeded, and a people repented and were spared? The plant was a soulless, temporary organism. Jonah had done nothing to bring it about or make it flourish. God created every single person who lived in Nineveh—thousands of them. Each person in Nineveh was a soul created in His image, capable of redemption given God's grace, and yet Jonah couldn't see past his own prejudice against them.

A Spirit of Ingratitude

How many of us are guilty of the same thing? Yes, we rightfully judge that the behavior of violent criminals and evil terrorists is abhorrent. That doesn't mean they aren't beyond saving, or all of us would be. Let's take it closer to home. What about people who vote or worship differently than you do? Are there people in our lives that we have deemed unworthy of the mercy God has lavished on us?

According to a 2024 Gallup poll, America hit a record high for the number of citizens who believe that we are "greatly divided on the most important values"—a whopping 80 percent. That number was 10 points higher than when it was measured in previous presidential election years in 2004 and 2012. Just 18 percent of the country believed we were united. So, 8 in 10 of us think we have no cohesion on the things that are supposed to bind our country together. We've all seen the stories about people keying cars or stealing political signs, about skyrocketing road rage incidents and worse. People feel justified in their fury. But how far off track might that take us from witnessing to those who need God in all the same ways that we do?

Yes, God may ask us to do what feels outrageous and unreasonable to our human minds. But does He not have the right? Oh, that we would see all our fellow humans the way that He does.

Thinking again about the parallels between Christ's three days in darkness and Jonah's time in the big fish, there are also stark differences. Jonah fought God's command, but Christ came to earth without hesitation, knowing what He would suffer. Jonah didn't want to see salvation for the brutal, barbaric Ninevites—yet Jesus died for every single one of them, knowing what they had done. In fact, Christ came to earth to suffer horrific torture and eventual death to cover every single sin that will ever be committed. He knew there was no other way to give us eternal life.

> Going a little farther, he fell with his face to the ground and prayed, "My Father, if it is possible, may this cup be taken from me. Yet not as I will, but as you will."
>
> Matthew 26:39

Yes, He sacrificed for the very worst among us, so who are we to question where God bestows His mercy? The message of Christ's forgiveness for all was a radical one in the first century, as Paul wrote to the Christian church in the city of Colossae.

> Here there is no Gentile or Jew, circumcised or uncircumcised, barbarian, Scythian, slave or free, but Christ is all, and is in all.
> Therefore, as God's chosen people, holy and dearly loved, clothe yourselves with compassion, kindness, humility, gentleness and patience. Bear with each other and forgive one another if any of you has a grievance against someone. Forgive as the Lord forgave you. And over all these virtues put on love, which binds them all together in perfect unity.
>
> Colossians 3:11–14

God's truth and benevolence wipes out every single barrier and prejudice. Who are we to do anything less?

Now Jonah may have felt some level of smugness had he been around roughly a century later when Nahum described God's eventual judgment and destruction of Nineveh this way:

> Woe to the city of blood,
>   full of lies,

full of plunder,
>never without victims!
The crack of whips,
>the clatter of wheels,
galloping horses
>and jolting chariots!
Charging cavalry,
>flashing swords
>and glittering spears!
Many casualties,
>piles of dead,
bodies without number,
>people stumbling over the corpses—
all because of the wanton lust of a prostitute,
>alluring, the mistress of sorceries,
who enslaved nations by her prostitution
>and peoples by her witchcraft.
"I am against you," declares the LORD Almighty.
"I will lift your skirts over your face.
I will show the nations your nakedness
and the kingdoms your shame.

Nothing can heal you;
>your wound is fatal.
>All who hear the news about you
>clap their hands at your fall,
>for who has not felt
>your endless cruelty?

Nahum 3:1–5, 19

God had thrown the Ninevites a lifeline. In Jonah's day, and despite his attitude, they humbled themselves and turned to Him. But subsequent generations' return to evil would ultimately be their downfall. That's why the story of redemption will never be over until God makes all things new. Until then, He'll keep calling for Jonahs to go to the Ninevehs of the world. Let's plan on saying yes.

Study Questions

1. Even among the prophets, we sometimes see a leaning toward a more pagan understanding of God (vindictive) than His true identity (compassionate). Why would God use prophets who didn't fully and accurately comprehend His true nature?
2. Think of a time you've run from God's leading. What was your motivation? Have you tried to negotiate with God? How did that go?
3. Have you ever spent time "in the belly of the fish"? What did you learn there while you were sidelined with time to consider both God's authority and mercy?
4. Be honest, are there those you believe are unworthy of God's forgiveness? Do you hesitate to see them as created in His image?
5. How are you bridging divides with people who worship, vote, or live differently than you do?

DANIEL'S INTEGRITY

Resisting the Culture When It Conflicts with Your Convictions

Daniel 1–6

I love to travel. It's something we didn't really have the time or resources to do while I was growing up, so I've been making up for lost time ever since. Early in our marriage, when we didn't have the budget for international travel, Sheldon and I stumbled into the deal of a lifetime. We were living in North Carolina when Lufthansa Airlines announced it was launching direct service from Charlotte to Munich, with rock-bottom fares the first week or so. We'd always wanted to visit Germany, and for $250 each, we got round-trip tickets and started planning! Deep inside, I'm a travel agent just waiting to burst out. I take enormous joy in planning trips for family and friends that I hope they will thoroughly enjoy. If you're the type who wants to do nothing more than pack a bag and show up at the airport, I'm the fellow traveler for you! I research every hotel, restaurant, cathedral, beach, and museum to within an inch of its life. Bring your passport, and I'll have your itinerary ready to roll.

Because I hadn't been out of the country much at that point, I was determined to have the full in-country experience as we adventured through Germany and Austria. For Sheldon, that meant renting a Mercedes and attempting a new land-speed record on the autobahn.

For me, it was a plan to do anything and everything *except* revert to something I could do in the States—like eat at McDonald's. We had a blast learning some conversational German in advance and spent nine days eating, drinking, and sleeping like locals. But as the days wore on, I began to grow tired of the effort it took to communicate clearly and to find something I recognized on the menus.

On our final day in Munich, we decided to do some shopping, and I was shocked to find that in one fancy department store, there was zero personal space. People flung open the curtains to the communal dressing room with no concern for what state of undress I was in, and I was certain as they laughed and spoke their native language that I was becoming the butt of their jokes. Suddenly, my broken attempts to ask for directions in German made no sense, and I started to sweat. While I knew just about everyone in Munich could speak much better English than my minimal, flawed German, this group in the dressing room seemed to be having a little too much fun with my struggle. When I finally found my way out and ran toward Sheldon, I pointed to a familiar sign and blurted out, "We are going to eat there right now!" Within thirty minutes, I was enjoying my personal pan pizza at Pizza Hut, slurping down a Pepsi, and feeling like I'd failed at this trip. I couldn't deny that when I finally reached my limit, what I really wanted was the comforts of home. And while I would soon return to what I knew and loved, God's faithful servant Daniel would never get that chance.

When I look at Daniel's exile in Babylon, I realize my experience of cultural discomfort was pretty mild compared to his. It's possible my own imagination exaggerated all the looks and snickering. But everything feels a lot more sinister when you're far away from home.

Imagine being a young student living at a university and far from your childhood small town for the first time. You're suddenly encountering new temptations that feel a lot more appealing because you're lonely. Giving in will make you part of the "in" crowd. You can't easily run to an outpost of home, like I did at that Pizza Hut in Munich. In fact, the temptations you're facing in this new place probably promise a false sense of comfort—of being somewhere that feels like belonging. Being a prisoner of war exiled to an ancient imperial capital was that experience on steroids. So how did Daniel find his spiritual comfort food when he wasn't just cut off from Israel—but he knew God's will was that likely he would never return?

Finding Community in Exile

Most scholars believe that Daniel and his three friends—Hananiah, Mishael, and Azariah—were roughly between fifteen and eighteen years old when they were carried away from Jerusalem to Babylon. Whatever was comfortable and familiar to them was left hundreds of miles away, forever. But they were dealing with more than just distance from their homeland—they were also facing a concerted effort to pry their affections away from their people, land, and God.

Rather than subjugating or physically tormenting their prisoners as the Assyrians did, the Babylonians had a much more palatable way of turning their captives away from their families, cultural customs, and religious beliefs. As in the case of Daniel and his friends, the Babylonians took the best and brightest young men from the lands they conquered and then showed them the beauty of their majestic city. They plied them with fine foods and delicious wines, trying to convince them that surrendering to a new life in Babylon wouldn't be difficult at all.

Throughout history, reeducating or brainwashing young people has been a way to alter their loyalties. And in that way, oppressors changed important foundational structures without using much violence—if at all. The United States Holocaust Memorial Museum outlines how Adolf Hitler bragged of beginning the indoctrination of young people at the tender age of ten, then continuing to reinforce false narratives and destructive lies well into their twenties.

> Schools played an important role in spreading Nazi ideas to German youth. . . . German educators introduced new textbooks that taught students love for Hitler, obedience to state authority, militarism, racism, and antisemitism.
>
> From their first days in school, German children were imbued with the cult of Adolf Hitler. His portrait was a standard fixture in classrooms. . . . Board games and toys for children served as another way to spread racial and political propaganda. . . .

Groups like Hitler Youth and Reich Labor Service filled these young minds with disinformation and sought to erase any moral conviction that conflicted with Hitler's twisted worldview.

Daniel and his friends also underwent a process designed to completely reshape the young men they had been when they were kidnapped. Everything would be different: their language, their names, the food they ate, and the books they studied. But these teenagers were different. Did they have some natural ability to resist? No, actually, it didn't have anything to do with a literal connection to home—but it did have everything to do with love for the God who *gave them their home.*

Someone in the lives of these Jewish teenagers had so embedded the God of Abraham, Isaac, and Jacob in their hearts and minds that they were not going to cave to peer pressure, despite what it might cost them. And when they decided to stand firm on the truth,

God made sure they were under the authority of someone willing to honor their obedience to Him.

> But Daniel resolved not to defile himself with the royal food and wine, and he asked the chief official for permission not to defile himself this way. Now God had caused the official to show favor and compassion to Daniel . . .
>
> Daniel 1:8–9

When we look at the stories of godly people who suffered in ways that seem wholly unjustified to our human minds, we almost always learn later why they were specifically assigned to live in those unfair situations. So often the Lord placed His servants into positions where their unique giftings would allow them to serve others and bring glory to Him as a result. God regularly blessed these biblical heroes with kind superiors, people who showed them respect and support despite their positions as exiles.

Remember Joseph, who was sold into captivity as a teenager many years before Daniel, yet he was consistently honored wherever he landed—even behind bars. He went from being a slave to having authority over everything in the home of one of Pharaoh's top officials.

> The LORD was with Joseph so that he prospered, and he lived in the house of his Egyptian master. . . .
> Joseph found favor in his eyes and became his attendant.
>
> Genesis 39:2, 4

And when Joseph ended up in jail for a crime he didn't commit, God made sure he once again rose to the top. The Lord:

> ... showed him kindness and granted him favor in the eyes of the prison warden. ...
> ... the LORD was with Joseph and gave him success in whatever he did.
>
> Genesis 39:21, 23

Years after Daniel's faithfulness in Babylon, we see that Esther, who risked her life to save the Jewish people, also repeatedly found compassion and kindness as a young woman hiding a secret that could have cost her dearly. Of the man who would oversee her entry into the palace:

> She pleased him and won his favor. ...
> And Esther won the favor of everyone who saw her.
>
> Esther 2:9, 15

This same respect flowed to Obadiah as he served in the court of the wicked King Ahab, and it's clear in the story of Nehemiah (more on that story in the next chapter).

Nothing is a surprise to God. The Lord knew Daniel and his friends would be stripped away from their families and the lives they knew and taken to Babylon. It wasn't a turn of events meant to punish them. Instead, as you'll see in the pages ahead, it set up numerous opportunities for the Lord to be glorified far beyond the borders of where the Jewish people were living at the time. But it required Daniel to stand firm in the faith of his fathers, even when his very life was at risk.

That first real test came when Daniel was presented with food and wine that was almost certainly offered to idols King Nebuchadnezzar worshiped. For Daniel to eat that food wasn't kosher—literally or figuratively. But Ashpenaz, the chief eunuch entrusted with Daniel's care, worried that he'd be the one to pay the price if he presented these young men back to the king looking sickly or unprepared compared to the others. "You would endanger my life with the king," he told Daniel.

But Daniel made a deal with the guard assigned to him.

> "Please test your servants for ten days: Give us nothing but vegetables to eat and water to drink. Then compare our appearance with that of the young men who eat the royal food, and treat your servants in accordance with what you see." So he agreed to this and tested them for ten days.
>
> At the end of the ten days they looked healthier and better nourished than any of the young men who ate the royal food. So the guard took away their choice food and the wine they were to drink and gave them vegetables instead.
>
> Daniel 1:12–16

Healthier and better nourished than those eating the royal food. Daniel's humble refusal to compromise was rewarded, and this was probably the beginning of those in the king's court realizing that there was something different about these Jewish exiles and the God they served. After all, this wasn't in the days when vegetarians had access to good nutritional options that would help them overcome the lack of protein in their normal diet. The people of the city must have been struck by the unlikely sight of young, growing boys outdoing others on a diet of vegetables and water!

It wasn't just the physical; we're told that the Lord also blessed these faithful young men with all kinds of knowledge and understanding. Daniel was gifted to understand dreams and visions as well. These four were at the top of their class by the time they were finally presented to the king.

> In every matter of wisdom and understanding about which the king questioned them, he found them ten times better than all the magicians and enchanters in his whole kingdom.
>
> Daniel 1:20

This really struck me. So many times in Washington I'm in a room full of brainiacs, people with all kinds of degrees and accolades from the top universities and programs on the planet. It continually reminds me to go to God for the wisdom and discernment I so desperately need. Scripture tells us it is there for the asking.

> To the person who pleases him, God gives wisdom.
>
> Ecclesiastes 2:26

> We continually ask God to fill you with the knowledge of his will through all the wisdom and understanding that the Spirit gives.
>
> Colossians 1:9

> If any of you lacks wisdom, you should ask God, who gives generously to all without finding fault, and it will be given to you.
>
> James 1:5

The Lord equipped Daniel and his friends with wisdom far beyond their years, and it wouldn't be long before it was put to the test.

Daniel's Wisdom from God

In Daniel 2, the king had troubling dreams that robbed him of sleep. He called for all the advisors at his disposal to come and stand before him. Scripture tells us it was a collection of "magicians, enchanters, sorcerers and astrologers" (Daniel 2:2). But the assignment was especially difficult because the king wanted them to tell him *what* he had dreamed before they attempted to decipher it. It should come as no surprise that the request sent them into an absolute panic.

"This is what I have firmly decided: If you do not tell me what my dream was and interpret it, I will have you cut into pieces and your houses turned into piles of rubble."

Daniel 2:5

I sometimes use the Christian Standard Bible, which says he threatened to turn their houses into garbage dumps—descriptive!

Again, the king's advisors begged for mercy, but none was coming. The king was "so angry and furious" that he ordered the execution of every single wise man who was serving in Babylon—including Daniel and his friends (Daniel 2:12). It doesn't appear they had any chance to attempt what the king was asking, but that didn't matter. Their names were on the kill list, but Daniel wasn't willing to accept that fate.

DANIEL'S INTEGRITY

> When Arioch, the commander of the king's guard, had gone out to put to death the wise men of Babylon, Daniel spoke to him with wisdom and tact. He asked the king's officer, "Why did the king issue such a harsh decree?" Arioch then explained the matter to Daniel. At this, Daniel went in to the king and asked for time, so that he might interpret the dream for him.
>
> Daniel 2:14–16

Once again, we see young Daniel acting with discernment. Because the king did not immediately deny Daniel's request for time, we can only assume that the king held Daniel in special regard—no doubt because of God's protection.

Daniel quickly returned home and called his friends into a prayer meeting. They asked God for mercy concerning the king's mysterious dream so that they would not be executed. During the night, the Lord revealed all to Daniel in a vision. He immediately thanked his heavenly Father and directed all praise to Him. Daniel was highly favored and respected, yet he turned all glory back to God. Others in the Bible weren't so humble. It's tempting to take a victory lap when you know the adulation of man is coming, but the temporary high will quickly fade.

When Daniel rushed back to Arioch, he didn't plead only for his life and the lives of his friends; Scripture says he called on the king not to destroy any of the wise men of Babylon. Instead, he asked to see the king and reveal both the dream and what it meant. When the king asked if he would truly be able to deliver, Daniel assured him that he would—but not of his own power or ability.

> Daniel replied, "No wise man, enchanter, magician or diviner can explain to the king the mystery he has asked about,

but there is a God in heaven who reveals mysteries. He has shown King Nebuchadnezzar what will happen in days to come."

Daniel 2:27–28

Daniel proceeded to outline every detail of the dream and its meaning. There could be no doubt in the king's mind that it was divine inspiration.

> Then King Nebuchadnezzar fell prostrate before Daniel and paid him honor and ordered that an offering and incense be presented to him. The king said to Daniel, "Surely your God is the God of gods and the Lord of kings and a revealer of mysteries, for you were able to reveal this mystery."
>
> Then the king placed Daniel in a high position and lavished many gifts on him. He made him ruler over the entire province of Babylon and placed him in charge of all its wise men.

Daniel 2:46–48

From death sentence to key ruler in Babylon in less than twenty-four hours! Let's be honest, if speaking up for God always guaranteed that sort of reward and acceptance, we all might be bolder. And to be fair, Daniel had acted under risk to his life. He had nothing to lose.

Still, the fact that King Nebuchadnezzar granted him time implies that Daniel's faith was not desperate or tentative. Rather, Daniel's faith in God was deeply grounded in his life of prayer and humility.

There's the first lesson for a person far from home: As long as you have a community of prayer, you can forge community wherever you are. Daniel made sure to give back to that faith family, too.

Daniel also requested that his friends be promoted to manage Babylon, which the king granted. But for the abduction of all four of them, would Nebuchadnezzar have come to see the power and truth of the God they served? The king wasn't exactly done with his spiritual journey. It's one thing to acknowledge the God of the universe. It's another thing entirely to commit your life to His authority.

The Fiery Furnace: God Is with You in the Flames

As these young exiles grew in stature and position in Babylon, the testing of their faith continued. Daniel 3 focuses on the renamed Shadrach, Meshach, and Abednego and their refusal to bow to a giant, lifeless idol that the king created. In *Love Stories of the Bible*, I wrote of the bravery these men found in their relationship with God and friendship with one another. Though Daniel isn't part of this particular story, you likely know it well. It illustrates that Daniel wasn't an outlier in his community—these Jewish young men were all faithful together.

And this time, the test wasn't about bringing good news to the king but resisting him. The trio didn't deny they were disobeying the decree to worship the golden statue, and the furious king mocked the ability of any "god" to save them from his "hand" (Daniel 3:15). The men didn't flinch. They declared the Lord's unmistakable ability to rescue them from the fiery furnace Nebuchadnezzar was about to throw them into, but they also vowed that even if God did not choose to rescue them, they would never serve or bow to the king's idols.

The king was "filled with rage" and ordered the furnace cranked up so high that the fire killed the men who threw Shadrach, Meshach, and Abednego into the blistering flames (Daniel 3:22). Bound and tossed in, they weren't alone for long. Nebuchadnezzar jumped up with alarm when he saw four "men" in the fire, and he quickly called for Daniel's friends to come out. Whether the fourth figure in the fire was an angel or an incarnation of God Himself, the trio was protected by divine intervention. When they walked out of the fire unharmed, Scripture tells us they didn't even bear the smell of smoke. Nebuchadnezzar was astonished, and for a second time he declared the power of the God of the Jewish captives in his court.

"Praise be to the God of Shadrach, Meshach and Abednego, who has sent his angel and rescued his servants! They trusted in him and defied the king's command and were willing to give up their lives rather than serve or worship any god except their own God. Therefore I decree that the people of any nation or language who say anything against the God of Shadrach, Meshach and Abednego be cut into pieces and their houses be turned into piles of rubble, for no other god can save in this way."

Daniel 3:28–29

In this story, we see a vital second lesson in maintaining your integrity far from home. Community can help guard your heart and maintain your prayer life, but even more important is the fact that God will be with you in the fire. The church and God Himself can be our home wherever we are.

What must this have looked like to those outside the body of believers? Nebuchadnezzar can show us. Had the king finally gotten it through his thick skull that none of the idols he worshiped, including himself at times, would ever be able to save him? Not exactly, and God wasn't through trying to reach him.

It's likely several years later by the time we catch up with the king in Daniel 4. He's had another troubling dream, and no one could interpret it for him—until Daniel arrived. Nebuchadnezzar acknowledged to his chief wise man, "[N]o mystery is too difficult for you" (Daniel 4:9). Once the dream was shared, Daniel's "thoughts terrified him" (Daniel 4:19). He knew that he wasn't going to be delivering good news to the king, and that's a frightening task for a member of a tyrant's court. Apparently, the king saw Daniel's hesitation and urged him to share the interpretation. It would not be easy for the king to digest.

The mighty tree that the king saw in his dream represented him. It was strong and flourishing, but it would be cut down. It's key to note that the tree wasn't going to be completely destroyed; the stump and roots were left intact. Daniel continued to interpret this image, revealing that this meant the king would live as a wild animal and go insane for seven years. But once he acknowledged God was the true Ruler over all kingdoms, Nebuchadnezzar would be restored. Risking his own position (and maybe more), Daniel urged the king to take action.

> "Therefore, Your Majesty, be pleased to accept my advice: Renounce your sins by doing what is right, and your wickedness by being kind to the oppressed. It may be that then your prosperity will continue."
>
> Daniel 4:27

This king had unmistakably seen and acknowledged the power and authority of Daniel's God numerous times before. He trusted Daniel's wisdom and knew it to be spot-on. But in his arrogance, this time, the king refused to follow his trusted advisor's advice.

A King, Exiled

A full year after Daniel dropped some tough love and truth on the king, Nebuchadnezzar was strutting around on the palace rooftop and basking in "his" accomplishments.

> [H]e said, "Is not this the great Babylon I have built as the royal residence, by my mighty power and for the glory of my majesty?"
> Even as the words were on his lips, a voice came from heaven, "This is what is decreed for you, King Nebuchadnezzar: Your royal authority has been taken from you."
>
> Daniel 4:30–31

The dream Daniel had interpreted for the king was about to become a nightmare.

Everything Daniel had boldly warned him about came to be. Nebuchadnezzar was "driven away" from normal people and society. He ate grass like an ox. His hair grew like "the feathers of an eagle and his nails like the claws of a bird" (Daniel 4:33).

Seven long years later, just as predicted, Nebuchadnezzar finally raised his eyes to heaven and his "sanity was restored." He openly praised God and "became even greater than before" (Daniel 4:36). He spent years in mental illness and a literal wilderness before he could finally proclaim of the Lord:

> His dominion is an eternal dominion;
> his kingdom endures from generation to generation.
> All the peoples of the earth
> are regarded as nothing.
> He does as he pleases
> with the powers of heaven
> and the peoples of the earth.
> No one can hold back his hand
> or say to him: "What have you done?" . . .
> Now I, Nebuchadnezzar, praise and exalt and glorify the King of heaven, because everything he does is right and all his ways are just. And those who walk in pride he is able to humble.
>
> Daniel 4:34–35, 37

Remember that in the king's dream, the powerful tree that was cut down (Nebuchadnezzar) was left with its stump and roots? Nebuchadnezzar's kingdom was waiting, preserved by the Lord, until he was willing to humble himself, but like a stump, it could still regrow. How many times did God prove Himself to the king through Daniel's testimony and gifting? How many times had the king acknowledged that yet failed to personalize it? Nebuchadnezzar finally admitted that God is able to humble.

Scripture is filled with warnings about pride, and the minute we think we couldn't possibly struggle with that sin—we probably already are.

> He mocks proud mockers
> but shows favor to the humble and oppressed.
>
> Proverbs 3:34

> For those who exalt themselves will be humbled, and those who humble themselves will be exalted.
>
> Matthew 23:12

After King Nebuchadnezzar was restored to his position, this is the last we hear of him. But he surprisingly reveals a third lesson about God's design for community. It's not about blood or land—Nebuchadnezzar found his way into the community of Israel through faith. The most unlikely person in the world, the *least* exiled person, identified with God's exiles after experiencing an exile of his own.

Visions Return: Daniel Back in the King's Service

You might think this was the end of Daniel's story. What could be a bigger climax than aiding in changing the heart of a king? But at the end of the day, Nebuchadnezzar's arc is a subplot in the longer tale.

After the king's death around 562 BC, there was a power struggle to assume the throne. It lasted years and involved several male relatives of Nebuchadnezzar. When the dust finally settled, his son-in-law Nabonidus took the throne. Scholars say Nabonidus was more interested in the trappings (and vacation home) of the throne than he was in actually serving as king. He essentially left the kingdom under the care of his son, Belshazzar, who was a wicked king indeed.

When we meet Belshazzar in the book of Daniel, he is throwing a massive party with a thousand nobles, his wives, and his concubines. This was no red Solo cup affair. Belshazzar had ordered the golden goblets taken from the temple in Jerusalem to be used that night. And as they drank from those sacred vessels, Belshazzar

DANIEL'S INTEGRITY

and his entourage praised lifeless idols made by human hands. In the midst of their blasphemous bash, a terrifying warning shocked them into silence.

> Suddenly the fingers of a human hand appeared and wrote on the plaster of the wall, near the lampstand in the royal palace. The king watched the hand as it wrote. His face turned pale and he was so frightened that his legs became weak and his knees were knocking.
>
> The king summoned the enchanters, astrologers and diviners. Then he said to these wise men of Babylon, "Whoever reads this writing and tells me what it means will be clothed in purple and have a gold chain placed around his neck, and he will be made the third highest ruler in the kingdom."
>
> Then all the king's wise men came in, but they could not read the writing or tell the king what it meant. So King Belshazzar became even more terrified and his face grew more pale. His nobles were baffled.
>
> Daniel 5:5–9

You may think to yourself—as I did the first time I read this—*Why wasn't Daniel the first person summoned?!* It appears several decades have passed since he was front and center, and that was under the reign of a different king. Daniel was probably in his early eighties at this point. But when the queen heard the commotion, she reminded Belshazzar about Daniel, and he was summoned.

The king vowed to reward Daniel lavishly if he could explain the frightening apparition. Did Daniel already have some sense that he was about to deliver some devastating news? I wonder because he told the king upfront:

"You may keep your gifts for yourself and give your rewards to someone else. Nevertheless, I will read the writing for the king and tell him what it means."

Daniel 5:17

What it meant was that time was just about up for Belshazzar. Daniel began by singing the praises of King Nebuchadnezzar, but he reminded the audience how prideful Nebuchadnezzar had once been and the enormous price it had cost him. No doubt, Belshazzar would know well the story of how Nebuchadnezzar had lived for years as an animal "until he acknowledged that the Most High God is sovereign over all kingdoms on earth and sets over them anyone [h]e wishes" (Daniel 5:21).

If the younger Daniel showed some hesitation about giving bad news to the king, this now-elderly Daniel had no hesitation at all. Daniel continued to lower the boom, calling out Belshazzar for his pride and the audacity he'd displayed in using the treasures of the temple for a raucous evening of debauchery. As for the words the mysterious hand wrote, they were: MENE, MENE, TEKEL, PARSIN. Daniel translated them to inform the king that he had been "weighed on the scales and found wanting," that his reign was coming to an end, and that the kingdom would be divided and given to new leaders.

That very night Belshazzar, king of the Babylonians, was slain, and Darius the Mede took over the kingdom, at the age of sixty-two.

Daniel 5:30–31

I love when there are records in secular history sources that complement what we already know to be true in the Word of God. That includes the fall of Belshazzar. Historians tell us the Babylonians diverted the Euphrates River so that it flowed under the walls of the city, and it also surrounded the city as a moat. By sabotaging the river's flow, Babylon's enemies were able to completely bypass attacks on the city walls, which stood more than thirty stories tall and eighty feet thick. The fall of Babylon was recorded by the ancient historians Herodotus, Berossus, and Xenophon.

Going forward, the Medes and Persians jointly ruled over what had been the vast, powerful Babylonian Empire. As Daniel had prophesied, Belshazzar's reign was over, and his kingdom was divided. Enter Darius and Cyrus.

The Lion's Den

While the man on the throne in Babylon changed, Daniel's esteem within the kingdom did not. Early in Daniel 6, we learn that Darius set up his administration with 120 satraps (princes) and three administrators over all those men. King Darius was so impressed with Daniel that he considered placing him over the entire kingdom (Daniel 6:3). And that's when the haters began to scheme.

> At this, the administrators and the satraps tried to find grounds for charges against Daniel in his conduct of government affairs, but they were unable to do so. They could find no corruption in him, because he was trustworthy and neither

corrupt nor negligent. Finally these men said, "We will never find any basis for charges against this man Daniel unless it has something to do with the law of his God."

Daniel 6:4–5

These leaders went straight to the place they were sure Daniel would never compromise: his faith and devotion to the Lord. It's as if his enemies had perceived the first lesson in this chapter: Daniel's strength was in his prayers. What a twist to a lifetime of faithful living! No matter what Daniel did, he couldn't win with the pagans. Despite being popular with the literal king of the land, the leader of the in-crowd, his rivals were able to turn Daniel's faithfulness into a legal trap.

I don't know about you, but as a kid in Sunday school, I pictured Daniel as a young man when he faced this showdown. That's not the case. As mentioned earlier, he was into his eighties by this point and hadn't buckled for roughly seven decades. What these enemies viewed as Daniel's weak spot was his greatest source of strength.

The leaders ran to the king, puffed him up with a heavy dose of flattery, and then unveiled their duplicitous plan. They convinced Darius to issue a formal decree that anyone who prayed to anyone or anything but the king for thirty days would be thrown into the lions' den. They knew, executed precisely, the command could not be revoked "in accordance with the law of the Medes and Persians" (Daniel 6:8). They laid a treacherous trap for the king and wanted to make sure he could show no mercy to Daniel when he discovered what they were up to.

What did Daniel do when he heard about the decree?

> [H]e went home to his upstairs room where the windows opened toward Jerusalem. Three times a day he got down on

his knees and prayed, giving thanks to his God, just as he had done before.

Daniel 6:10

He knew that there was a death sentence on the other side of his actions. Daniel didn't try to rationalize: *I'll just pray in private for the next thirty days.* This was a man who had been in exile for roughly seventy years, ripped away from the foundations of his faith and family. We may only read about the major trials he suffered as a Jewish man in captivity, but we can imagine there were smaller tests and challenges to his beliefs sprinkled throughout his life in Babylon. We never see anything in Daniel's life but faithfulness and the confidence that compromise simply wasn't an option.

Sure enough, Daniel's enemies went right to where they knew he would be.

Then these men went as a group and found Daniel praying and asking God for help.

Daniel 6:11

It encourages my heart to see Scripture note that Daniel was "asking God for help." He wasn't living with blinders on, pretending there was no threat to his life. He was remaining consistent in his prayers, while petitioning his heavenly Father. As Christians, we aren't called to be so heavenly minded that we can't acknowledge the reality of life on this flawed planet. Yes, we will face trouble. But we will never be alone.

The schemers ran straight to Darius and reminded him of the irrevocable decree he'd issued, gleefully pointing out that Daniel was praying to someone other than the king. Darius must have immediately realized these leaders weren't concerned about celebrating him; their plot had always been to destroy Daniel, the man the king respected most.

> When the king heard this, he was greatly distressed; he was determined to rescue Daniel and made every effort until sundown to save him.
>
> Daniel 6:14

But Darius's hands were tied, and he gave the order for elderly Daniel to be thrown to the lions. Before a stone was placed over the den and sealed with the king's signet ring, Darius called out to Daniel, "May your God, whom you serve continually, rescue you!" (Daniel 6:16).

The king couldn't eat or sleep and rushed back to the lions' den at the break of dawn. He shouted to Daniel again. This time Scripture tells us it was with an "anguished voice."

> "Daniel, servant of the living God, has your God, whom you serve continually, been able to rescue you from the lions?"
> Daniel answered, "May the king live forever! My God sent his angel, and he shut the mouths of the lions. They have not hurt me, because I was found innocent in his sight. Nor have I ever done any wrong before you, Your Majesty."
> The king was overjoyed and gave orders to lift Daniel out of the den. And when Daniel was lifted from the den, no wound was found on him, because he had trusted in his God.
>
> Daniel 6:20–23

What a mix of emotions Darius must have felt—joy that his most respected advisor had miraculously escaped death and rage that those scheming leaders had conned him into such a devious plot. Retribution was swift. Those underhanded leaders were thrown into the lions' den, suffering the very fate they'd planned for Daniel.

It reminds me of Queen Esther's story and the wicked Haman, who had conspired to destroy not only Mordecai (the man who'd raised and protected Esther) but also every other Jewish person in the kingdom. Instead, Haman was killed on the very pole he'd constructed for the purpose of impaling Mordecai! Ramifications in the Old Testament may be difficult to digest, but they were certainly just.

Again, Daniel's steadfast, humble faith led a powerful king to declare the glory of the Lord.

> "I issue a decree that in every part of my kingdom people must fear and reverence the God of Daniel.
>
> "For he is the living God
> and he endures forever;
> his kingdom will not be destroyed,
> his dominion will never end.
> He rescues and he saves;
> he performs signs and wonders
> in the heavens and on the earth.
> He has rescued Daniel
> from the power of the lions."
>
> So Daniel prospered during the reign of Darius and the reign of Cyrus the Persian.
>
> Daniel 6:26–28

Daniel never tried to bargain with his enemies—or God. He didn't confront the backstabbing officials or try to exact his own revenge. He quietly led a devoted, honorable life, bolstered by the community of God. He refused to cave or crumble. A foreigner in a strange land, he held to what he knew was true, because he understood that God was always with him. He used his remarkable gifts to direct all praise to the Lord. And ultimately, he found that the community of God can open its doors even to those who seem most unlikely to enter it.

Daniel found a home in Babylon because he knew that security and integrity come not from a physical place but from a heavenly Father.

We, too, are strangers in a land that is not our home. May we be willing to stand firm in uncomfortable situations, knowing our heavenly Father is on the journey with us—one that will eventually take us home to Him.

Study Questions

1. How does Daniel model grace and faith in a place that's ripped him away from his roots, his family, and his way of life?
2. As a believer, this world is not your home. So how do you find comfort and peace for your earthly journey? What are some verses you can commit to memory for when homesickness hits?
3. How is God Himself our home?
4. What kinds of peer pressure have you experienced

whether as a young person or into adulthood? How does the world try to capture our hearts like a modern-day Babylon?
5. What more can you be doing to build a community of believers to strengthen, challenge, and support your faith?

NEHEMIAH'S WISDOM

Dreaming Big in the Face of Opposition

Nehemiah 1–13

Have you ever cherished a dream in your heart? One that didn't make sense to anyone else but you? Maybe you treasured it so deeply that you didn't even share it with anyone but the Lord. That far-off hope might have come directly from Him and not even fully make sense to you!

As a little girl, I loved to watch the Miss America pageant with Mom and Grandma Nell, and some part of me fantasized that maybe one day I could be on that stage: sparkling evening gown, big ambitions, perfect poise. But *no one* would have imagined that future for me if they'd seen me back in the day. I had braces and wore hand-me-downs, and I often startled people with excited talk of Jesus and belting out show tunes.

I treasured and nurtured that unlikely hope for years, keeping it really close to the vest. All through my awkward years of skinned knees, pool-chlorine-stained green hair, and my goofball behavior, there was a tiny whisper in my heart that I was going to end up somewhere impossible. Fast-forward a couple of decades, and somehow the Lord dropped me right onto that stage and into the Miss America finals. All credit goes to my heavenly Father because I sure couldn't have gotten there on my own!

Nehemiah had a dream, too, a much bigger one. He had a deep longing to go to a faraway city he'd never even seen. Nehemiah was a godly man, displaced from his people and his homeland. Nearly a century and a half earlier, the Babylonians had destroyed Jerusalem, and many of the city's inhabitants either fled or were carried off to Babylon (as we saw in the story of Daniel). Tens of thousands of Jews were still living in the capital when the Babylonian Empire was overthrown by the Persians in 539 BC.

Eventually, Cyrus the Great, the first king of the Persian Empire, issued a decree that allowed Jews to return home to rebuild their temple (Ezra 1:1–4). So a group of more than 42,000 Jews returned to Jerusalem, led by Zerubbabel, a descendant of David (Ezra 2:64; Nehemiah 7:66). Roughly eighty years later, Ezra the priest took a second, smaller group of around 2,000 Jews to Jerusalem (Ezra 7–8).

How Nehemiah's Peace Came from Prayer

Ezra and Nehemiah were contemporaries, and they often worked together in guiding God's people. So by the time the books of Ezra and Nehemiah were written, the Jews had had almost eight decades of attempting to rebuild Jerusalem after the exile. Which raises the question: Why did it take so long? You might remember the story of Nehemiah because of the "dream come true" aspect of the Jews returning to their homeland, but actually, after some initial quick progress, it's a story about how to deal with constant setbacks and challenges and how to keep trusting God when He seems totally absent.

Nehemiah's role started with a deep desire in his heart, but it had been years in the making. Long before Nehemiah could have known about his heavenly assignment, God was directing his path to be just where He needed him to be.

> The words of Nehemiah son of Hakaliah:
> In the month of Kislev in the twentieth year, while I was in the citadel of Susa, Hanani, one of my brothers, came from Judah with some other men, and I questioned them about the Jewish remnant that had survived the exile, and also about Jerusalem.
> They said to me, "Those who survived the exile and are back in the province are in great trouble and disgrace. The wall of Jerusalem is broken down, and its gates have been burned with fire."
> When I heard these things, I sat down and wept. For some days I mourned and fasted and prayed before the God of heaven.
>
> Nehemiah 1:1–4

This faithful man of God was born in captivity. He'd probably never set foot in Jerusalem, but when he heard his brother Hanani describe the depressing condition of the city where his fellow Jews were trying to rebuild their lives, he was grieved. He didn't simply sit and fret, though. As you'll see throughout his story, Nehemiah's first response was always to get on his knees. He wept, he fasted, and then he poured out his heart to the Lord.

> Then I said:
> "Lord, the God of heaven, the great and awesome God, who keeps his covenant of love with those who love him and keep his commandments, let your ear be attentive and your eyes open to hear the prayer your servant is praying before you day and night for your servants, the people of Israel. I confess the sins we Israelites, including myself and my father's family, have committed against you. We have acted very wickedly

toward you. We have not obeyed the commands, decrees and laws you gave your servant Moses.

"Remember the instruction you gave your servant Moses, saying, 'If you are unfaithful, I will scatter you among the nations, but if you return to me and obey my commands, then even if your exiled people are at the farthest horizon, I will gather them from there and bring them to the place I have chosen as a dwelling for my Name.'

"They are your servants and your people, whom you redeemed by your great strength and your mighty hand. LORD, let your ear be attentive to the prayer of this your servant and to the prayer of your servants who delight in revering your name."

Nehemiah 1:5–11

Nehemiah wasted no time praising the Lord, also acknowledging the Israelites' role in the trouble they were facing. He confesses his own sin, and his people's sin collectively. He then hearkens back to the promises God made. Yes, He would scatter the Jewish people because of their disobedience, but also He would bring them back together if they would return to His commands. Nehemiah repeatedly asked the Lord to hear his prayers.

> "Give your servant success today by granting him favor in the presence of this man. I was cupbearer to the king."

Nehemiah 1:11

Talk about burying the lead! Nehemiah wasn't just any old Jewish exile living in Babylon-turned-Persia; he happened to be living in the palace as one of the closest companions and most trusted advisors of the current king of Persia, King Artaxerxes. As cupbearer, Nehemiah was perfectly positioned to ask the king for the impossible.

Clearly, Nehemiah's life up until this point hadn't been one of quiet piety. He had risen from the obscurity of an exiled people to become a power player in the court of the most powerful empire on earth. Biblehub.com gives us this context:

> Cupbearers were more than mere servants; they were confidants and advisors to the king. Their proximity to the monarch allowed them to influence decisions and policies. The position required a person of integrity and discretion, as they were privy to the king's private moments and discussions. . . . The role of the cupbearer is emblematic of the broader theme of service and stewardship found throughout the Bible. It illustrates the potential for individuals in seemingly subordinate positions to effect significant change and contribute to God's purposes.

If this seems unlikely, remember all the other stories where God wove together both tragedy and triumph to have His servants in places of honor so they could fight for His people: Esther, Joseph, Obadiah, and Moses are just a few. Nehemiah shared those characters' savvy ability to move in elite circles. As we'll see, he had incredible leadership and diplomatic skills, which he must have developed while navigating the courtroom intrigues of Susa.

Prayer and Preparation Go Together

About four months passed after Nehemiah received the disheartening news about Jerusalem before he would get his chance to speak with the king.

> In the month of Nisan in the twentieth year of King Artaxerxes, when wine was brought for him, I took the wine and gave it to the king. I had not been sad in his presence before, so the king asked me, "Why does your face look so sad when you are not ill? This can be nothing but sadness of heart."
>
> I was very much afraid, but I said to the king, "May the king live forever! Why should my face not look sad when the city where my ancestors are buried lies in ruins, and its gates have been destroyed by fire?"
>
> The king said to me, "What is it you want?"
>
> Then I prayed to the God of heaven . . .
>
> Nehemiah 2:1–4

In those times it was disfavored, if not downright illegal, to enter the king's presence in a less than cheerful mood. Remember Esther? (Sidenote: Some scholars believe Esther was the stepmother of Artaxerxes, the king Nehemiah served. It's very possible that she would have met Artaxerxes on the palace grounds and possibly even Nehemiah, but regardless, they would have both been familiar with her story.) Esther had risked her life by entering King Xerxes's presence without an invitation. But in doing so, she saved the Jewish people from annihilation. Now Nehemiah was approaching Esther's stepson with another unique request on behalf of the Jews. And King Artaxerxes had such respect for Nehemiah that he was open to it.

Note that Nehemiah, who had been fasting and praying for four months, quickly sent up a cry for help. This is characteristic of Nehemiah, and an important lesson for us to apply from his story: He always turned to God first. There was no time to return to his room for a long-form, eloquent conversation with God. Nehemiah was already walking so closely with his heavenly Father that he likely whispered the quickest of requests—and then he made his case.

> I answered the king, "If it pleases the king and if your servant has found favor in his sight, let him send me to the city in Judah where my ancestors are buried so that I can rebuild it."
>
> Then the king, with the queen sitting beside him, asked me, "How long will your journey take, and when will you get back?" It pleased the king to send me; so I set a time.
>
> I also said to him, "If it pleases the king, may I have letters to the governors of Trans-Euphrates, so that they will provide me safe-conduct until I arrive in Judah? And may I have a letter to Asaph, keeper of the royal park, so he will give me timber to make beams for the gates of the citadel by the temple and for the city wall and for the residence I will occupy?" And because the gracious hand of my God was on me, the king granted my requests. So I went to the governors of Trans-Euphrates and gave them the king's letters. The king had also sent army officers and cavalry with me.
>
> Nehemiah 2:5–9

Nehemiah had clearly served the king so well that the king not only granted his request but also sent Nehemiah on his way to Jerusalem with his blessing and protection. Whether Nehemiah was given the words to say in that exact moment or whether his four months of fasting and praying had given him the wisdom to craft a plan, he was ready when the king said yes. Even if God gave him supernatural favor—and Nehemiah was convinced this was so—it's clear he had the facts at hand in case his request met with favor. He knew how long it would take to complete his mission, and he knew the names of the appropriate officials to ensure his safety on the road. Nehemiah's preparation made it easy for the king to act, even though only God could truly incline the king's heart to say yes.

There's a second lesson: Pray, but don't act without preparation. Don't assume God will save the situation if you haven't done your homework. Fast, pray, and prepare. Nehemiah's faith showed a hopefulness that God would intervene *and* that he would be ready if that came to fruition.

Trap One: Nehemiah's Enemies

It can be difficult and frustrating to know what God is up to when we are in seasons of grief and/or waiting. Nehemiah didn't waste the time. It seems apparent that he was living up to the admonition in Colossians 3:23:

> Whatever you do, work at it with all your heart, as working for the Lord, not for human masters.

King Artaxerxes trusted, valued, and respected Nehemiah.
Even though Nehemiah had the support of the king, he wasn't welcomed back to Jerusalem with open arms by everyone living in the area.

> When Sanballat the Horonite and Tobiah the Ammonite official heard about this, they were very much disturbed that someone had come to promote the welfare of the Israelites.
>
> Nehemiah 2:10

Very much disturbed. Sanballat and Tobiah were foreign leaders who were not on board with the rebuilding of Jerusalem's wall, and you'll see all the different ways they tried to keep that from happening as you stay tuned.

Nehemiah wisely began an assessment of what needed to be done before diving into the work.

> I went to Jerusalem, and after staying there three days I set out during the night with a few others. I had not told anyone what my God had put in my heart to do for Jerusalem. There were no mounts with me except the one I was riding on.
>
> Nehemiah 2:11–12

Nehemiah was on the ground in Jerusalem, with the king's blessing, and yet his plan was still under wraps. In the verses that follow, we journey through the night with Nehemiah as he takes stock of just how bad the disrepair is. He didn't make a big announcement. He didn't take along a camera crew (to which I would have said "darn it!" at the time!). Even the leaders in the region weren't tipped off until Nehemiah himself had determined what needed to be done. Again, we see the sort of person Nehemiah was. He was careful and deliberate. He didn't seek out the spotlight, and he didn't even take credit for his plan to secretly survey the land; instead, he said it was all God's idea.

Don't ever feel like you need to be rushed along when God is leading your steps. Once he had taken a careful assessment, Nehemiah gathered the people who would join the mission he was leading.

> Then I said to them, "You see the trouble we are in: Jerusalem lies in ruins, and its gates have been burned with fire.

Come, let us rebuild the wall of Jerusalem, and we will no longer be in disgrace." I also told them about the gracious hand of my God on me and what the king had said to me.

They replied, "Let us start rebuilding." So they began this good work.

Nehemiah 2:17–18

Nehemiah once again pointed to the glory to God, and the Jews were immediately on board—much to the displeasure of Nehemiah's enemies. These foreign leaders got to work trying to undermine Nehemiah's authority.

But when Sanballat the Horonite, Tobiah the Ammonite official and Geshem the Arab heard about it, they mocked and ridiculed us. "What is this you are doing?" they asked. "Are you rebelling against the king?"

I answered them by saying, "The God of heaven will give us success. We his servants will start rebuilding, but as for you, you have no share in Jerusalem or any claim or historic right to it."

Nehemiah 2:19–20

It is almost guaranteed that when God calls you to something and you begin the work, the enemy is going to throw up obstacles in nearly every direction you turn. I love how Nehemiah responded to these guys. He could have easily said, "The most powerful ruler on earth has given me his backing, so sit down and shut up." (Maybe I'm channeling what *I* would have said!) Instead, Nehemiah went all the way to the top, saying, in essence, "Almighty God is with me, and you have no say in this."

There's a final lesson for us about Nehemiah. He was not only patient and prepared, but he was also pious—knowing that his true King was not Artaxerxes. As a result, he wasn't distracted by petty accusations or sidetracked into quarreling with his enemies on their own terms. He rejected the whole premise of their argument. Their issue wasn't about the king of Persia. It was about their attempt to deny the power of God.

In Nehemiah 3, we get to meet the dedicated men and women who began to restore Jerusalem's walls, gates, and infrastructure (and some who chose not to). Tens of thousands of displaced Jews had traveled back to Jerusalem generations earlier, but think about what they'd returned to. Businesses and homes had been decimated. What about cultivated fields for crop production so that they had reliable food sources? Irrigation systems? Even as these things began to return to function, the inhabitants of Jerusalem faced constant danger without city walls to keep invaders out. This vulnerability—coupled with political challenges—is why the work had faltered after the first generation of exiles returned on Cyrus's orders (2 Chronicles 36:22-23).

In many cases, the people worked on projects near their homes. It gave them a personal interest in the work and kept them from having to travel to get to their assignments. And while they were faithful and industrious, their opponents were scheming.

> When Sanballat heard that we were rebuilding the wall, he became angry and was greatly incensed. He ridiculed the Jews, and in the presence of his associates and the army of Samaria, he said, "What are those feeble Jews doing? Will they restore their wall? Will they offer sacrifices? Will they finish in a day? Can they bring the stones back to life from those heaps of rubble—burned as they are?"

Tobiah the Ammonite, who was at his side, said, "What they are building—even a fox climbing up on it would break down their wall of stones!"

Nehemiah 4:1-3

In my mind, these two guys are standing around like Cinderella's ugly stepsisters, just trash-talking and sulking. They were setting a trap for Nehemiah, hoping that their words would prompt him to overreact and give them an excuse to report him. Instead, their taunts sparked another prayer from Nehemiah. It demonstrates how near the danger was that he took a break from recording his enemies' insults to write a prayer in his account, switching to the present tense.

Hear us, our God, for we are despised. Turn their insults back on their own heads. Give them over as plunder in a land of captivity. Do not cover up their guilt or blot out their sins from your sight, for they have thrown insults in the face of the builders.

Nehemiah 4:4-5

Then, in classic Nehemiah style, he got back to work. His very next words were:

So we rebuilt the wall till all of it reached half its height, for the people worked with all their heart.

Nehemiah 4:6

Please tell me you're fist-pumping like I am as I read these verses. I'm gonna bookmark this prayer for my future run-ins with the enemy. *Turn their insults back on their own heads!* Oh, and by the way, the people just kept working their hearts out to rebuild the wall.

In the verses that follow, we learn that Sanballat and Tobiah and some of their friends were really ticked about the progress Nehemiah and the Israelites were making, and they began to plot against them. Nehemiah responded to their threats as he so often did.

> But we prayed to our God and posted a guard day and night to meet this threat.
>
> Nehemiah 4:9

He prayed *and* he acted. Despite that, some of the Jewish people were still afraid. They were overwhelmed by the scope of the work (Nehemiah 4:10) and the attacks on them (Nehemiah 4:12). Nehemiah stationed people at various parts of the city wall with weapons and gathered them together for a pep talk.

> After I looked things over, I stood up and said to the nobles, the officials and the rest of the people, "Don't be afraid of them. Remember the Lord, who is great and awesome, and fight for your families, your sons and your daughters, your wives and your homes."
>
> When our enemies heard that we were aware of their plot and that God had frustrated it, we all returned to the wall, each to our own work.
>
> Nehemiah 4:14–15

The people knew that, under Nehemiah's leadership, nothing was going to stop what God had ordained. You and I can take the same comfort and confidence when He is leading us. It doesn't have to make sense on paper or by the world's perspective. Remember Paul's admonition in Romans:

> What, then, shall we say in response to these things? If God is for us, who can be against us?
>
> Romans 8:31

Nehemiah's efforts contained all the right ingredients: humility, prayer, fasting, wise planning, reliance on the Lord, and hard work. From that point forward, he assigned people both to labor and protect; sometimes they did both at once (Nehemiah 4:17)! He also stayed vigilant.

> But the man who sounded the trumpet stayed with me.
> Then I said to the nobles, the officials and the rest of the people, "The work is extensive and spread out, and we are widely separated from each other along the wall. Wherever you hear the sound of the trumpet, join us there. Our God will fight for us!"
>
> Nehemiah 4:18–20

Nehemiah told the people to stay inside Jerusalem overnight so they could act as workers by day and guards by night. We learn that no one on security duty, including Nehemiah, was ever without a weapon (Nehemiah 4:23). We would be wise to take note and be sure we are always ready with our spiritual armaments.

Be alert and of sober mind. Your enemy the devil prowls around like a roaring lion looking for someone to devour. Resist him, standing firm in the faith, because you know that the family of believers throughout the world is undergoing the same kind of sufferings. And the God of all grace, who called you to his eternal glory in Christ, after you have suffered a little while, will himself restore you and make you strong, firm and steadfast.

1 Peter 5:8–10

The Lord never promises us we won't face opposition. He warns us that we *will*. But He expects us to equip ourselves, and He will help us to stand firm.

Trap Two: Nehemiah's Friends

Nehemiah had overcome the first trap his enemies set—the temptation to overreact or preemptively start a battle—but he was about to face a second potential snare. As is often the case, if the enemy can't get to us via outside forces, he's more than happy to sow some internal dissension. While Nehemiah was humbly leading the people to rebuild the physical walls of Jerusalem, there was also spiritual renewal that needed to happen. After all, in light of the whole biblical narrative, rebuilding Jerusalem was a way to enable the true work of building the kingdom of God in the people's hearts.

In Nehemiah 5, Nehemiah had to turn his attention to those concerns when it became evident that, mimicking the vicious tactics of their neighbors, some in the Jewish community were taking advantage of their brothers and sisters who were trying desperately to rebuild their lives while also being obligated to pay taxes to the Persian Empire.

> Now the men and their wives raised a great outcry against their fellow Jews. Some were saying, "We and our sons and daughters are numerous; in order for us to eat and stay alive, we must get grain."
> Others were saying, "We are mortgaging our fields, our vineyards and our homes to get grain during the famine."
> Still others were saying, "We have had to borrow money to pay the king's tax on our fields and vineyards. Although we are of the same flesh and blood as our fellow Jews and though our children are as good as theirs, yet we have to subject our sons and daughters to slavery. Some of our daughters have already been enslaved, but we are powerless, because our fields and our vineyards belong to others."
> When I heard their outcry and these charges, I was very angry.
>
> Nehemiah 5:1–6

Nehemiah was a just and godly man, so it's no surprise that he was livid about some of his fellow Israelites taking advantage of others in the community. But notice that Nehemiah was not mastered by his anger. Rather than lashing out, verse 7 tells us that he first "pondered" the cries for help that he'd heard. One translation says it was only "after seriously considering the matter" (CSB) that Nehemiah acted.

Have you ever wished you'd paused before lashing out at someone? I'm raising my hand up from the keyboard. My first impulse is often to respond with heat, especially if I'm fired up. I recently found out about a betrayal by someone I trusted as a friend. I didn't know the whole story, but an unlikely source had tipped me off to something brewing behind my back. I was livid. I said words I shouldn't have, but luckily that was just in my bathroom venting to my husband. I rehearsed a blistering takedown I couldn't wait to unleash on this person, and boy did I fill it with venom. But each time I went to pick up the phone some other matter required my immediate attention. It was several days before I could confront the person, and by then I had a lot more facts to work with. I would truly have regretted that confrontation I'd originally plotted. I both cringe (at the words I wouldn't have been able to take back) and sigh with relief (that delays kept me from responding in that first flash of anger).

It wasn't Nehemiah's style to fly off the handle. Instead, he modeled wisdom and discernment, and we would be smart to follow his example.

Having considered his options, Nehemiah got down to business and called out the nobles and officials behind the lopsided financial deal benefiting the richest and oppressing the poorest. Nehemiah decided it was time to let the people see his anger, paired with a demonstration of his mercy.

> So I called together a large meeting to deal with them and said: "As far as possible, we have bought back our fellow Jews who were sold to the Gentiles. Now you are selling your own people, only for them to be sold back to us!" They kept quiet, because they could find nothing to say.
>
> So I continued, "What you are doing is not right. Shouldn't you walk in the fear of our God to avoid the reproach of our

Gentile enemies? I and my brothers and my men are also lending the people money and grain. But let us stop charging interest! Give back to them immediately their fields, vineyards, olive groves and houses, and also the interest you are charging them—one percent of the money, grain, new wine and olive oil."

"We will give it back," they said. "And we will not demand anything more from them. We will do as you say."

Nehemiah 5:7–12

As the saying goes, "Trust but verify." Nehemiah called all the offenders together and made them take an oath to promise they would stop exploiting the people (Nehemiah 5:12). He also shook his robe and warned that God would shake out the homes and possessions of anyone who didn't keep the promise.

At this the whole assembly said, "Amen," and praised the LORD. And the people did as they had promised.

Nehemiah 5:13

It may feel easier at times to tackle the problems being caused by people outside your community. There's camaraderie when you have a common enemy. It's often more difficult to look around at the people you love and trust and to address the internal disputes. But Nehemiah didn't shy away from tackling anything that stood in the way of what God had placed on his heart.

This victory must have cemented Nehemiah's reputation as a wise and charismatic leader. After all, he was able to pressure powerful slave owners into giving up their property and sticking to their word.

Trap Three: The Temptation of Power

With the blessing and protection of King Artaxerxes, Nehemiah had been appointed governor to serve for more than a decade in Jerusalem, ultimately serving twelve years. Perhaps worried that he would be tempted by the perks of ancient leadership, during that entire time, he decided not to enjoy the benefits that came with the job—food, wine, and luxuries—funded by taxes on the people. "Out of reverence for God," Nehemiah chose the humble route instead and devoted himself "to the work on this wall" (Nehemiah 5:15–16). He knew the burdens on the people were already heavy, and though he legally could have, he opted not to live an elevated life while on his heavenly assignment. All he asked was that God remember him with favor (Nehemiah 5:19).

Though he was focused on the task at hand and not the trappings that came with it, Nehemiah's enemies weren't done scheming. They saw the progress that the people continued to make and wanted to lay a trap for Nehemiah. They repeatedly invited him to meet in a nearby village, but Nehemiah was on to them. He sent the same reply four times: *I'm busy doing something important, and I can't take a break.* (Nehemiah 6:3–4). They didn't give up so easily.

> Then, the fifth time, Sanballat sent his aide to me with the same message, and in his hand was an unsealed letter in which was written:
> "It is reported among the nations—and Geshem says it is true—that you and the Jews are plotting to revolt, and therefore you are building the wall. Moreover, according to these reports you are about to become their king and have even appointed prophets to make this proclamation about you in

Jerusalem: 'There is a king in Judah!' Now this report will get back to the king; so come, let us meet together."

I sent him this reply: "Nothing like what you are saying is happening; you are just making it up out of your head."

They were all trying to frighten us, thinking, "Their hands will get too weak for the work, and it will not be completed."

But I prayed, "Now strengthen my hands."

Nehemiah 6:5–9

In the face of a lot of threats and attempts to create fear, Nehemiah stood strong and focused. And once again, he prayed. It seems Nehemiah had also lived in such a way that he wasn't worried about word getting back to King Artaxerxes. He was trusted and honorable. It's something I like to say half-jokingly these days: I want to be a person known for integrity so when the "incriminating" AI deepfakes show up, no one will believe them!

By the way, old Sanballat and Tobiah were still at it. They hired someone to prophesy against Nehemiah and try to convince him he needed to abandon the project because his life was in danger. They wanted him to run and hide, to be discredited. Not only did Nehemiah resist, but he also asked God to handle his enemies—while he kept on working.

> Remember Tobiah and Sanballat, my God, because of what they have done; remember also the prophet Noadiah and how she and the rest of the prophets have been trying to intimidate me. So the wall was completed on the twenty-fifth of Elul, in fifty-two days.

Nehemiah 6:14–15

You read that right: fifty-two days!

> When all our enemies heard about this, all the surrounding nations were afraid and lost their self-confidence, because they realized that this work had been done with the help of our God.
>
> Nehemiah 6:16

No way could mere human hands have pulled off a feat like this. Don't you love it when God shows up and gets the glory? We, flawed vessels, get to partner with Him. That means we also get to *rely* on Him. It takes the pressure off, doesn't it? Yes, we are expected to be industrious, like Nehemiah, but we can rest in God's timing and provision for the results.

A Spiritual Homecoming

Remember, the city wall was just part of what Nehemiah wanted to rebuild in Jerusalem. He also wanted to restore the spiritual condition and morale of the people. There was a hunger and thirst for the truth of God's Word. In Nehemiah 8, the people gathered together and asked Ezra to bring out the Book of the Law of Moses and read it to them. This is a people who had strayed countless times from the Lord and His commands. They'd chased foreign idols and false gods, yet the reconstruction of the temple and the walls of their cherished city seems to have awakened something deep within their hearts.

So on the first day of the seventh month Ezra the priest brought the Law before the assembly, which was made up of men and women and all who were able to understand. He read it aloud from daybreak till noon as he faced the square before the Water Gate in the presence of the men, women and others who could understand. And all the people listened attentively to the Book of the Law.

Ezra the teacher of the Law stood on a high wooden platform built for the occasion. . . .

Ezra opened the book. All the people could see him because he was standing above them; and as he opened it, the people all stood up. Ezra praised the LORD, the great God; and all the people lifted their hands and responded, "Amen! Amen!" Then they bowed down and worshiped the LORD with their faces to the ground.

Nehemiah 8:2-4, 5-6

The people were dialed in, retuning their souls to God's principles. The following verses tell us that many godly men instructed the people, helping them to interpret what they were hearing so that they could understand it. Keep in mind, many of these returning Jewish exiles may never have learned to speak or understand Hebrew (we can see from Ezra that Aramaic was the common language in the Persian Empire by this point). And while they were hungry to hear the Word, they also began weeping—likely because they realized how far they had strayed from God's plans. Nehemiah told them not to mourn or weep but to remember the day as holy and to celebrate "for the joy of the LORD is your strength" (Nehemiah 8:10).

The people did rejoice, and they also began to revive their festivals and other traditions because the Law had been made known to them.

> From the days of Joshua son of Nun until that day, the Israelites had not celebrated it like this. And their joy was very great.
>
> Nehemiah 8:17

Their jubilation was also marked by deep repentance. They recognized their sins, they confessed them, and—most important—they turned away from them (Nehemiah 9:2). They also continued to study the Law and worship the Lord. Then several Levites (priests) called the people to stand as they offered up what is truly an epic prayer. For thirty-three verses, they praised God, confessed where they had all failed, revisited the beautiful history of Israel, and asked God to protect them as they started anew. It's worth your time to read through, and here's how it wraps up:

> "In all that has happened to us, you have remained righteous; you have acted faithfully, while we acted wickedly. Our kings, our leaders, our priests and our ancestors did not follow your law; they did not pay attention to your commands or the statutes you warned them to keep. Even while they were in their kingdom, enjoying your great goodness to them in the spacious and fertile land you gave them, they did not serve you or turn from their evil ways.
>
> "But see, we are slaves today, slaves in the land you gave our ancestors so they could eat its fruit and the other good things it produces. Because of our sins, its abundant harvest goes to the kings you have placed over us. They rule over our bodies and our cattle as they please. We are in great distress.
>
> "In view of all this, we are making a binding agreement,

putting it in writing, and our leaders, our Levites and our priests are affixing their seals to it."

Nehemiah 9:33–38

The people knew that though they had broken covenant with God, He was always faithful. They were deeply aware of how much they needed His protection and guidance, and they vowed to keep His commands. Later, in Nehemiah 10:30–39, we see the specific promises they made to the Lord.

With the physical walls and the spiritual framework in place, it was time for families to begin repopulating Jerusalem. One in ten were chosen to move back in, while the others stayed close by in other towns. Eventually, it was time to celebrate the glorious results of Nehemiah's bravery, faithfulness, and commitment to the dream God had placed in his heart long before. There were songs of thanksgiving with musical instruments, and singers. Nehemiah assigned two big choirs to march in different directions on the top of the wall. Clearly it withstood much more than the foxes that Tobiah had predicted would topple it.

> And on that day they offered great sacrifices, rejoicing because God had given them great joy. The women and children also rejoiced. The sound of rejoicing in Jerusalem could be heard far away.
>
> Nehemiah 12:43

I myself have always loved giant musical productions at church. It was something I longed to join when I was just a kid. Somehow, I talked my way into singing in the adult choir at the ripe old age of twelve.

I can only assume because my momma was a respected vocalist (and I was always waiting around for her during choir practice) that they caved to my begging. But I'm quite sure no choir performance I ever participated in came close to the joyful noise that was so loud on those Jerusalem walls that it could be heard well beyond the city.

As beautiful as those worship sessions were, the people weren't beyond backsliding. In the absence of good leadership, they drifted.

After Nehemiah had returned to Persia and was back in service to King Artaxerxes, he heard of trouble brewing in Jerusalem. Remember that vow everybody made and signed on to? Not everyone was sticking to it. In fact, the high priest, Eliashib, allowed Tobiah (yes, *that* guy!) to have a room "in the courts of the house of God" (Nehemiah 13:7). This same high priest had a grandson who married the daughter of our old friend Sanballat the Horonite, demonstrating just how determined those foreign enemies were to undermine the people of Israel.

On the other hand, it was hard to be a priest in those days. The people hadn't been supporting the Levites and the musicians as they had pledged to do. So Nehemiah headed back to Jerusalem and started cleaning house—literally. He spotted people violating the Sabbath and marrying outside their religious community. It got ugly.

> I rebuked them and called curses down on them. I beat some of the men and pulled out their hair. I made them take an oath in God's name.
>
> Nehemiah 13:25

Why was Nehemiah so angry? He seems more heated here than anywhere else in the book. See, there was a difference between the repentance of Nehemiah and the false repentance of those people in Jerusalem. They thought the goal was just to physically rebuild Jerusalem, and then they could continue living exactly like—and with!—their neighbors. Nehemiah understood that the goal of restoration was not just rebuilding a city but rebuilding a relationship with God, which meant living a distinct lifestyle. He understood just how fragile everything was—if the people abandoned God again, all their work could go down the drain. He probably had in mind these words of the psalmist:

> Unless the LORD builds the house,
> the builders labor in vain.
> Unless the LORD watches over the city,
> the guards stand watch in vain.
>
> Psalm 127:1

Nehemiah could have stayed at the king's palace in Persia. He could have plausibly argued that he'd already done the work God called him to. *I did my part; enforcing this is going to be up to someone else.* But he didn't. The journey to Jerusalem wasn't a short one—it was roughly nine hundred miles away from the Persian city of Susa, where he served King Artaxerxes. But Nehemiah was committed to overcoming oppression, whether external or internal. So he went all the way back to Jerusalem to make things right in the sight of God.

Throughout the final chapter of Nehemiah, we see him seeking reassurance—repeatedly praying that God would remember his faithfulness and view him with favor. It's hard to imagine that He wouldn't, but it's also a good reminder that even Nehemiah's calm wasn't unshakable—like all of us, he was capable of very human frustration.

Nehemiah didn't shy away from difficult assignments, and his story reminds us that we are all prone to wander—even after genuine spiritual revival. So while Nehemiah's repeated attempts to restore the Jewish people's spiritual connection with God were likely never finished, the One who would come centuries later would finally restore the people's hearts to God once and for all—as He will for all who will come to Him.

Study Questions

1. What homework might you need to do regarding dreams in your heart? How can you prepare for the moment when a door opens?
2. Nehemiah never seems to take the bait laid for him by his enemies. How would you rate your ability to do the same? Read and reflect on Galatians 5:22–23.
3. So often we have an impulse to immediately throttle our enemies. Why is stability and calmness such an important characteristic of a leader, spouse, friend?
4. What is true repentance and how should it lay the foundation for long-term spiritual maturity?
5. When is anger righteous or appropriate?

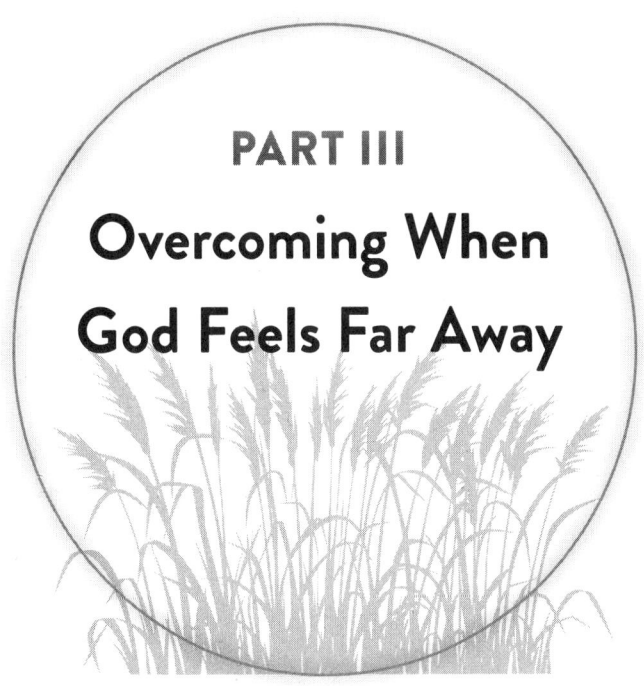

PART III
Overcoming When God Feels Far Away

Scripture is full of God's promises that He is with us. So why does He so often feel far away? So many thinkers have written about the "hiddenness" of God. That term refers to various things, from God's invisibility to—what seem to us to be—unanswered prayers.

Waiting on God can sometimes feel like an endless test. God doesn't operate on our timetable. Both Noah and Joshua, despite being faithful, had to wait decades to see the fulfillment of God's promises. Did they experience this as a moment of sorrow, wishing God would act sooner? C. S. Lewis wrote in his grief over his wife's death that God seemed silent and uncaring. "Why is He so present a commander in our time of prosperity and so very absent a help in time of trouble?"

Of course, God does hide Himself from those who refuse to seek Him, or who live in egregious unrepentant sin. But even God's faithful can experience a felt sense of His absence. David was the first to pray, "My God, my God, why have you forsaken me?" And Christ would go on to pray this as He experienced the Father turning His face away.

We know that God is never truly absent. And the way He reveals Himself often has to do with teaching us to understand Him on His terms and not ours. Elijah had to learn that God isn't always in the fire. Jesus constantly had to warn people not to come to Him for miracles, but for Himself.

We won't fully understand these things on this side of heaven, but the story of Christians who went through those hard times—and even of God willingly putting Himself through an experience of "divine absence"—should comfort us that even if we *feel* like it, we're never truly alone.

NOAH'S PATIENCE

Waiting on God in Hard Times

People often lament "the times we're living in" or refer to the past with statements like "things were different then." The phrase usually is meant to suggest that things are beyond our control, and so we're just forced to go with the flow. Many of us, consciously or unconsciously, conform because we don't want to look foolish. But what we're really talking about is what's fashionable in society—what thinkers used to call the zeitgeist, or spirit of the age. This is the story of Noah, a man who, by God's grace, didn't simply yield to what was accepted. Whether or not he knew it, the future of humanity rode on his choices.

But for the grace of God, you wouldn't be reading these words right now. In Noah's day, "the times" were so bad that the whole world nearly came to an end. Humanity could have been wiped off the face of the earth long ago, no history books filled with generations of adventurers, no amazing discoveries or advances. There would be no traveling to outer space or finding ways to translate the Bible into every language on the planet. That's because relatively early in our existence, humans had gotten so far off track that the Lord regretted that He'd created us at all! That's where we start the story of Noah.

> The LORD saw how great the wickedness of the human race had become on the earth, and that every inclination of the

thoughts of the human heart was only evil all the time. The LORD regretted that he had made human beings on the earth, and his heart was deeply troubled. So the LORD said, "I will wipe from the face of the earth the human race I have created—and with them the animals, the birds and the creatures that move along the ground—for I regret that I have made them." . . .

Now the earth was corrupt in God's sight and was full of violence. God saw how corrupt the earth had become, for all the people on earth had corrupted their ways. So God said to Noah, "I am going to put an end to all people, for the earth is filled with violence because of them. I am surely going to destroy both them and the earth."

Genesis 6:5–7, 11–13

We were made in God's image, every one of us (Genesis 1:27). He intended that we would walk with Him, enjoy and care for His creation, and reflect His glory. Instead, we got woefully off track. Not just dabbling in comfortable sins and being garden-variety selfish. We're all capable of that pretty much from birth. The times of Noah were something else entirely. *"Every* inclination of the thoughts of the human heart was *only evil all the time* . . . *all* the people on the earth had corrupted their ways." That doesn't seem to leave room for much redemption—then comes verse 8.

But Noah found favor in the eyes of the LORD.

Genesis 6:8

Because of Noah's faith, you and I are here. There was enough belief in this one man that God spared us all. Not that it came out of nowhere. Noah must have been guided by the example of the forerunners of faith in his own family line. He descended from Adam and Eve's son Seth, and that lineage includes the legendary Enoch. We're told in Genesis 5:24 that Enoch walked with God and "then he was no more, because God took him away." We see his faithfulness mentioned again in the New Testament:

> By faith Enoch was taken from this life, so that he did not experience death: "He could not be found, because God had taken him away."
>
> Hebrews 11:5

Noah honored that legacy in his own life. He wasn't perfect (more on that later), but that didn't keep the Lord from using Noah—an encouragement for every one of us flawed children of God.

Before the Ark: Noah's Years of Daring to Be Different

We often think of peer pressure in terms of kids or teens, and I was sad to discover it actually continues into adulthood. I was raised in a home that encouraged me to be as countercultural as necessary to stay true to my faith—"Be a modern-day Noah"! Did that make for some awkward moments while I was growing up? Heck yeah. I didn't go where other kids did. I didn't listen to the same music or watch the shows everyone gossiped about. Even as a kid my parents had somehow convinced me to wear my "otherness" as a badge of honor. So there is a part of me that will always feel a bit like I'm looking in from the outside. But like Noah, I've been human and made plenty of mistakes.

Every hero we meet in the Bible is shown for who he or she really is. Their stories aren't sanitized or glossed over. We see their failures, witness their sin. But we also see how God welcomes their repentance, restoring their brokenness into something that brings Him glory. Stories of God's judgment should not lead us to despair. Don't ever let anyone—including yourself—tell you that you're too far gone, that your story is too messy to be redeemed. That's a lie of the enemy. The pages of your Bible will tell you the truth.

What comes next in Noah's story may be the first concrete expression of the Lord's generous and loving grace toward Noah. "So make yourself an ark . . ." (Genesis 6:14a). God in His infinite mercy, as He always does, provided the way out. Humanity was actually facing two threats at this point: overwhelming evil and the impending flood. For Noah, God mapped out a way to overcome both. Second Peter 2:5 tells us God "protected Noah" because:

> . . . the Lord knows how to rescue the godly from trials and to hold the unrighteous for punishment on the day of judgment.
>
> 2 Peter 2:9

It's a picture we see over and over again, neatly woven all through the Bible. God desires redemption for us. He meets us right where we are.

> For it is by grace you have been saved, through faith—and this is not from yourselves, it is the gift of God—not by works, so that no one can boast.
>
> Ephesians 2:8–9

Grace through faith. That's Noah's story, and it can be ours, too. By the way—Ephesians 2:10 goes on to say:

> For we are God's handiwork, created in Christ Jesus to do good works, which God prepared in advance for us to do.

And boy, did Noah have some work to do.

The Lord set out the exact parameters for Noah's once-in-a-lifetime vessel, to be built on dry land.

> So make yourself an ark of cypress wood; make rooms in it and coat it with pitch inside and out. This is how you are to build it: The ark is to be three hundred cubits long, fifty cubits wide and thirty cubits high. Make a roof for it, leaving below the roof an opening one cubit high all around. Put a door in the side of the ark and make lower, middle and upper decks.
>
> Genesis 6:14–16

I always find it helpful to translate these numbers into something that allows me to picture the ark in a modern context. The length was about 450 feet, or nearly 1.5 football fields. It was 75 feet wide and about 45 feet high. This was not an elegant sailing ship. It was more like a giant barge. There was no propulsion system and no apparent way to guide or steer it. It was designed to float, but its direction was at the mercy of the elements. And as the story will go on to show, the Lord is master of the sky and the sea.

Noah was building something that made no sense by human standards—and that he had no power to control. Have you ever sensed the Lord asking you to do something like that? Have you been willing to take it on? Those are the questions at the core of

Noah's story. Maybe it's trying to repair a broken relationship. Maybe it's giving in a way that's going to cost you financially, and you aren't sure how you'll make up the difference. What if it's finally taking concrete steps toward a dream the Father has put on your heart? It doesn't have to line up with the world's logic if the Creator of the universe is asking you to move.

We don't always get a road map, but the Lord did tell Noah some more about what was eventually coming.

> I am going to bring floodwaters on the earth to destroy all life under the heavens, every creature that has the breath of life in it. Everything on earth will perish. But I will establish my covenant with you, and you will enter the ark—you and your sons and your wife and your sons' wives with you.
>
> Genesis 6:17–18

I often wonder if Noah felt sorrow over what the Lord told him was coming. Was he relieved that he and his family would be saved, but grieved over the death and destruction of every other living thing? I feel like I had the tiniest experience with this feeling during the early days of the pandemic back in 2020.

Because of the work I do, we'd been tracking the initial reporting on the mysterious illness beginning to sweep through pockets of China. I had access to many doctors, researchers, and intelligence experts—and what they were telling me was truly frightening. I remember crying in my shower one day, beginning to realize what was about to happen to the world. I ached that so much destruction was likely on the way and that there was absolutely nothing I could do to stop it. I knew our viewers and their loved ones would begin to understand the full impact in the weeks ahead, but for a period of time I felt like I was carrying around a lead weight in my chest. I grasped what was imminent, though billions around the world carried on with their lives, unaware of the coming catastrophe. It felt like an asteroid was on a collision course with Earth, but no one could comprehend the reality of what was about to hit.

In Noah's case, he knew almost no one would survive the Flood. But God had a plan for rebuilding the creation that had (mostly) forsaken Him, and that meant giving more unique instructions for His faithful servant.

> "You are to bring into the ark two of all living creatures, male and female, to keep them alive with you. Two of every kind of bird, of every kind of animal and of every kind of creature that moves along the ground will come to you to be kept alive. You are to take every kind of food that is to be eaten and store it away as food for you and for them."
>
> Noah did everything just as God commanded him.
>
> Genesis 6:19–22

No hesitation. Noah may not have understood exactly how God's plan would unfold, and he didn't demand that God fill him in before he acted in obedience. Many of us can probably picture what Noah must have seemed like—an eccentric with a boondoggle of a boat-building hobby, droning on about how God told him the apocalypse was near. If he lived today, we'd probably dismiss him as an obsessive or a crank. We'd roll our eyes when he started gushing about boatbuilding at family dinners, and sigh when he got on his moral high horse about our flaws. *How awkward*, we might whisper to each other, *that he doesn't mind his own business. Who is he to judge us?*

Most of us would like to think we're the Noah in the room, but more often than not, we're sitting there quietly going along with the flow, laughing at the rude jokes our boss makes, or joining in on the company gossip.

Reading the Skies: Obeying God When No One Else Sees What We See

So what was it that enabled Noah to step out of line, take a risk, and follow God when no one else did? It was the fact that Noah knew that, even if no one else could see what he could see, God could. The author of Hebrews describes this sort of expectant faith:

> Now faith is confidence in what we hope for and assurance about what we do not see. . . .
> By faith Noah, when warned about things not yet seen, in holy fear built an ark to save his family.
>
> Hebrews 11:1, 7a

"Things not yet seen." As I'm writing these words, I'm looking out the window by my desk at a stormy sky. I know what rain is, but there's a good chance the people of Noah's day didn't. When the sky darkened with an oncoming torrent, no one knew what it meant. Did it just seem like an oddly colored horizon, a clear blue turning bruised and purple? Why would it have been so mysterious? Back in Genesis 2, before God had created Adam and Eve we see this explanation:

> ... the Lord God had not sent rain on the earth ... streams came up from the earth and watered the whole surface of the ground.
>
> Genesis 2:5–6

Some translations say "mist" or "vapor" or "dew." We can't know for sure if it had rained prior to the ark, but we do know the Lord was about to send a flood unlike anything seen on the face of the earth. Just as the people couldn't see how their sin had corrupted creation, they couldn't read the signs of the sky—the darkening horizon that said that judgment was coming. Jesus will later use this turn of phrase himself to warn the Pharisees and Sadducees to stop asking God to prove Himself. By that time, mankind knew what to look for when rain was coming, but they still hadn't learned to "interpret the signs of the times" (Matthew 16:3), which is to say, to understand that God Himself had come to them in the form of a man. Instead of interpreting the truth, they let themselves be led astray by groupthink.

Noah shows the answer: instead of being led by the times, we must interpret them rightly. The first step toward doing that is being in relationship with God—obeying Him, even before we understand His plans and purposes.

And part of walking with God is that He lets us do the walking! Have you ever wondered why God didn't just build the ark Himself? It likely required decades of labor by a man who was probably several hundred years old at the point he started on the massive project. It certainly would have attracted attention, so was construction of the ark an opportunity to witness to a desperately lost world? Peter would later call Noah "a preacher of righteousness" (2 Peter 2:5). It must have sparked conversation with anyone who happened upon this most unusual construction site. Interestingly, though, we don't see a single word from Noah recorded in Genesis. He's not debating with God, like Gideon or Moses. He's simply acting, and sometimes that's our most powerful witness of all.

Noah confirmed what the Lord already knew about him, that he was a faithful, obedient man. God always has the ability to fast-forward what He's asking us to do. He doesn't need our help. But He does invite us to partner with Him in the work of building His kingdom. What an honor. We are made more Christ-like in the process as we share His hope with others.

C. S. Lewis asked the question: why *does* God choose to delay and hand the keys to us? We're such bad drivers! Lewis wrote that God...

> ... seems to do nothing of Himself which He can possibly delegate to His creatures. He commands us to do slowly and blunderingly what He could do perfectly and in the twinkling of an eye. He allows us to neglect what He would have us do, or to fail. Perhaps we do not fully realize the problem, so to call it, of enabling finite free wills to co-exist with Omnipotence. It seems to involve at every moment almost sort of a divine abdication. We are not mere recipients or spectators. We are either privileged to share in the game or compelled to collaborate in the work, "to wield our little tridents." Is this amazing process simply Creation going on before our eyes?

This is a startling way to read Genesis—every time God calls us to work with him, He's continuing Creation. In calling Noah, God was trying—yet again—to appoint a second Adam, a leader who would this time overcome the temptations of sin and cultivate a new world. But with Noah there's something different from the original creation story. This time, new life would come forth in the wake of destruction. Noah's story reminds me of someone else who built a bit of an ark herself: Jochebed. You met her in the chapter about her son, Moses. She built a baby ark and sent her child out onto the very waters where he would have otherwise been sent to die. Like Noah, she couldn't control that watercraft she'd created or know where it would end up. All she could do was trust God. What Jochebed and Noah's stories shared was their status as faithful heroes. They saw the entire world chasing after evil and chose to go against the flow because of the hope they could not see. But for Noah . . . faith would, in part, become sight.

Finally, the time Noah had faithfully worked toward arrived.

> The LORD then said to Noah, "Go into the ark, you and your whole family, because I have found you righteous in this generation. . . . Seven days from now I will send rain on the earth for forty days and forty nights, and I will wipe from the face of the earth every living creature I have made."
>
> And Noah did all that the LORD commanded him.
>
> Genesis 7:1, 4–5

At this point, Noah was six hundred years old. He had toiled long and hard without question or hesitation, but that's when the waiting began. That promised flood was coming.

When I was a kid, one of my favorite things at church was kids' choir. At least a couple times a year we'd put on a musical, and I looked forward to every bit of the preparation. I loved learning the lyrics, the harmonies and—yes—all the cheesy, Baptist-approved "choreography." There is one song in particular that often pops into my mind when I get stuck in Washington, DC, traffic. It's about Herbert the Snail, and the chorus goes like this:

> Have patience,
> Have patience
> Don't be in such a hurry
> When you get—impatient, you only start to worry.

We would alternate between singing the words as quickly as they would tumble out of our little mouths, and then eventually shift gears down to a painfully slooooooooooow cadence—as if Herbert himself was leading the performance. Haaaaaaaaaaaaaaave paaaaaaaaaaaatience. It may sound silly, but it's stuck with me for decades. I'm still working on it!

We see not a single flinch from Noah, though. The Lord instructed him on final preparations and told him what He'd promised was just seven days away. Whatever naysayers may have mocked Noah while he was building the ark must have thought he'd really lost it when he started loading up every kind of animal known to man. And the Bible tells us Noah didn't have to round up a single one. They all came to him. What a sight that must have been!

It's a position we are likely to find ourselves in at some point, looking foolish to the world for following God's law. The Lord doesn't owe us an explanation when He asks us to obey. Scripture makes clear that some of the greatest heroes of the faith didn't get to see what they hoped for actually come to fruition in their lifetimes, people like Abraham and Sarah.

> All these people were still living by faith when they died. They did not receive the things promised; they only saw them

and welcomed them from a distance, admitting that they were foreigners and strangers on earth.

Hebrews 11:13

But even if God doesn't provide all the details about why we're supposed to obey Him, he does provide a reason for *why* we're expected to obey Him, by revealing His character as that of a loving father. Obedience and love are bound up together, Jesus explained:

> Whoever has my commands and keeps them is the one who loves me. The one who loves me will be loved by my Father, and I too will love them and show myself to them.

John 14:21

Even though Noah didn't have the same total view of God's plan that we do in light of Jesus's resurrection, he intuited that his Creator was Someone he could trust and follow. And God, in His mercy, let Noah see the fulfillment of his crazy boat-building mission.

Noah, counted among those Hebrews heroes of the faith, was about to see exactly what God had promised him.

> In the six hundredth year of Noah's life, on the seventeenth day of the second month—on that day all the springs of the great deep burst forth, and the floodgates of the heavens were opened. And rain fell on the earth forty days and forty nights. . . .
>
> For forty days the flood kept coming on the earth, and

as the waters increased they lifted the ark high above the earth. The waters rose and increased greatly on the earth, and the ark floated on the surface of the water. They rose greatly on the earth, and all the high mountains under the entire heavens were covered. The waters rose and covered the mountains to a depth of more than fifteen cubits. Every living thing that moved on land perished—birds, livestock, wild animals, all the creatures that swarm over the earth, and all mankind. Everything on dry land that had the breath of life in its nostrils died. Every living thing on the face of the earth was wiped out; people and animals and the creatures that move along the ground and the birds were wiped from the earth. Only Noah was left, and those with him in the ark.

The waters flooded the earth for a hundred and fifty days.

Genesis 7:11–12, 17–24

Complete and total destruction.

And then . . . more waiting. What was life like inside that floating farm? Were the storms frightening in their fury, or were Noah and his family calm in the assurance that the Lord was preserving their lives? Did they wonder where they were? How did they divide up the care (and cleanup) related to all those animals? Oh, the questions I have for this family!

Genesis 8 starts by telling us that God remembered Noah and every living thing on the ark and "sent a wind over the earth" (v.1) so that the waters began to recede. This was the turning point. The old ways, the wickedness, the human failing that so grieved God was behind. A new start was unfolding.

A New Promise and Covenant

Eventually, the ark came to rest on the "mountains of Ararat" (Genesis 8:4) and finally the tops of the mountains started to be visible. What follows echoes the creation sequence, as God again separated the earth from the water in set periods of time. Little by little, God began to show Noah signs of the life to come. Some of those were in the form of a dove. The first time Noah sent the dove out it returned to the ark because there was nowhere for it to land that wasn't covered in water.

> He waited seven more days and again sent out the dove from the ark. When the dove returned to him in the evening, there in its beak was a freshly plucked olive leaf! Then Noah knew that the water had receded from the earth. He waited seven more days and sent the dove out again, but this time it did not return to him.
>
> Genesis 8:10–12

Noah waited and watched as the earth continued to dry out. By most calculations, it was roughly a year after Noah had entered the ark when he finally heard these words:

> Then God said to Noah, "Come out of the ark, you and your wife and your sons and their wives. Bring out every kind of living creature that is with you—the birds, the animals, and all the creatures that move along the ground—so they can multiply on the earth and be fruitful and increase in number on it."
>
> So Noah came out, together with his sons and his wife and

his sons' wives. All the animals and all the creatures that move along the ground and all the birds—everything that moves on land—came out of the ark, one kind after another.

Then Noah built an altar to the LORD and, taking some of all the clean animals and clean birds, he sacrificed burnt offerings on it. The LORD smelled the pleasing aroma and said in his heart: "Never again will I curse the ground because of humans, even though every inclination of the human heart is evil from childhood. And never again will I destroy all living creatures, as I have done.

"As long as the earth endures,
seedtime and harvest,
cold and heat,
summer and winter,
day and night
will never cease."

Genesis 8:15–22

Noah, faithful from the start, began his new life—the restart for humanity—by building an altar and honoring the Lord.

This is the first mention of an altar in the Bible. We know there were other sacrifices, but this is our earliest look at a structure for sacrifice, built by a human who was coming before God with reverence and thanksgiving. Throughout Scripture, altars were where mankind brought his sins and shortcomings to lay before God's holiness. At that place, the meeting of two wildly different positions, God poured out His redemption.

After all Noah and his family had been through, before they took a single step forward in their brand-new lives—they stopped to honor the Lord. Noah had been told to build the ark, and with great detail. He followed God's commands. This time, Noah took the initiative to build the altar. He wasn't prompted or nudged. He chose to set that marker and offer up those sacrifices.

It's a beautiful illustration of thanking and praising God for each storm he brings us through. Sometimes when we've weathered a difficult season it's almost a challenge for our brains to see that we made it to the other side. If you've been fighting and scraping, it may be unfamiliar to be in a place of relief and rest. It may take time to let the realization settle into your heart and mind that you are in a place of peace and restoration. What a season of overwhelming thanksgiving it can be. There are very painful journeys in my life I would never have chosen, but I can thank God for what He accomplished and for His presence in the valley. Altars were places of remembrance in times of old, and we should build spiritual symbols in our own lives, too. While, under the new covenant, we don't need an altar, Christians use crosses as a reminder of gratitude for the final sacrifice that Christ made—those Roman crossbeams acting as an altar for the sacrifice of the Son of God. Noah's altar, then, was a foreshadowing, or a "sign," of that moment.

Remember that Noah had limited resources when he stepped off that ark. His family had only what they'd taken on with them, but he didn't hesitate to sacrifice what he had. Noah had seen God do the impossible, so we can assume that he wasn't worried about offering up what was already God's anyway. Noah came from a lineage of godly forefathers, and he was modeling that for his sons and their families moving forward. That altar would have been a permanent fixture in their lives and community—a testament to God's rescue and to their thanks for it.

It was also an action that moved the Lord. He smelled the "pleasing aroma" of the sacrifices and "said in His heart" that he would never again curse the ground or destroy every living thing

(Genesis 8:21). Our offerings resonate with the Lord. It matters to Him that we turn our thanksgiving and praise in His direction, that we can say after a storm: thank you. In Noah's case it prompted an eternal covenant.

Genesis 9 begins with the Lord giving Noah and his descendants dominion over everything on the earth. He also warned that human life was precious.

> And from each human being, too, I will demand an accounting for the life of another human being.
> "Whoever sheds human blood,
> by humans shall their blood be shed;
> for in the image of God
> has God made mankind.
> As for you, be fruitful and increase in number; multiply on the earth and increase upon it."
>
> Genesis 9:5b–7

The message is clear, to take a human life is to desecrate something made in God's very image. It's the one thing most like God Himself that a human can violate.

After this warning, our Creator outlined His covenant with the one righteous family He chose to save, a promise that resembles the later promises to Abraham, Israel, and the church, in its affirmation of God's unchanging character.

> "I now establish my covenant with you and with your descendants after you and with every living creature that was with you—the birds, the livestock and all the wild animals, all those that came out of the ark with you—every living creature

on earth. I establish my covenant with you: Never again will all life be destroyed by the waters of a flood; never again will there be a flood to destroy the earth."

Genesis 9:9–11

This language is echoed and the promise reaffirmed in Isaiah 54.

> "To me this is like the days of Noah,
> when I swore that the waters of Noah would never again cover the earth.
> So now I have sworn not to be angry with you,
> never to rebuke you again.
> Though the mountains be shaken
> and the hills be removed,
> yet my unfailing love for you will not be shaken
> nor my covenant of peace be removed,"
> says the LORD, who has compassion on you.

Isaiah 54: 9–10

His promise to Noah was the first of several key covenants God would make with humanity, and He marked it with something He knew could be a constant—and beautiful—reminder.

And God said, "This is the sign of the covenant I am making between me and you and every living creature with you, a covenant for all generations to come: I have set my rainbow in the clouds, and it will be the sign of the covenant between me and the earth. Whenever I bring clouds over the earth and the rainbow appears in the clouds, I will remember my covenant between me and you and all living creatures of every kind. Never again will the waters become a flood to destroy all life. Whenever the rainbow appears in the clouds, I will see it and remember the everlasting covenant between God and all living creatures of every kind on the earth."

So God said to Noah, "This is the sign of the covenant I have established between me and all life on the earth."

Genesis 9:12–17

Remember that passage earlier about reading the signs of the sky? Now, humanity knew what a rainy sky looked like—a sign of God's judgment—but also what a rainbow was—a sign of His mercy. Rainbows are a fascinating phenomenon. It makes sense—that if it hadn't rained before the flood, in God's providence, they would only appear afterward. You have to have rain in the skies to get to that colorful arc. Here's a little bit more about how it works, courtesy of the U.S. Geological Survey's (USGS) Water Science School:

> Sunlight is white light, but white light actually contains all of the colors of the rainbow all ready for you to see, but blended together. Light has wavelengths and each color of light has a different wavelength. When the light enters [a prism], which is denser than air, it slows down and is bent, with the different wavelengths that make up white light bending at different angles (red on one side to violet on the other). . . .
>
> Just why do rainbows have colors? It is because . . . the raindrops refract the light from the sun into a color spectrum. . . .
>
> The water drop is acting like a prism, except the light is being refracted at three different points (some of the light bounces off the back of the raindrop and back out to you as you watch).

Each time the light beam bounces, it gets wider, and the rainbow you see is a combination of millions of these light beams coming back to you.

Millions of little light beams bouncing off raindrops so God can remind you of the covenant He made with Noah. And here's a nugget I love. The USGS says the brightest, biggest rainbows come from the heaviest rainstorms with the largest raindrops. So the wildest storms give you the clearest, most colorful picture of that covenant!

And there would be more covenants to come, including Christ's sacrifice, which provides us the ultimate in forgiveness and redemption. In days of old, sacrifices were the norm and they were repetitive. In the Old Testament, no one was able to make a sacrifice and find lifelong atonement. There had to be regular offerings, whether individually or on behalf of the nation. All of them, including Noah's offerings on the altar he built, pointed to the day God's only Son would pay that debt once and for all.

The Ark Is a Sign: Looking to the Future

The ark was also a picture of the salvation that would come through Christ. Just as then, the world is now marred by evil. Everywhere you look, there are distortions of the peace and splendor God had planned for us. Jesus spoke of the parallels while addressing his disciples on the Mount of Olives.

> As it was in the days of Noah, so it will be at the coming of the Son of Man. For in the days before the flood, people were eating and drinking, marrying and giving in marriage, up to the day Noah entered the ark; and they knew nothing about

what would happen until the flood came and took them all away. That is how it will be at the coming of the Son of Man.

Matthew 24:37–39

Yes, there is corruption all around, but there is also now a permanent way of escape. Just get into the ark and you will be saved. Christ is our vessel of deliverance. Do we share the urgency that Noah must have felt? Do we look around at the lost and brokenhearted and grieve for them? Or do we look at our ark (Christ) and simply feel thankful that we have a way out?

Before we leave Noah, I think it's important to touch on the fact that he was human. We never reach perfection in our walk of faith, and he didn't either—despite a righteousness solid enough to motivate God to spare him at a time the Almighty had decided it was time to nearly wipe humanity from the face of the earth.

> Noah, a man of the soil, proceeded to plant a vineyard. When he drank some of its wine, he became drunk and lay uncovered inside his tent. Ham, the father of Canaan, saw his father naked and told his two brothers outside. But Shem and Japheth took a garment and laid it across their shoulders; then they walked in backward and covered their father's naked body. Their faces were turned the other way so that they would not see their father naked.
>
> When Noah awoke from his wine and found out what his youngest son had done to him, he said,
>
> "Cursed be Canaan!
> The lowest of slaves
> will he be to his brothers."
> He also said,

> "Praise be to the LORD, the God of Shem!
> May Canaan be the slave of Shem.
> May God extend Japheth's territory;
> may Japheth live in the tents of Shem,
> and may Canaan be the slave of Japheth."
>
> Genesis 9:20–27

Yes, even this family with a rich legacy of honorable men had its own messes. Was the curse regarding Canaan a prophecy or was it a punishment? In either case, what Noah said played out in the generations to come. Canaan's descendants later occupied the land known by the same name. In Genesis 12:6-7, the Lord promised that land to Abraham's descendants. It wasn't until hundreds of years later that the pledge was fulfilled, and there was plenty of conflict and struggle in the interim. The Canaanites were eventually subjugated, just as Noah had said they would be.

Even after Noah's humble obedience, mankind still had plenty of *overcoming* to do. Noah lived another 350 years after the flood, for a total of 950 years (Genesis 9:28–29). His life shows us that even an imperfect man can be capable of integrity worthy of God's praise. It's often when things around us are darkest that—by contrast—our testimony will shine brightest. Like Noah, Lot—"A righteous man"—was "rescued" by God because he stood out in a time of what Peter writes of as "lawless" (2 Peter 2:7). We can learn from Noah that it is possible to stand up for the truth when no one else will, if we do as he did: trust God's call, obey even when we look foolish, hold to the hope set before us, and remember the cross.

May the choices we make in times of compromise, and our willingness to obey when we can't see the clear path ahead, lead God to find us just as he did Noah and Lot: righteous. It's from that place that we *overcome*, with God's provision, the evil around us.

Study Questions

1. What is God asking you to do that resonates in your spirit, but may make no sense to the world?
2. How can your faithfulness in that "thing" be a witness to both believers and non-believers in your life?
3. Even after the storm stopped, Noah waited for roughly a year in the ark before God told him to get out. We see no record of God communicating directly with Noah during that time. How do you keep moving forward when you're in a holding pattern?
4. As righteous as he was, Noah had his own failings. How does that knowledge impact you as a believer saved by grace?
5. The next time you see a rainbow, remember God's covenant and share the story with someone who doesn't know the biblical promise.

JOSHUA'S OBEDIENCE

Staying an Optimist in a Pessimist's World

Numbers 13–14, Joshua 1–6

I don't know about you, but when someone tells me I can't do something, I'm probably going to sprain a body part trying to prove them wrong. It's not a vengeful thing; it's a determination thing. I actually enjoy being underestimated. It helps you to surprise people! When I was a twenty-something attorney with a baby face, visitors to my firm often assumed I was the one making the coffee or taking notes when they showed up for a meeting or deposition. It didn't bother me one bit. It was fun when I got to introduce myself as the attorney handling the matter and then watch them fall all over themselves trying to pretend they'd known that was the case all along.

Same thing with the heavy Southern accent I had before I had to tone it down for broadcasting. I had more than one person tell me no one would take me seriously or assess me as intelligent if I showed up with that voice. Fine by me! I prefer the element of surprise anyway. Doubters can sideline you or they can spur you on. And when there's fear in the mix, it's more often the former than the latter.

But then there are those people who *do* know you and still question your abilities. Those actually hurt. My agent was in the midst of negotiations for me decades ago, talking to my then-employer about the professional ambitions I hoped to achieve. By her telling, my then-boss replied with a bit of a laugh, "She's not network material." Ouch! (And this is a different boss than the one who fired me from my first TV job!)

The story of Joshua is a story of people doubting someone they should have known beyond all doubt was capable. And it wasn't Joshua! It was the One he served. The way I felt about my boss's rejection was nothing compared to this—the people of Israel were rejecting the God who had just saved them with miracles and wonders from one of the mightiest empires in the world. But this is also a story about some people who resisted doubt. How did those believers maintain their faith in God when everyone around them had slipped into pessimism? The answer isn't as obvious as you might think.

Taking God for Granted in the Wilderness

We probably shouldn't feel too superior to the doubting Israelites. Our human minds can easily default to worst-case scenarios, and it can be hard for optimistic messages to break through. That's exactly what happened to the newly freed people of Israel who struggled to believe all that the Lord had promised them would truly come to fruition—despite having witnessed a series of stunning miracles. Remember, these folks had just seen the waters of the Red Sea peeled back and turned into solid walls so the people could walk through on dry land. It's hard to imagine experiencing that and not being permanently in amazement of God's power and goodness. And yet . . .

Much as we are capable of doing in our own lives, the people of Israel were quick to forget what God had done for them when they were confronted with another seemingly impossible challenge. By most scholars' estimates, it was roughly fifteen months after the miracle of the Red Sea parting that the people had finally arrived at the cusp of the promised land. The Lord had been guiding them there with a cloud by day and pillar of fire by night (Exodus 13:21–22). How had that daily miracle of God's visible presence leading the way become so commonplace to them that they were dulled to just how incredible it truly was?

Did you ever go to an amusement park as a kid? I remember the tingles all the way down to my toes when we started the approach to Disney World. We saw billboards for miles on the interstate before we got to the actual park, telling us about all the unbelievable things we were going to see and do. Even once we got to the park grounds, it seemed the road stretched on forever. We were so close I could almost taste that turkey leg in the Frontier Land section of the park. I was psyched! How seldom do we as adults rise out of our jaded daily lives to feel such excitement?

You might think that childlike anticipation would be an accurate reflection of the Israelites' feelings, approaching a land of plenty beyond their wildest dreams. That's not exactly how we find the Israelites in Numbers 13.

> The LORD said to Moses, "Send some men to explore the land of Canaan, which I am giving to the Israelites. From each ancestral tribe send one of its leaders."
>
> Numbers 13:1–2

Notice God did not say, "Go check things out to see if you've got a chance against these guys." No, He told Moses clearly that the land would be theirs. Twelve men—one from each of the twelve tribes—

were selected to do reconnaissance on the abundance in the land of Canaan.

Caleb and Joshua's Understanding of God's Character

Among these spies were Caleb and Hoshea. Hoshea means "salvation." Moses changed his name to Joshua, meaning "Yahweh is salvation" (Numbers 13:16). That little switch underlines the heart of the story: Salvation won't come from the might of Israel—that ragged band of freed slaves who'd never had to operate as an army—but from their God, Yahweh. Israel needed to relate to God less like a mafia boss they could call in a pinch, and more like a loving Father they rely on because they trusted Him. As we'll see, understanding this correctly is part of what made Joshua different from most of the other spies.

The chosen twelve men were going to scout out something much bigger and better than any theme park. Moses told them to check out the soil, the people, and the cities and towns. He urged them to be courageous and to bring back some fruit for them to size up. The spies understood their assignment, taking note of all the relevant details. While they were checking out the land, they even cut down a cluster of grapes that was so enormous they put it on a pole that had to be carried by two men. For forty days, they gathered information about the land of Canaan to take back to the people.

When the spies finally returned, the Israelites were eager to hear what they'd discovered. They saw the oversized fruit and listened as the scouts told them of a land that "does flow with milk and honey"—meaning it was a place of great abundance (Numbers 13:27). Then ten of the twelve spies dropped the bomb of discouragement.

But the people who live there are powerful, and the cities are fortified and very large. We even saw descendants of Anak there. The Amalekites live in the Negev; the Hittites, Jebusites and Amorites live in the hill country; and the Canaanites live near the sea and along the Jordan.

Numbers 13:28-29

Just a couple of verses later, they ramped up their negativity.

"We can't attack those people; they are stronger than we are." And they spread among the Israelites a bad report about the land they had explored. They said, "The land we explored devours those living in it. All the people we saw there are of great size. We saw the Nephilim there (the descendants of Anak come from the Nephilim). We seemed like grasshoppers in our own eyes, and we looked the same to them."

Numbers 13:31-33

The spy from the tribe of Judah, Caleb, had been on that same forty-day scouting mission, yet he came away with a totally different perspective. The Bible says he "silenced the people" and then made his pitch.

We should go up and take possession of the land, for we can certainly do it.

Numbers 13:30

We see Caleb's childlike faith—he didn't feel the need to make a complex, detailed explanation of his position. To him, it was totally obvious that God would come through for His people. But while God had already told them the land was theirs, fear and doubt were ruling the day. Only Joshua and Caleb believed that the God who had dropped ten devastating plagues on the Egyptians, guided His people by supernatural cloud and fire, and parted the Red Sea could also handle the humans who inhabited the land promised to Abraham, Isaac, and Jacob. The rumors spread by the naysayers caused a camp-wide meltdown.

> That night all the members of the community raised their voices and wept aloud. All the Israelites grumbled against Moses and Aaron, and the whole assembly said to them, "If only we had died in Egypt! Or in this wilderness! Why is the LORD bringing us to this land only to let us fall by the sword? Our wives and children will be taken as plunder. Wouldn't it be better for us to go back to Egypt?" And they said to each other, "We should choose a leader and go back to Egypt."
>
> Numbers 14:1–4

Every time I've had a personal struggle with sin or a stronghold in my life, I hear myself having this same conversation when it gets tough. *It would be so much easier to just go back to slavery!* No, no, it wouldn't. Remember how miserable and trapped you were there? How you dreamed of the day you could break free and go live a life of hope and promise? Make decisions without a slave master dragging you back to captivity and oppression?

The people were so overcome with fear that they decided they'd pick someone to take them back to that dreadful place where their heavenly Father had unleashed hell to set them free. Let's not make that same mistake. On that note, be careful what you ask for. The people imagined it would be better to die in slavery or in the wilderness than in a battle. Because of their disbelief and rebellion, God was eventually going to grant that request.

Joshua and Caleb weren't done making their case just yet.

> [They] tore their clothes and said to the entire Israelite assembly, "The land we passed through and explored is exceedingly good. If the LORD is pleased with us, he will lead us into that land, a land flowing with milk and honey, and will give it to us. Only do not rebel against the LORD. And do not be afraid of the people of the land, because we will devour them. Their protection is gone, but the LORD is with us. Do not be afraid of them."
>
> Numbers 14:6–9

Those people don't have the God who created and sustains the universe—we do! They're the ones who should be afraid.

Their words were not well-received. Instead, Scripture tells us the people were getting ready to stone Joshua and Caleb when the Lord Himself showed up.

The Prince Who Became a Shepherd Intercedes for His Sheep

> The LORD said to Moses, "How long will these people treat me with contempt? How long will they refuse to believe in me, in spite of all the signs I have performed among them?"
>
> Numbers 14:11

Moses knew the wrath of God was real and powerful, and he immediately began interceding on behalf of the people. Lord, what will the Egyptians think if they hear You decided to wipe out all Your people before even getting them to the land You've promised them?

"Now may the Lord's strength be displayed, just as you have declared: 'The LORD is slow to anger, abounding in love and forgiving sin and rebellion. Yet he does not leave the guilty unpunished; he punishes the children for the sin of the parents to the third and fourth generation.' In accordance with your great love, forgive the sin of these people, just as you have pardoned them from the time they left Egypt until now."

Numbers 14:17–19

Note here the knowledge of God's character that Moses displayed. It's clear that despite the dramatic judgments that occurred during the book of Exodus, Moses had discerned that at His heart, God is love. God's sword is His Word, which cuts the heart but for the purpose of pouring in His steadfast love. It's also clear that despite Moses's frustrations with the people of Israel, he loved them, too, inspiring him to stand "in the breach before" God (Psalm 106:23) for them. The Lord had mercy on His people, but there would be consequences.

The LORD replied, "I have forgiven them, as you asked. Nevertheless, as surely as I live and as surely as the glory of the LORD fills the whole earth, not one of those who saw my glory and the signs I performed in Egypt and in the wilderness but who disobeyed me and tested me ten times—not one of them will ever see the land I promised on oath to their ancestors. No one who has treated me with contempt will ever see it."

Numbers 14:20–23

The Lord was angry with His people for their disobedience, and they would pay the price. Throughout Scripture, you'll see references to what happened when they refused to move forward on His assurance about this land He'd pledged to them and guided them to.

> "Do not harden your hearts as you did at Meribah,
> as you did that day at Massah in the wilderness,
> where your ancestors tested me;
> they tried me, though they had seen what I did.
> For forty years I was angry with that generation;
> I said, 'They are a people whose hearts go astray,
> and they have not known my ways.'
> So I declared on oath in my anger,
> 'They shall never enter my rest.'"

Psalm 95:8–11

An entire unbelieving generation of Israelites (except Joshua and Caleb) missed the opportunity to dwell in the promised land because they refused to take God at His word. There are times in all our lives when it seems much easier to follow the majority, especially if we ourselves are unmoored from the truth. As followers of Christ, we will always be in the minority in some respect, and we should embrace the discomfort that can come with that. As Jesus said:

"Enter through the narrow gate. For wide is the gate and broad is the road that leads to destruction, and many enter through it. But small is the gate and narrow the road that leads to life, and only a few find it."

Matthew 7:13–14

Faithfulness in the Wilderness: Keeping Rooted in the Deep Waters of God's Word

John told us we are "not of the world" (John 17:14–16). Peter reminded us we are "foreigners" and "exiles" (1 Peter 2:11). Paul urged us not to "conform to the pattern of this world" (Romans 12:2). Bottom line: We should be comfortable breaking from the majority and choosing to trust God, just as Caleb and Joshua did. As you will see later in Elijah's story, the Lord is fully capable of preserving His people—especially a minority that stays bound to Him in faithfulness, even when mistakenly believing they are alone.

But it's easy to *say* we should be like Caleb and Joshua. It's a lot harder to actually *do* it. The process of doing that might just involve some time in the wilderness. God doesn't promise we won't face periods of dryness, just that He'll be with us through them.

> "But blessed is the one who trusts in the LORD,
> whose confidence is in him.
> They will be like a tree planted by the water
> that sends out its roots by the stream.
> It does not fear when heat comes;
> its leaves are always green.

It has no worries in a year of drought
and never fails to bear fruit."

Jeremiah 17:7–8

On the other hand, those whose spiritual roots don't reach the deep water of God's Word will experience the wilderness not as a chance to grow but as a place of hopelessness.

In the face of the Israelites' unwillingness to move forward, the Lord decided to send them *backward*. He told Moses, *Head for the wilderness* (Numbers 14:25). He also gave Moses and Aaron a harsh and difficult message to give to the people: No one aged twenty years or older (with the exception of Joshua and Caleb) would enter the promised land (Numbers 14:29). Their grumbling wish to die in the wilderness would be granted.

> "But as for you, your bodies will fall in this wilderness. Your children will be shepherds here for forty years, suffering for your unfaithfulness, until the last of your bodies lies in the wilderness. For forty years—one year for each of the forty days you explored the land—you will suffer for your sins and know what it is like to have me against you. I, the Lord, have spoken, and I will surely do these things to this whole wicked community, which has banded together against me. They will meet their end in this wilderness; here they will die."

Numbers 14:32–35

God struck down the ten spies who had brought back the negative report that sparked the people's defiance. Given their forty-year sentence and the death of the ten spies, the people were reeling. They suddenly had a change of heart, but it was too late.

We're told they got up the next day and decided they *would* go into "the land the Lord promised" (Numbers 14:40). Various Scripture versions say they admitted they had sinned or had "done wrong." But Moses warned them, *We have new orders from God, and you will not succeed if you disobey them.* Even with his caution ringing in their ears, they decided to attempt a coup, and it failed spectacularly. Their effort to take enemy territory ended in disaster, as the Canaanites and Amalekites soundly defeated the people, who had abandoned Moses and the ark of the covenant.

The ark was sacred, the physical place where God's presence resided with His people. Dr. Daniel R. Hyde writes of its majesty this way:

> The eternal God who is not constrained by the existence of time, the infinite God who is not bound by the constraints of space, the transcendent God who dwells above and beyond all time and space, and the immense God who fills all time and space condescended to the weakness of His people and became manifest for their benefit in one locale. . . . The fact that the ark was the place of the Lord's presence among His people brought great assurance to the people of God. This high, lofty, majestic, and resplendent King dwelt among His grumbling, complaining, bickering, and sinful people.

But the people had walked away from the presence of God in more than one way. Their disobedience shows they'd missed the point. Taking the promised land wasn't about feeling confident that they could do so. It was about respecting and loving the God who had pledged to give it to them. Confidence is no good if you're rebelling against Yahweh.

As Joshua and Caleb had said, they would be blessed "if the LORD is pleased with us" (Numbers 14:8). Many of the Israelites didn't love and trust God, which shows their hearts hadn't truly changed—their repentance was skin-deep. They were only regretful because of the punishment, not because they wanted to be reconciled to God. See, again, how badly they'd misread His character. They'd have forty years to replay the defeat as they stumbled through the desert.

> Do not be deceived: God cannot be mocked. A man reaps what he sows.
>
> Galatians 6:7

During their decades of wandering, the Israelites continued to try God's patience. There was idol worship, disobedience to His direct guidance, sexual immorality with foreign women, endless complaining and quarreling, and outright opposition to what the people knew to be holy. Even Moses was banned from entering the promised land with the people because of his disobedience (Numbers 20:12). As the Israelites trudged through the wilderness, the Lord instructed Moses to designate Joshua as his successor (Numbers 27:18–23). He also gave Moses specific instructions that the people were to follow when they finally arrived in Canaan.

> . . . drive out all the inhabitants of the land before you. Destroy all their carved images and their cast idols, and demolish all their high places. Take possession of the land and settle in it, for I have given you the land to possess.
>
> Numbers 33:52–53

There would be no compromise, no room to worship anything or anyone but God Almighty. It's a principle we would be wise to practice ourselves. The Lord knew the Israelites would need to be reminded; He'd seen their unfaithfulness despite His miraculous rescues time and again. It can be easy to judge the Israelites in hindsight, while ignoring my own faults. How often I must take note of the idols in my own life and toss them aside so they don't corrupt my promised land.

The Second Spy Mission: Joshua Takes Charge

Forty long years passed. I wonder if Moses thought back to his forty years as a shepherd in Midian. He must have felt a strange sense of déjà vu. Before Moses passed away, God did allow him to get a look at the land "flowing with milk and honey" where the people would eventually claim their divine guarantee (Deuteronomy 34:1–4). Finally, after four decades, it was time for God's people to move boldly ahead in faith.

With Joshua now leading the Israelites, there were new challenges and adventures ahead. As the book of Joshua opens, the Lord lavishes his servant with encouragement.

"I will give you every place where you set your foot, as I promised Moses. . . .

"No one will be able to stand against you all the days of your life. As I was with Moses, so I will be with you; I will never leave you nor forsake you. Be strong and courageous, because you will lead these people to inherit the land I swore to their ancestors to give them.

"Be strong and very courageous.

"Have I not commanded you? Be strong and courageous.

Do not be afraid; do not be discouraged, for the LORD your God will be with you wherever you go."

Joshua 1:3, 5–7, 9

Do you sense a theme? Joshua had already shown himself to be strong and courageous, but even God's most devoted children need assurance from time to time. Joshua was following in the footsteps of one of the world's greatest leaders. Moses, emboldened by the Lord, had stood up to the most powerful man in Egypt—someone who could have easily wiped him out but for God's supernatural protection. He had led a disgruntled, disobedient nation through decades of struggle and strife. Moses repeatedly petitioned the Lord on behalf of the people, and he had finally led them to the cusp of where they'd always been meant to be. But it would be Joshua who would take them across the finish line.

God tucked the keys to success into His directions to Joshua: *Don't get distracted. Stay on target. Meditate on My truth day and night.* It's really a simple formula, if we'll just commit ourselves to it—and Joshua did. He went to the people and told them to get ready to cross the Jordan River. Some of the people would remain on the east side of the river long term, but Joshua directed their men to first help those who would cross over for good.

> ". . . all your fighting men, ready for battle, must cross over ahead of your fellow Israelites. You are to help them until the LORD gives them rest . . ."

Joshua 1:14–15

The men agreed without hesitation.

> "Whatever you have commanded us we will do, and wherever you send us we will go. . . . Only be strong and courageous!"
>
> Joshua 1:16, 18

What a contrast to the timid, grumbling Israelites of forty years prior. They'd had decades to consider their sin, and this generation was ready for the fight.

It was time for another scouting mission. I find it interesting that this time around, Joshua sent only two spies. They wound up at the home of a prostitute named Rahab. Her life story is one of my favorites, and I explored it in depth in my book *Women of the Bible Speak*. Rahab was critical to the mission of the Jewish people, risking her own life even though she was not one of them. And interestingly, we'll see that she's a recurring sort of character in the Bible—a believing Gentile who was held up as an example to the people of Israel. Rahab took in the two spies, and word soon got out.

> So the king of Jericho sent this message to Rahab: "Bring out the men who came to you and entered your house, because they have come to spy out the whole land."
>
> But the woman had taken the two men and hidden them. She said, "Yes, the men came to me, but I did not know where they had come from. At dusk, when it was time to close the city gate, they left. I don't know which way they went. Go after them quickly. You may catch up with them." (But she had taken them up to the roof and hidden them under the stalks of flax she had laid out on the roof.)
>
> Joshua 2:3–6

That sent the men searching for the spies on a wild-goose chase. So, why did Rahab do it? It all aligned with the Lord's promises to His people. Word of His might and power had spread throughout the land, and it made Israel's enemies tremble. Yet it was more than just fear that was driving Rahab.

Rahab's Faith: Betting on God's Goodness

[Rahab] said to [the spies], "I know that the LORD has given you this land and that a great fear of you has fallen on us, so that all who live in this country are melting in fear because of you. We have heard how the LORD dried up the water of the Red Sea for you when you came out of Egypt, and what you did to Sihon and Og, the two kings of the Amorites east of the Jordan, whom you completely destroyed. When we heard of it, our hearts melted in fear and everyone's courage failed because of you, for the LORD your God is God in heaven above and on the earth below."

Joshua 2:9–11

How the tables had turned! Forty years before, when those ten Israelite spies returned full of fear and foreboding, the people crumbled under the thought of going into battle against the people indwelling the land God had promised them. But as they prepared to take the land under Joshua's leadership, it was the people they would soon confront who feared *them*. The inhabitants of Jericho rightly dreaded the approach of the Israelites.

Rahab was wise enough to recognize that the Israelites were protected and guided by the one true God. She asked the spies to save her family in return for her kindness to them. Rahab's home was part of the city wall, so the spies asked her to tie a red cord in her window to signify that she and all in her home would be saved. In the same way that the blood of the lamb had signaled to the Lord to pass over the righteous in Egypt, the red cord in Jericho would signal to God's people that they should spare Rahab. She let them down on a rope out her window and back they went to Joshua with their report. Like Joshua and Caleb had done decades before, the two spies predicted success.

> "The LORD has surely given the whole land into our hands; all the people are melting in fear because of us."
>
> Joshua 2:24

The next day, Joshua prepared the people. They were to follow the ark of the covenant at a distance and consecrate themselves for the battle ahead. Joshua told them, "tomorrow the LORD will do amazing things among you" (Joshua 3:5). He had the same belief and trust in God's promise that he'd had years earlier as he stood alongside Caleb and spoke of victory. And he followed the Lord's guidance to a tee, directing the priests to carry the ark and step into the Jordan.

Yet as soon as the priests who carried the ark reached the Jordan and their feet touched the water's edge, the water from upstream stopped flowing. It piled up in a heap a great distance away, at a town called Adam in the vicinity of Zarethan, while the water flowing down to the Sea of the Arabah (that is, the Dead Sea) was completely cut off. So the people crossed over opposite Jericho. The priests who carried the ark of the covenant of the LORD stopped in the middle of the Jordan and stood on dry ground, while all Israel passed by until the whole nation had completed the crossing on dry ground.

Joshua 3:15–17

Biblical scholars believe the town where the waters "piled up" was roughly sixteen to twenty miles upstream from where the Israelites were. I have to imagine there were plenty of other people living along the Jordan who saw that miracle and wondered what or who on heaven or earth could accomplish such a feat. If the people of Jericho were frightened before, when word of the Jordan crossing reached the city, it must have triggered all-out panic.

The people of Israel immediately took an important step upon crossing to the other side of the Jordan. They gathered twelve stones from the middle of the Jordan where the priests were standing with the ark. They were taken to make a memorial so that when future generations would ask what they meant, the story of God cutting off the Jordan would be passed down.

"[S]o that all the peoples of the earth might know that the hand of the LORD is powerful and so that you might always fear the LORD your God."

Joshua 4:24

Are there memorials or markers in your life? For a couple of my friends, it's a tattoo of a favorite Bible verse or song lyric. For others, it's a Scripture verse tacked on a bathroom mirror or a needlepoint canvas on the wall. Simple or elaborate, they can be guideposts to remind our weak hearts when we need a jolt of courage.

After everyone passed through safely, Joshua gave the command for the priests to proceed.

> And the priests came up out of the river carrying the ark of the covenant of the LORD. No sooner had they set their feet on the dry ground than the waters of the Jordan returned to their place and ran at flood stage as before.
>
> Joshua 4:18

As predicted, when word of the event began to spread, so did fear of the Lord. The Amorite and Canaanite kings "lost heart and their courage failed because of the Israelites" (Joshua 5:1, CSB).

Before the Israelites could forge ahead, they camped in Gilgal and took care of some business. None of the men born during the wandering in the wilderness had been circumcised, so the Lord called on Joshua to make sure the command was reinstated. Circumcision had long been a sign of God's covenant with Abraham and his future descendants (Genesis 17:11). The people stayed in camp while the men recovered. It was there that the Lord told them, "Today I have rolled away the disgrace of Egypt from you" (Joshua 5:9). *Gilgal* is related to the Hebrew word *galal*, meaning to roll. The Lord had spun away the past, and His people seemed more determined than ever to meet their future.

Marching Around Jericho

The first of their big battles would come within weeks: Jericho. Scripture tells us it was a heavily fortified city. "Because of the Israelites," no one was coming or going from its protective walls. The

Lord's message to Joshua was clear: "I have delivered Jericho into your hands" (Joshua 6:2). And then He gave Joshua instructions that may have seemed odd by human standards. It certainly wasn't a traditional battle strategy, yet Joshua didn't try to reason with God or question His logic. He simply took the plan to the troops and began to prepare the people.

For six days, the fighting men of Israel would march around the city once. The processional started with an armed guard ahead of seven priests carrying seven trumpets, who were followed by the ark of the covenant. A rear guard followed the ark. Though the trumpets sounded, Joshua commanded the troops not to shout or say a word (Joshua 6:10–14).

But on the seventh day, all heaven broke loose!

> [T]hey got up at daybreak and marched around the city seven times in the same manner, except that on that day they circled the city seven times. The seventh time around, when the priests sounded the trumpet blast, Joshua commanded the army, "Shout! For the LORD has given you the city!" . . .
>
> When the trumpets sounded, the army shouted, and at the sound of the trumpet, when the men gave a loud shout, the wall collapsed; so everyone charged straight in, and they took the city.
>
> Joshua 6:15–16, 20

Every living thing in the city was destroyed, with the exception of Rahab and those who took refuge in her home. They were all taken to safety, and that's where her story really gets good!

In Matthew 1, we find Rahab in the lineage of Christ Himself.

> Salmon the father of Boaz, whose mother was Rahab,
> Boaz the father of Obed, whose mother was Ruth,
> Obed the father of Jesse,
> and Jesse the father of King David.
>
> Matthew 1:5–6

A Gentile prostitute who bravely risked her life because she believed in the God of Israel was not only grafted into the Jewish nation but was also a forerunner of the One who would make it possible for all of us to have the same opportunity. Rahab's son, Boaz, not only stars in one of the Bible's most beautiful love stories with Ruth, but he, too, serves as a foreshadowing of the power of redemption Christ offers each of us. You can read about their legacy in *Love Stories of the Bible Speak* if you'd like to know more.

Rahab is also at the center of James's teaching on how faith and works go together. Not that our deeds can or should save us. That principle is clear throughout the New Testament.

> For it is by grace you have been saved, through faith—and this is not from yourselves, it is the gift of God—not by works, so that no one can boast.
>
> Ephesians 2:8–9

James says that our faith should give birth to action. He cites the willingness of Abraham to place his beloved son Isaac on a literal altar before seeing God's salvation in the form of a nearby ram. And James applauds Rahab, too.

> In the same way, was not even Rahab the prostitute considered righteous for what she did when she gave lodging to the spies and sent them off in a different direction?
>
> James 2:25

Rahab is also celebrated among a long list of spiritual heroes in Hebrews.

> By faith the prostitute Rahab, because she welcomed the spies, was not killed with those who were disobedient.
>
> Hebrews 11:31

Next on that list? Gideon, the overcomer, whom you know well by now.

But the inspiring script of Rahab's life may never have come to be had Joshua and Caleb not taken a stand, resolved to band together as a small minority in the face of overwhelming opposition. And what was it that enabled them to do this? It was because they remembered who God was—a Savior, a gift-giver, a loving Father. Because they understood this, they didn't rebel, and they weren't afraid to enter the promised land. Rahab had the same sort of faith, recounting God's mighty deeds and trusting in His mercy. God tests hearts. Joshua, Caleb, and Rahab weren't superheroes, but they did earnestly seek the Lord, and that made all the difference.

They were surrounded by doubters who allowed their fear to drown out the promises God Almighty had made to the people. It took repeated acts of courage, over many decades, before the victory Joshua and Caleb believed in actually came to be. May we also be ready to hear—and follow—the One Voice that matters—buoyed by His command: "Be strong and courageous."

Study Questions

1. How do you view the command "be strong"? How is that directive more about remembering God's love and mercy vs. willpower or white-knuckling your way through a situation?
2. What is the purpose of periods of wilderness or wandering in life? How can those times be about growth when they're focused on God's goodness and faithfulness?
3. Where are you looking at a situation and fearing defeat rather than claiming a victory God has already guaranteed you—that He is with you or that He will walk you through?
4. How does viewing God as a loving Father change the way you relate to Him and His promises?
5. What is the best way to address doubters or those who operate out of fear?

ELIJAH'S DISCOURAGEMENT

How to Stop a Negative Spiral

1 Kings 16–19, 21; 2 Kings 1–2

I'm an introvert. There, I've said it! There's nowhere I'd rather be than at home on my couch with a stack of books. Many people assume, because of the work I do, that I'm a naturally outgoing person who loves chatting up strangers and being on the go. That's definitely part of what I do, but it's most certainly not my default setting. I *love* being alone. For me, the silver lining to the pandemic was all the quiet time.

But being alone and feeling lonely are two very different things. I have friends who struggled mightily during quarantine because of the very thing that gave me peace in the midst of such turmoil. They felt isolated and lonely. The truth is you can feel lonely even in a crowded room. It can put real pressure on your mental and emotional state, and that's at the heart of Elijah's story. Loneliness can evolve into a place of real discouragement when you're feeling completely unsupported in the midst of a trial.

This is a man who followed God so faithfully and so closely that he never actually faced death. Instead, God sent a heavenly chariot to pick him up and take him to his eternal home (2 Kings 2:11). He was a conduit for incredible miracles and had the Lord's hand on his life. James would later use him as the ultimate example of a righteous man whose prayers are heard (James 5:16-18). Yet Elijah experienced deep discouragement and a feeling that he was the only one fighting for what was right and good. We know he was never truly alone, and neither are you. So how do you keep going when your own mind has fooled you into thinking you're without backup? How do we learn to test our own thoughts against the truth?

Elijah's Dramatic Entrance

We meet Elijah in the context of real trouble for the divided nation of Israel. The kingdom to the north was technically Israel, and to the south, the land was called Judah. King Ahab was leading Israel, and not well.

> Ahab son of Omri did more evil in the eyes of the LORD than any of those before him. He not only considered it trivial to commit the sins of Jeroboam son of Nebat, but he also married Jezebel daughter of Ethbaal king of the Sidonians, and began to serve Baal and worship him. He set up an altar for Baal in the temple of Baal that he built in Samaria. Ahab also made an Asherah pole and did more to arouse the anger of the LORD, the God of Israel, than did all the kings of Israel before him.
>
> 1 Kings 16:30-33

Not only did Ahab not listen to or worship the Lord, but he also married the daughter of a man who served as a sort of priest to Baal. Far worse than that choice was Ahab's decision to set up an altar to Baal and Asherah and worship them himself. We can see here how God's ban on cultural intermarriage had everything to do with preserving spiritual faithfulness. It was never meant to imply that foreigners were any less made in the image of God. As we will see later in the story of Elijah, God blesses a different woman from Jezebel's people because of her faith.

That's why Jezebel's main sin, it is clear, is not being from Sidon, but tempting Ahab and the people of Israel away from their God, to worship her gods, Baal and Asherah. The false goddess, Asherah, was the female counterpart to Baal. Both were lifeless, meaningless small "g" gods whose followers did incredibly wicked things. The people of Israel had no business tolerating much less embracing Baal and Asherah.

God was angry with Ahab, and the king was about to find out just how much. The Lord deputized his faithful prophet Elijah to take a devastating message to one of the most powerful men in the world, and we see no hesitation from Elijah in the midst of a situation that would likely be—at the very least—stressful. That stands in contrast to initial pushback, in Gideon's case, and outright rebellion, in Jonah's—when God came to call. We'll see as we go how characteristic this is of Elijah. He is unfailingly bold in his confrontations with powerful leaders—at least at first.

> Now Elijah the Tishbite, from Tishbe in Gilead, said to Ahab, "As the Lord, the God of Israel, lives, whom I serve, there will be neither dew nor rain in the next few years except at my word."
>
> Then the word of the Lord came to Elijah: "Leave here, turn eastward and hide in the Kerith Ravine, east of the Jordan. You will drink from the brook, and I have directed the ravens to supply you with food there."
>
> So he did what the Lord had told him. He went to the Kerith Ravine, east of the Jordan, and stayed there. The ravens

brought him bread and meat in the morning and bread and meat in the evening, and he drank from the brook.

1 Kings 17:1–6

Elijah followed God's first set of directions: *Deliver my message to Ahab.* Scholars say drought was widely viewed as a spiritual punishment in those days. It had the ability to wipe out livestock, crops, humans; all of that weakened the political and military power of the area impacted by it. Ahab couldn't have been happy about the message. We'll come to see just how much he also resents the messenger.

Into the Wilderness: Elijah Trusts God for Nourishment

Elijah had delivered his message, but he was about to face a different sort of challenge. It was only once Elijah had obeyed that first command that he got the next piece of the puzzle. God directed Elijah to a very specific location, where he could hide and where his physical needs would also be met. Elijah obeyed. That took him to an initial period of isolation, but that's often where God works most deeply on our hearts—when He has our undivided attention. Elijah was completely dependent on the Lord and those ravens. Interestingly, ravens were considered unclean at that time (Deuteronomy 14:14). But that was the animal God chose to deliver sustenance to Elijah. It may be a hint, too, about the nature of the prophet that God had sent to his people—God's message is more important than the messenger. As bold as Elijah could be, he was also imperfect—prone to fickle moods, doubting God's goodness and his own worth.

One of the most lauded preachers in the Christian faith, Charles Spurgeon, underlined the use of unclean ravens as yet another reminder that God can use us despite our flaws.

These ravens never croaked out a single objection, but did as they were bidden! Their instincts did not rebel, but they submitted absolutely to God's will, and I daresay, were quite as diligent and quite as happy in carrying the bread and meat to Elijah as they would have been if they had been taking it to their own young or feasting upon it themselves!

How humbling!

Spurgeon also noted how God always provided for Elijah, but never in advance. While Elijah was spared from the land's famine, he wasn't eating fancy meals, and he wasn't storing up more food for later. He had to rely on God's daily mercy, delivered by animals that he may have felt embarrassed to be dependent on.

A Foreign Widow

Eventually, Elijah's time at the Kerith Ravine (in some translations also known as the brook of Cherith) would be over. Like much of the land suffering under the drought, the brook there dried up. It was time for another puzzle piece. Just like the ravens, God was about to provide for Elijah, through yet another unlikely source of help. God told Elijah to leave Israel, and to go to the region where Jezebel was from!

> Then the word of the LORD came to him: "Go at once to Zarephath in the region of Sidon and stay there. I have di-

rected a widow there to supply you with food." So he went to Zarephath. . . .

What do we do when our brooks dry up? Health, job, status, family, comforts—what about when they aren't what they once were? Elijah must have seen that every day the brook was providing less water. But rather than panic when it stopped altogether, he turned his eyes to the One who had provided it. Elijah wasn't dependent on the blessing itself, but on the One from whom the blessing came. He trusted God's plan.

> When he came to the town gate, a widow was there gathering sticks. He called to her and asked, "Would you bring me a little water in a jar so I may have a drink?" As she was going to get it, he called, "And bring me, please, a piece of bread."
>
> "As surely as the LORD your God lives," she replied, "I don't have any bread—only a handful of flour in a jar and a little olive oil in a jug. I am gathering a few sticks to take home and make a meal for myself and my son, that we may eat it—and die."
>
> Elijah said to her, "Don't be afraid. Go home and do as you have said. But first make a small loaf of bread for me from what you have and bring it to me, and then make something for yourself and your son. For this is what the LORD, the God of Israel, says: 'The jar of flour will not be used up and the jug of oil will not run dry until the day the LORD sends rain on the land.'"
>
> She went away and did as Elijah had told her. So there was food every day for Elijah and for the woman and her family. For the jar of flour was not used up and the jug of oil did not run dry, in keeping with the word of the LORD spoken by Elijah.
>
> 1 Kings 17:8–16

I wrote extensively about this story in my book *The Mothers and Daughters of the Bible Speak*. There's beauty in the fact that the Lord used a Gentile woman who would have been among the most destitute to provide for Elijah. In the beginning, she refers to God as Elijah's God—not hers. But she responds in humility and trust. God, in turn, honors the promise that her limited means would *miraculously* not run dry. Notice here, how she is the complete opposite of Jezebel. While Jezebel tempts Ahab into idol worship, the widow of Zarephath obeys the word of the Lord, ultimately identifying with God's people. And she'll be rewarded by becoming an early "type," or foreshadowing, of the Messiah's mother!

If you keep reading, you'll see that the woman's son dies while Elijah is staying with them, and through God's power, the boy is miraculously raised back to life. By the way, this is the first time we see someone raised from the dead in Scripture. First Kings 17:21 tells us Elijah cried out to God and that the Lord heard him and answered his prayers. Something else to notice is how personal Elijah's prayer is. He doesn't just use God's name, but adds "my God." He sees God as someone with whom he can have a personal relationship. You don't see anyone talking about Baal that way! Followers of these false gods would know nothing about a compassionate relationship with them. Their worship was based mostly on fear.

This intimacy is returned by God. You will see throughout Elijah's story that his prayers packed a punch. James writes of Elijah in the New Testament:

> The prayer of a righteous person is powerful and effective.
>
> James 5:16b

That grieving widow found out firsthand.

> Then the woman said to Elijah, "Now I know that you are a man of God and that the word of the LORD from your mouth is the truth."
>
> 1 Kings 17:24

Suffering across Israel had been building for roughly three years at this point and the Lord had a fresh command for Elijah: Go back to Ahab. It was almost time for the rains to return.

Elijah Meets the Remnant

This is where we meet another brave man of God named Obadiah (note that this is a different guy than the prophet of the same name). Ahab and Jezebel had continued their wicked ways, with the queen specifically targeting God's prophets for death. But Obadiah, who was the administrator of Ahab's palace, "was a devout believer in the LORD" (1 Kings 18:3).

Working directly against Jezebel's murderous campaign, Obadiah was hiding one hundred of the Lord's prophets in caves and making sure they had food and water. I'm fascinated by Obadiah's ability and willingness to undermine Jezebel, a decision I'm sure could have cost him his life!

Still, King Ahab trusted Obadiah. He suggested that the two of them go searching for sources of water in order to keep the royal animals alive, and they set off in two different directions. That's when, to Obadiah's awe and dismay, he ran into Public Enemy Number One—the man his boss hated more than any other.

As Obadiah was walking along, Elijah met him. Obadiah recognized him, bowed down to the ground, and said, "Is it really you, my lord Elijah?"

"Yes," he replied. "Go tell your master, 'Elijah is here.'"

"What have I done wrong," asked Obadiah, "that you are handing your servant over to Ahab to be put to death? As surely as the LORD your God lives, there is not a nation or kingdom where my master has not sent someone to look for you. And whenever a nation or kingdom claimed you were not there, he made them swear they could not find you. But now you tell me to go to my master and say, 'Elijah is here.' I don't know where the Spirit of the LORD may carry you when I leave you. If I go and tell Ahab and he doesn't find you, he will kill me. Yet I your servant have worshiped the LORD since my youth. Haven't you heard, my lord, what I did while Jezebel was killing the prophets of the LORD? I hid a hundred of the LORD's prophets in two caves, fifty in each, and supplied them with food and water. And now you tell me to go to my master and say, 'Elijah is here.' He will kill me!"

1 Kings 18:7–14

We see the reverence Obadiah has for Elijah. Clearly, Elijah's reputation as a man of God precedes him. He's also the man that everyone must have credited—or blamed—for the famine. You can see why people may respond with fear instead of reverence. Even if you were a faithful person who understood the famine as a just judgment of God, it must have been hard to like the bringer of judgment, which is what Elijah represented. Perhaps that's why Obadiah hesitated to do what Elijah asked of him: *Just tell Ahab I'm back.*

Obadiah, who has likely risked life and limb to hide God's prophets, does not want to deliver that message. *What have I done wrong? Why are you trying to get me killed?!*

Elijah was insistent that he was going to find Ahab that very same day. So Obadiah went to broker the meeting, and it was quickly apparent that Ahab wasn't the least bit happy to see Elijah—years after he'd prophesied the drought that was crippling Israel.

> When he saw Elijah, he said to him, "Is that you, you troubler of Israel?"
>
> "I have not made trouble for Israel," Elijah replied. "But you and your father's family have. You have abandoned the LORD's commands and have followed the Baals. Now summon the people from all over Israel to meet me on Mount Carmel. And bring the four hundred and fifty prophets of Baal and the four hundred prophets of Asherah, who eat at Jezebel's table."
>
> 1 Kings 18:17–19

We never see Elijah cower or defer to Ahab. Instead, he speaks boldly and sets up what will be an epic showdown.

God Revealed on the Mountain

In the very next verse, we see that Ahab follows Elijah's command. He gathered the people of Israel and all those godless prophets on Mount Carmel, and then Elijah issued a challenge.

Elijah went before the people and said, "How long will you waver between two opinions? If the LORD is God, follow him; but if Baal is God, follow him."

But the people said nothing.

1 Kings 18:21

Tough crowd! Little did they know they would soon see the power of God Almighty on that mountaintop. First, Elijah laid out the conditions for a moment of truth with Baal's followers. Keep in mind, that group was likely composed of most of Israel at that point.

"Get two bulls for us. Let Baal's prophets choose one for themselves, and let them cut it into pieces and put it on the wood but not set fire to it. I will prepare the other bull and put it on the wood but not set fire to it. Then you call on the name of your god, and I will call on the name of the LORD. The god who answers by fire—he is God."

Then all the people said, "What you say is good."

1 Kings 18:23-24

The people agreed that was a legitimate bargain: Whoever's god shows up wins.

Remember, Ahab blamed Elijah for the drought. He didn't like the messages the prophet of God brought. Yet he respected him enough to allow this spectacle to take place. We see elsewhere in the Bible (1 Kings 22:1-28) that Ahab surrounds himself with "yes men" prophets who tell him what he wants to hear. But even though he hates the Lord's prophets because they always criticize him, he seems to know they're also more reliable. When a reliable prophet predicts his death, Ahab scoffs at the prophecy, but he also goes out of his way to disguise himself as he goes to battle. We see similar grudging respect for the Lord's prophet here. Ahab's seen the power of Elijah's prayers, and at least reveres him as what he might have considered a powerful rival wizard. *Maybe it's worth seeing what this annoyingly contrary prophet has to say?*

Similarly, the prophets of Baal followed Elijah's directives. Somehow, Elijah's unwavering faithfulness had earned him the right to make his case to his enemies.

> Elijah said to the prophets of Baal, "Choose one of the bulls and prepare it first, since there are so many of you. Call on the name of your god, but do not light the fire." So they took the bull given them and prepared it.
>
> Then they called on the name of Baal from morning till noon. "Baal, answer us!" they shouted. But there was no response; no one answered. And they danced around the altar they had made.
>
> At noon Elijah began to taunt them. "Shout louder!" he said. "Surely he is a god! Perhaps he is deep in thought, or busy, or traveling. Maybe he is sleeping and must be awakened." So they shouted louder and slashed themselves with swords and spears, as was their custom, until their blood flowed. Midday passed, and they continued their frantic prophesying until the time for the evening sacrifice. But there was no response, no one answered, no one paid attention.
>
> 1 Kings 18:25–29

The servants of Baal did their best, but their false god never showed up. It got so bad that Elijah even resorted to some trash-talking. They were cutting themselves, frantic, and yet . . . nothing.

Then Elijah said to all the people, "Come here to me." They came to him, and he repaired the altar of the LORD, which had been torn down. Elijah took twelve stones, one for each of the tribes descended from Jacob, to whom the word of the LORD had come, saying, "Your name shall be Israel." With the stones he built an altar in the name of the LORD, and he dug a trench around it large enough to hold two seahs of seed.

1 Kings 18:30–32

Elijah called together the people who had abandoned their God. He had total and complete confidence that the Lord was going to show up. He didn't simply throw together a sacrifice; Elijah "repaired the altar of the LORD," which had been destroyed at some point. He specifically gathered stones to represent each tribe, calling the people to remember who they were—*Whose* they were. And Elijah was going to make the demonstration as clear as possible.

He arranged the wood, cut the bull into pieces and laid it on the wood. Then he said to them, "Fill four large jars with water and pour it on the offering and on the wood."

"Do it again," he said, and they did it again.

"Do it a third time," he ordered, and they did it the third time. The water ran down around the altar and even filled the trench.

1 Kings 18:33–35

Only supernatural intervention would allow that bull to be burned up. Elijah's preparations pointed all the credit to God alone. There could be no human intervention or trickery that would bring fire to that altar. Having done that, Elijah geared up his powerful prayers.

"LORD, the God of Abraham, Isaac and Israel, let it be known today that you are God in Israel and that I am your servant and have done all these things at your command. Answer me, LORD, answer me, so these people will know that you, LORD, are God, and that you are turning their hearts back again."

Then the fire of the LORD fell and burned up the sacrifice, the wood, the stones and the soil, and also licked up the water in the trench.

When all the people saw this, they fell prostrate and cried, "The LORD—he is God! The LORD—he is God!"

1 Kings 18:36b–39

Lord, this is all about You. Bring them back to You. And He did! Everything was consumed by God's holy fire and the people fell down in worship. Oh, to be a fly on the wall when Ahab realized what had happened!

Ahab is not a take-charge sort of guy. When he sees that the supernatural winds have shifted, his response is, notably, to do nothing. Elijah is clearly in charge of the situation, and he wasted no time executing the wicked prophets of Baal and sending a new message to Ahab.

And Elijah said to Ahab, "Go, eat and drink, for there is the sound of a heavy rain." So Ahab went off to eat and drink, but Elijah climbed to the top of Carmel, bent down to the ground and put his face between his knees.

"Go and look toward the sea," he told his servant. And he went up and looked.

"There is nothing there," he said.

Seven times Elijah said, "Go back."

The seventh time the servant reported, "A cloud as small as a man's hand is rising from the sea."

So Elijah said, "Go and tell Ahab, 'Hitch up your chariot and go down before the rain stops you.'"

Meanwhile, the sky grew black with clouds, the wind rose, a heavy rain started falling and Ahab rode off to Jezreel. The power of the LORD came on Elijah and, tucking his cloak into his belt, he ran ahead of Ahab all the way to Jezreel.

1 Kings 18:41–46

Everyone there must have been waiting on pins and needles for the result of Elijah's prayer. Finally, after years of empty skies, they see the first cloud coming in from the sea. Ahab rode back to his queen on the wings of a storm, but then—so did Elijah.

Back into the Wilderness

I can only assume the two men were racing back to the royal palace (which was then located in Jezreel) with very different expectations, one eager to see Jezebel's reaction to the slaughter of Baal's prophets—the other . . . not so much. Elijah hadn't been intimidated by Ahab. But Jezebel was a different story.

Now Ahab told Jezebel everything Elijah had done and how he had killed all the prophets with the sword. So Jezebel sent a messenger to Elijah to say, "May the gods deal with me, be it ever so severely, if by this time tomorrow I do not make your life like that of one of them."

Elijah was afraid and ran for his life. When he came to Beersheba in Judah, he left his servant there, while he himself went a day's journey into the wilderness. He came to a broom bush, sat down under it and prayed that he might die. "I have had enough, Lord," he said. "Take my life; I am no better than my ancestors." Then he lay down under the bush and fell asleep.

1 Kings 19:1–5a

To this point, Elijah has faithfully followed God's direction. He's delivered hard truths. He's been helped by the most unlikely sources (ravens and a destitute widow), sent directly by the Lord. He's literally witnessed fire from heaven come down in such a commanding way that the people of Israel who witnessed it turned back to God in revival. And yet there's something about Jezebel that sends him running. Who can blame him? This homicidal leader made it her mission to put his fellow prophets to death, and now she's got her sights set on Elijah himself. He knows God is mightier than the queen, but he fears her still.

His first reactions are interesting. He runs and abandons his servant, going into the wilderness, hiding under a bush, and praying for death.

I've seen God move in incredible ways in my life, in my valleys—and yet I'm human. I'm still capable of fear and doubt. I used to think that if I could just achieve a certain level of spiritual maturity, I'd no longer struggle with those things. I thought other believers had it all figured out, and that my emotions were sins I somehow needed to overcome. It's what drove me to seek out a wise, Christian counselor. Sometimes what we need most is to be vulnerable with a trusted friend or advisor. They can be professionals, but they certainly don't have to be. Loneliness, fear, isolation—they're all fertile breeding grounds for the enemy's lies. Perspective and truth do a wonderful job of putting a stop to the deception. There is nothing wrong with seeking medical and/or therapeutic intervention when life becomes unmanageable.

Feelings aren't wrong, but they also aren't facts. We are fallible. Remember, Christ came and experienced everything we do—so He has great compassion on us. But unlike us, there was never a time He lacked the capacity to override His emotions with discernment, wisdom, and truth.

Another important piece of context is that it doesn't seem that Elijah is *supposed* to be in the wilderness this time. Elijah and God have been so aligned up until this point that something seems dramatically wrong. Elijah's fear and flight might seem strange to us. Why was he afraid of Jezebel when he had just seen God's awesome power over fire and water on Mount Carmel? How could you not have perfect courage if you'd seen such power?

But if all faith required was seeing God do a miracle, Ahab would have had the same faith as Elijah. So something more mysterious is happening here.

Let's look at what happens next. Elijah was hungry and lonely. But his response to those things was not to seek out their appropriate solution, but to let them determine his behavior. Like Elijah, we need proper nourishment and rest. Our spiritual health, physical wellness, and mental health are intertwined.

We can't ignore those needs—and if anyone tells you that you should, that's a lie! Obviously we shouldn't be gluttons, but a starvation diet is a mistake in the opposite direction. Elijah responded to his physical, social, and spiritual hunger by essentially going on a hunger strike—isolating himself from food, friends, and faith. Have you ever made that mistake? You feel lonely, so you choose to sulk and suffer instead of calling a friend. You're hangry, but instead of seeing it as a signal to enjoy some food, you snap at your spouse.

God created us knowing we'd need to recharge and regroup, and food, rest, and fellowship are the gifts He offers us to bring about those blessings. See His tender provision for Elijah.

> All at once an angel touched him and said, "Get up and eat." He looked around, and there by his head was some bread baked over hot coals, and a jar of water. He ate and drank and then lay down again.
>
> The angel of the Lord came back a second time and touched him and said, "Get up and eat, for the journey is too much for you." So he got up and ate and drank. Strengthened by that food, he traveled forty days and forty nights until he reached Horeb, the mountain of God. There he went into a cave and spent the night.
>
> 1 Kings 19:5b–9a

I love how personal this is. Elijah is frightened and alone. After so many years of boldness, he's run out of energy right before a final confrontation. Yet instead of rebuking him, God sends an angel not once, but twice, to attend to his very real needs and to prepare him for the trip ahead. What was the significance of Mount Horeb and the long trip to get there?

You may know the mountain more familiarly as Mount Sinai. Ring any bells? It's where Moses, having also run into the wilderness out of fear, heard from God in the burning bush. It's where he was given the Ten Commandments and where the people of Israel dishonored the Lord and built that golden calf. It's where Moses experienced the presence of God and a covenant was made with Israel, plans for the Tabernacle were outlined, and the art of the covenant was crafted. It's where God had some questions for his faithful servant Elijah.

> And the word of the LORD came to him: "What are you doing here, Elijah?"
> He replied, "I have been very zealous for the LORD God Almighty. The Israelites have rejected your covenant, torn down your altars, and put your prophets to death with the sword. I am the only one left, and now they are trying to kill me too."
>
> 1 Kings 19:9b–10

The Lord never asks us a question He doesn't already know the answer to. It reminds me of God's questions to Adam and Eve in Genesis 3 after they had sinned and were avoiding Him.

Where are you?

Who told you that you were naked?

Have you eaten from the tree that I commanded you not to eat from?

What is this you have done?

The Creator of the universe knew every single answer, so what was He really doing? I believe He prods us so that we examine our own hearts, just as he did with Elijah. He wanted Elijah to make clear the source of his fear. It wasn't actually about being alone, or being in danger. He'd faced those things before.

No, Elijah's worry was tied up in the idea that he was the only faithful person left in Israel. He had experienced Jezebel's words not just as a personal attack but as a plausible threat to wipe out the faith entirely.

How often do we make the same mistake, thinking we're the only person on Earth that God can use? If I were Elijah and had been responsible for creating droughts and calling fire from the sky, I'd probably have made the same error, thinking I was the only one who could fix a faithless country. Elijah had gone to the very place where God made a covenant with Israel, the people who'd rejected him in favor of Baal and Asherah. But unlike Moses, who stood in the same place and interceded for the people of Israel, Elijah sees this as an opportunity to criticize the faithless people. He reminded God about their sin, how he'd tried to speak truth to them, and how alone, afraid, and discouraged he felt. God met him where he was—literally and figuratively.

> The LORD said, "Go out and stand on the mountain in the presence of the LORD, for the LORD is about to pass by."
> Then a great and powerful wind tore the mountains apart and shattered the rocks before the LORD, but the LORD was not in the wind. After the wind there was an earthquake, but the LORD was not in the earthquake. After the earthquake came a fire, but the LORD was not in the fire. And after the fire came a gentle whisper. When Elijah heard it, he pulled his cloak over his face and went out and stood at the mouth of the cave.
>
> 1 Kings 19:11–13a

How often do we miss what our heavenly Father is saying because we're focused on fireworks: an emotional experience, a flashy display, or miraculous sign? Yes, He can be and is in all those things. But more often, He's in the daily routines of our lives. I was recently headed to work very early in the morning. It was still dark out, and a driver who obviously didn't see me pulled right out in front of me. I swerved to miss the car, and thank the Lord there was no one in the lane next to me. I took a moment to say, "Thank you for protecting me—all the times I'm aware of and the millions I'm not!" It can be far too easy for us to barrel through our busy days and nights, missing where God is whispering to us, providing for us, protecting us.

The enemy wants to turn God's working through us into a matter for our own pride and self-congratulation. Elijah took his eyes off God just long enough to fall into fear. That's why God needed to remind his suffering servant that he was not the only remnant of the people of God. But what a blessing that when God humbles us, He does so by giving us the best possible news of grace!

God seemed to want Elijah to understand that divine faithfulness doesn't have to look like mightiness. It can look like scraps of bread in a raven's beak. Once Elijah tuned into that still, small voice—God spoke again.

> Then a voice said to him, "What are you doing here, Elijah?"
> He replied, "I have been very zealous for the LORD God Almighty. The Israelites have rejected your covenant, torn down your altars, and put your prophets to death with the sword. I am the only one left, and now they are trying to kill me too."
>
> 1 Kings 19:13b–14

Elijah repeated his woes, as if God hadn't heard him the first time. Elijah still hadn't gotten the point—but don't judge him! We're talking about a man who will eventually have the honor of being one of the two historical figures to appear on a mountain to commune with the Son of God in the Transfiguration.

Recognizing Elijah's emotional and spiritual state, the Lord immediately gave him an assignment, which might not have made sense in the short run (though it would much later). It provided purpose for Elijah, a way to move him out of isolation and forward with God's blessing. Depression is real, and it can be paralyzing. (David is just one of many other examples of men of God who cried out to Him in despair, lamenting their lives and tragedies.) It can also distort the truth of our circumstances. The Lord spoke truth to Elijah that he needed to hear.

> "Yet I reserve seven thousand in Israel—all whose knees have not bowed down to Baal and whose mouths have not kissed him."
>
> 1 Kings 19:18

Elijah, get up; you are not alone!

There's the message for Elijah and for us: it's not just on you. You don't have to carry this burden alone. From there, we see Elijah take action, following God's directions. He comes upon Elisha, the young man who would serve with him for years and eventually continue his ministry. Not only did God assure Elijah that thousands were faithfully believing in Israel, but He gave him the presence of a confidant to continue the journey with him. We aren't meant to walk this journey by ourselves. In community—whether it's Bible study or as part of a faithful church body—we find restoration, encouragement, and support. Elisha brought a gust of fresh enthusiasm to the mission.

A Plot and a Vineyard: Jezebel Gets Up to More Mischief

Part of Elijah's earthly work would once again involve confronting Ahab and Jezebel's wicked ways. Ahab wanted a vineyard near his palace and first offered the owner either an even better piece of land or whatever price he would ask. The man refused, citing the family inheritance tied to the vineyard. Ahab was furious and went home to complain to Jezebel. The Bible literally tells us he was sullen and angry. "He lay on his bed sulking and refused to eat" (1 Kings 21:4). Jezebel had a plan and told him to cheer up! She cooked up some false witnesses to testify against Naboth, the owner of the vineyard. They did and the man was stoned to death. Jezebel gleefully reported the news to Ahab, who went and took possession.

Enter Elijah . . .

> Then the word of the LORD came to Elijah the Tishbite: "Go down to meet Ahab king of Israel, who rules in Samaria. He is now in Naboth's vineyard, where he has gone to take possession of it. Say to him, 'This is what the LORD says: Have you not murdered a man and seized his property?' Then say to him, 'This is what the LORD says: In the place where dogs licked up Naboth's blood, dogs will lick up your blood—yes, yours!'"
>
> Ahab said to Elijah, "So you have found me, my enemy!"
>
> "I have found you," he answered, "because you have sold yourself to do evil in the eyes of the LORD. He says, 'I am going to bring disaster on you. I will wipe out your descendants and cut off from Ahab every last male in Israel—slave or free. I will make your house like that of Jeroboam son of Nebat and that

of Baasha son of Ahijah, because you have aroused my anger and have caused Israel to sin.'

"And also concerning Jezebel the LORD says: 'Dogs will devour Jezebel by the wall of Jezreel.'

"Dogs will eat those belonging to Ahab who die in the city, and the birds will feed on those who die in the country."

(There was never anyone like Ahab, who sold himself to do evil in the eyes of the LORD, urged on by Jezebel his wife. He behaved in the vilest manner by going after idols, like the Amorites the LORD drove out before Israel.)

1 Kings 21:17–26

Ahab and Jezebel were going to pay, big time. Once again, Elijah got to be the bearer of bad news. But notice that he didn't hesitate to share God's word of truth, even after being greeted by Ahab as his "enemy."

You may be shocked at how Ahab responded.

When Ahab heard these words, he tore his clothes, put on sackcloth and fasted. He lay in sackcloth and went around meekly.

Then the word of the LORD came to Elijah the Tishbite: "Have you noticed how Ahab has humbled himself before me? Because he has humbled himself, I will not bring this disaster in his day, but I will bring it on his house in the days of his son."

1 Kings 21:27–29

Make no mistake, there are consequences for our sins. But God is merciful and has compassion on those who humble themselves

(James 4:6), just as we saw in the case of the Ninevites. And as God promised, the ramifications of Ahab's sins would come later. (If you want to see just how much Ahab's son carries on the family tradition of disliking Elijah, read 2 Kings 1.)

Eventually, Elijah's earthly ministry would come to an end and Elisha would take up his mantle—literally. Elijah asked what he could do for the man who'd served faithfully with him for years and Elisha asked, "Let me inherit a double portion of your spirit" (2 Kings 2:9). It was quite a request, and it would seem God granted it. There is no one recorded in Scripture who performed more miracles than Elisha, other than Jesus Himself. Elijah's work would continue via yet another godly man unafraid to follow God's leading.

Elijah was never actually alone, but God was sensitive to his irrational fears and needs as a human vessel. He equipped Elijah to go on both physically and spiritually. Elijah overcame his isolation and despair, going boldly into situations that could have cost him his life. And don't forget—he never really died.

> As they were walking along and talking together, suddenly a chariot of fire and horses of fire appeared and separated the two of them, and Elijah went up to heaven in a whirlwind.
>
> 2 Kings 2:11

A man who struggled with depression and despair was so esteemed by God that He gave him a special ride to his heavenly home.

Just as Elijah fought with feelings of discouragement and isolation, we, too, can believe the lies of the enemy. It can be lonely to take a stand in our homes, neighborhoods, schools, or places of work. We can look around and wrongly believe we are the only ones standing in the gap, doing the work God has called us to. Remember what Paul wrote to the early Christians in Rome, who likely faced growing feelings of exclusion.

> Don't you know what Scripture says in the passage about Elijah—how he appealed to God against Israel: "Lord, they have killed your prophets and torn down your altars; I am the only one left, and they are trying to kill me"? And what was God's answer to him? "I have reserved for myself seven thousand who have not bowed the knee to Baal." So too, at the present time there is a remnant chosen by grace.
>
> Romans 11:2b–5

You, too, are part of the "remnant chosen by grace." Be encouraged!

Study Questions

1. Why do you think Elijah disregarded the faith of people like Obadiah and the widow of Zarephath in claiming that he alone was faithful in the fight for what was right and true?
2. How do you think it was possible Elijah could see literal miracles and still be so discouraged and doubting? Have you done the same thing?
3. What is the hardest thing about reaching out for help when you are suffering from the belief that no one else is standing for the righteous commands God gives us?
4. How has the Lord sent you ravens just when you needed them?

5. Why was Elijah so bold in his messages for Ahab and yet so fearful of Jezebel? Do we assess God's ability to defend us based on the enemy that we're facing? How can we view all our challenges through His eyes? What promises from Scripture cover all threats?

JESUS

God with Us Is the Ultimate Overcomer

One of my favorite places in Washington, DC, is the Library of Congress. I would live there if they would allow it, but sadly, *they will not*. It's just down the block from the US Supreme Court (which, by the way, has its own impressive library), where I've spent years as a journalist covering the justices. Books have always been a refuge for me, an escape from whatever challenge I was facing. As a kid, that included the dreaded monster of boredom. Books let me travel the world, go along on daring adventures, solve crimes, and dream beyond what I knew.

The Library of Congress reports it has more than 39 million books and other printed materials in its catalog. If every line of every page of every book there was about Jesus, there would still be more to experience. Since the first book was ever printed, it's estimated that around 150 million books have been published. But no book could ever capture the full essence of Jesus Christ. Even when it comes to the Bible, I think we get the absolute best glimpse we can—but the God-breathed words written there are just an introduction to truly knowing and experiencing Jesus. Even after recording His astonishing life and miracles, the apostle John wrote at the end of his Gospel account of Jesus's life:

Jesus did many other things as well. If every one of them were written down, I suppose that even the whole world would not have room for the books that would be written.

John 21:25

So, a single chapter here is my best attempt to talk about just one sliver of His greatness—that He is the ultimate Overcomer. By crushing sin and death, Jesus gave us eternal life and hope. He was so filled with compassion that He left the glories of heaven to descend to us, knowing the disregard and torture He would suffer before being executed like a common criminal. Who does that? The God of the universe—the One who created you in His own image, breathed His life into you, and then gave you the opportunity to decide whether you would ultimately choose Him. Jesus created the bridge, taking on every sin that will ever be committed, bearing the weight of everything that separated us from our heavenly Father.

Earlier in this book, I wrote about how God's answer to my chronic illness was ultimately not a physical healing, but the presence of God. If you've never experienced a close feeling of His presence, holding this out as the solution to suffering might seem callous. But it's His nearness that speaks into our pain, walks us through what feels humanly impossible, and binds up our wounds. What is it about "presence" that makes such a big difference? A story might help.

I hate it when my husband is gone on super long trips—especially the hunting trips that take him into the wilds where only a satellite phone works. I can't call him, so I have to wait for the nightly/scratchy three-minute call just to know that he and everyone in camp are safe and alive. I swear to you something tough happens every time he's gone. Once I found out I'd been subpoenaed and dragged into a legal fight and had to find an attorney ASAP. Another time, I had to leave on an emergency work trip—with no one to care for the dog. There was also the night all the Wi-Fi and power shut down in our house while I was on a deadline that couldn't be extended. No one could figure out how to fix it! Again, these may be silly fears—but it just made me miss him even more. The house (and the issues) felt overwhelming by myself. I'm always so relieved the minute he steps through the door and I know we're reunited!

My husband being there wouldn't have made the problems go away, or meant that I was automatically happy, but the comfort of his presence would have transformed the situation. That's what the presence of God is like. It's not fuzzy feelings or the absence of trouble, but the presence of a relationship with a real person.

It's the relationship part that's important here. After all, isn't God always present? God is certainly everywhere! But the Bible's idea of presence is a lot more than physically inhabiting the same space as God. In the Old Testament, God's glory was everywhere, but *especially* in the Tabernacle (and eventually in the temple in Jerusalem), behind the curtain in a room separate from the rest of the sanctuary called the Holy of Holies.

Why couldn't God's presence come out of the Holy of Holies? It's because His intimacy with humanity was prevented by our sin and guilt.

The Holy of Holies was where the ark of the covenant (the law of Moses) was housed. God gave Moses these instructions:

> Make a curtain of blue, purple and scarlet yarn and finely twisted linen, with cherubim woven into it by a skilled worker. Hang it with gold hooks on four posts of acacia wood overlaid with gold and standing on four silver bases. Hang the curtain from the clasps and place the ark of the covenant law behind

the curtain. The curtain will separate the Holy Place from the Most Holy Place.

Exodus 26:31–33

Only the high priest could enter the Holy of Holies, and he could do that *only once a year,* on the Day of Atonement (Leviticus 16:34).

God is so holy that He can't have a relationship with a sinful people. But God wouldn't be satisfied to let that separation continue. He allowed His own Son to be beaten, mocked, whipped, publicly humiliated, and nailed to a cross. All for us. All for you. It was a necessary payment. It was the only way the separation between God and us could be bridged. And why did He do it?

For God so loved the world that he gave his only Son . . .

John 3:16

He who did not spare his own Son, but gave him up for us all—how will he not also, along with him, graciously give us all things?

Romans 8:32

Our response to this should not be feeling crushed by guilt—that's what the enemy wants, because he wants us to think we're unforgivable—but rather to praise God, who says no one is too far gone for His hand to reach.

While Jesus's sacrifice doesn't prevent us from going through hard things, it does powerfully comfort us because we know God has a purpose for everything, even when it looks for all the world like He's forgotten us. So when I report on horrific suffering and loss, as I have for twenty-five years now, when I walk through my own dark valleys, when I see people I love in pain, I remember that God Himself allowed—and took on—a brutality that had purpose but that looked like the ultimate moment of pointless suffering. I'm sure in the hours around Jesus's death, His followers couldn't make any sense of it. Where was the kingdom they'd heard so much about? If Jesus was divine, why was His life slipping away as He hung between two disgraced thieves? Why was the enemy winning? At that moment, they could not yet see that every drop of blood, every jeering taunt, and every piece of torn flesh was making a way for our ultimate salvation.

We are so used to knowing the end of the story that it can be difficult to remember that—at the time—Jesus's victory over death looked like the worst defeat in history! But shouldn't His disciples have known? It's not like there weren't signs—not to mention flat-out warnings by Jesus Himself.

For centuries, God's prophets had been pointing the world to the Messiah to come. When He arrived, most Jews expected the coming Messiah to be a worldly ruler with an earthly kingdom. They couldn't fathom that a humble builder who walked the countryside telling stories they struggled to understand was God Himself. But there were clues along the way.

VIRGIN BIRTH

Therefore the Lord himself will give you a sign: The virgin will conceive and give birth to a son, and will call him Immanuel.

Isaiah 7:14

This is how the birth of Jesus the Messiah came about: His mother Mary was pledged to be married to Joseph, but before they came together, she was found to be pregnant through the Holy Spirit. . . .

All this took place to fulfill what the Lord had said through the prophet: "The virgin will conceive and give birth to a son, and they will call him Immanuel."

Matthew 1:18, 22–23

BORN IN BETHLEHEM

"But you, Bethlehem Ephrathah,
though you are small among the clans of Judah,
out of you will come for me
one who will be ruler over Israel,
whose origins are from of old,
from ancient times."

Micah 5:2

After Jesus was born in Bethlehem in Judea, during the time of King Herod, Magi from the east came to Jerusalem.

Matthew 2:1

Remember, Mary and Joseph wouldn't have been in Bethlehem but for a census ordered by Caesar Augustus.

So Joseph also went up from the town of Nazareth in Galilee to Judea, to Bethlehem the town of David, because he belonged to the house and line of David.

Luke 2:4

A FORERUNNER WOULD PRECEDE HIM

A voice of one calling:
"In the wilderness prepare
the way for the LORD;
make straight in the desert
a highway for our God.
Every valley shall be raised up,
every mountain and hill made low;
the rough ground shall become level,
the rugged places a plain."

Isaiah 40:3–4

John [the Baptist] replied in the words of Isaiah the prophet, "I am the voice of one calling in the wilderness, 'Make straight the way for the Lord.'"

John 1:23

ENTRANCE TO JERUSALEM

Rejoice greatly, Daughter Zion!
Shout, Daughter Jerusalem!
See, your king comes to you,

righteous and victorious,
lowly and riding on a donkey,
on a colt, the foal of a donkey.

Zechariah 9:9

As they approached Jerusalem and came to Bethphage on the Mount of Olives, Jesus sent two disciples, saying to them, "Go to the village ahead of you, and at once you will find a donkey tied there, with her colt by her. Untie them and bring them to me. If anyone says anything to you, say that the Lord needs them, and he will send them right away."

This took place to fulfill what was spoken through the prophet . . .

The disciples went and did as Jesus had instructed them. They brought the donkey and the colt and placed their cloaks on them for Jesus to sit on.

Matthew 21:1–4, 6–7

BETRAYAL

I told them, 'If you think it best, give me my pay; but if not, keep it." So they paid me thirty pieces of silver.

And the LORD said to me, "Throw it to the potter"—the handsome price at which they valued me! So I took the thirty pieces of silver and threw them to the potter at the house of the LORD.

Zechariah 11:12–13

The chief priests picked up the coins and said, "It is against the law to put this into the treasury, since it is blood money." So they decided to use the money to buy the potter's field as a burial place for foreigners. That is why it has been called the Field of Blood to this day. Then what was spoken by Jeremiah the prophet was fulfilled: "They took the thirty pieces of silver, the price set on him by the people of Israel, and they used them to buy the potter's field, as the Lord commanded me."

Matthew 27:6–10

REJECTION BY THOSE HE CAME TO SAVE

He was despised and rejected by mankind,
a man of suffering, and familiar with pain.
Like one from whom people hide their faces
he was despised, and we held him in low esteem.

Isaiah 53:3

He came to that which was his own, but his own did not receive him.

John 1:11

WORDS ON THE CROSS

My God, my God, why have you forsaken me?
Why are you so far from saving me,
so far from my cries of anguish?

Psalm 22:1

About three in the afternoon Jesus cried out in a loud voice, *"Eli, Eli, lema sabachthani?"* (which means "My God, my God, why have you forsaken me?").

Matthew 27:46

Into your hands I commit my spirit;
deliver me, Lord, my faithful God.

Psalm 31:5

Jesus called out with a loud voice, "Father, into your hands I commit my spirit." When he had said this, he breathed his last.

Luke 23:46

He was unconventional. From the way He spoke with authority to His decision to include women in His ministry, Jesus upended norms. He called out religious leaders, and He chastised His own inner circle. He went to sinners where they were, not to condemn them, but to redeem them. He was building an eternal kingdom, and almost no one seemed to understand it.

Jesus often spoke in parables, stories that required people to pay attention to the underlying message. He explained why, as recorded in Matthew.

> This is why I speak to them in parables:
> "Though seeing, they do not see;
> though hearing, they do not hear or understand."
> In them is fulfilled the prophecy of Isaiah:
> "You will be ever hearing but never understanding;

you will be ever seeing but never perceiving.
For this people's heart has become calloused;
they hardly hear with their ears,
and they have closed their eyes.
Otherwise they might see with their eyes,
hear with their ears,
understand with their hearts
and turn, and I would heal them."

Matthew 13:13–15

Throughout the Bible, God resists giving simple pat answers to His people's questions. Even when Jesus explained Himself more plainly, people still expressed confusion. Even the disciples had trouble understanding what Jesus kept telling them about His ultimate plan to overcome sin and death by laying down His own life.

For as Jonah was three days and three nights in the belly of a huge fish, so the Son of Man will be three days and three nights in the heart of the earth.

Matthew 12:40

For even the Son of Man did not come to be served, but to serve, and to give his life as a ransom for many.

Mark 10:45

The Jews then responded to him, "What sign can you show us to prove your authority to do all this?"

Jesus answered them, "Destroy this temple, and I will raise it again in three days."

They replied, "It has taken forty-six years to build this temple, and you are going to raise it in three days?" But the temple he had spoken of was his body.

John 2:18–21

"I am the good shepherd. The good shepherd lays down his life for the sheep."

John 10:11

And if those word pictures weren't enough, Jesus gave details about His mission to overcome the seemingly impossible and what it would cost.

And he said, "The Son of Man must suffer many things and be rejected by the elders, the chief priests and the teachers of the law, and he must be killed and on the third day be raised to life."

Luke 9:22

When they came together in Galilee, he said to them, "The Son of Man is going to be delivered into the hands of men. They will kill him, and on the third day he will be raised to life." And the disciples were filled with grief.

Matthew 17:22–23

Rather than rejoicing over the news that he would defeat death and rise again, the disciples focused on Jesus's continued warning that He would be killed. That's understandable when He later spelled out His upcoming death in even more detail.

> Now Jesus was going up to Jerusalem. On the way, he took the Twelve aside and said to them, "We are going up to Jerusalem, and the Son of Man will be delivered over to the chief priests and the teachers of the law. They will condemn him to death and will hand him over to the Gentiles to be mocked and flogged and crucified . . ."
>
> Matthew 20:17–19

But again, they overlooked the best part of what Christ was saying to them:

> "On the third day he will be raised to life!"
>
> Matthew 20:19

So if you ever feel worried that you just can't understand God's plan, or that you keep misunderstanding it—be comforted. Even Jesus's disciples, who spent every day with Him, couldn't figure it out! God's salvation plan is so at odds with worldly logic that it looked like insanity. A lamb who saves? A king that becomes a servant? Death that brings life? You would have been confused, too! But we should still aspire to understand and trust God's plan, because it grieves Him when we don't trust Him.

It pained Jesus that He walked into His suffering without the understanding *or* the trust of His friends. Jesus dreaded the path He would have to walk. The beauty of Christ's being fully God and fully human is that He has walked through all the frailty we experience. He knows emotions, including sorrow.

> For we do not have a high priest who is unable to empathize with our weaknesses, but we have one who has been tempted in every way, just as we are—yet he did not sin.
>
> Hebrews 4:15

There must have never been a greater moment of loneliness than what happened that night to the One facing a trial like no other. In the moments that the apostles Peter, James, and John drifted off to sleep rather than joining Jesus in prayer in the garden of Gethsemane, we witness just how much He struggled the closer He inched to the agony of the sacrifice that would pay our debt of sin. His arrest was imminent.

> ... [he] began to be sorrowful and troubled. Then he said to them, "My soul is overwhelmed with sorrow to the point of death. Stay here and keep watch with me."
> Going a little farther, he fell with his face to the ground and prayed, "My Father, if it is possible, may this cup be taken from me. Yet not as I will, but as you will."
>
> Matthew 26:37–39

"Father, if you are willing, take this cup from me; yet not my will, but yours be done." An angel from heaven appeared to him and strengthened him. And being in anguish, he prayed more earnestly, and his sweat was like drops of blood falling to the ground.

Luke 22:42–44

Yes, Jesus prayed. All throughout Scripture, He made time to talk with His Father. In so many key moments, Christ modeled the power and necessity of prayer.

Then people brought little children to Jesus for him to place his hands on them and pray for them.

Matthew 19:13

Very early in the morning, while it was still dark, Jesus got up, left the house and went off to a solitary place, where he prayed.

Mark 1:35

But Jesus often withdrew to lonely places and prayed.

Luke 5:16

One of those days Jesus went out to a mountainside to pray, and spent the night praying to God.

Luke 6:12

> Then Jesus told his disciples a parable to show them that they should always pray and not give up.
>
> Luke 18:1

In His loneliness in the garden, Jesus reached for the presence of God. He knew that prayer is always our refuge in suffering. The entire chapter of John 17 is Jesus's prayer just prior to his arrest.

> "Father, the hour has come. Glorify your Son, that your Son may glorify you. For you granted him authority over all people that he might give eternal life to all those you have given him. Now this is eternal life: that they know you, the only true God, and Jesus Christ, whom you have sent."
>
> John 17:1–3

After Jesus prayed that He would glorify God, He then asked that the Lord watch over His believers:

> Holy Father, protect them by the power of your name, the name you gave me, so that they may be one as we are one.
>
> John 17:11

In other words, He prayed for them to gain more and more of the presence of God. But interestingly, He didn't ask for God to shield them against any and all trouble. Even though Christ acknowledged that "the world has hated" His followers, He did not ask God to remove them from that uncomfortable, dangerous situation. "My prayer is not that you take them out of the world but that you protect them from the evil one" (John 17:15). Jesus also prayed for those "who will believe in me through their message" (John 17:20)—a prayer that includes you and me!

But Jesus also experienced the pain of rejected prayer. When He asked the Father to take away the cup He must drink, He knew the answer He would receive. Jesus was fully aware there was no other way to make sure you and I could come into the presence of God, what the Old Testament calls living "face to face" with God, than that He experience a loss of His own presence of God, a turning away of God's face. Imagine it—a relationship that existed before time began, and on the cross, the Son who had never been separated from the Father experienced estrangement and abandonment for our sake.

This is why Jesus, resurrected, can be a champion for our cause—because He isn't just our defender but also our substitute.

Jesus continues to advocate for us, even now.

> ... if anybody does sin, we have an advocate with the Father—Jesus Christ, the Righteous One.
>
> 1 John 2:1

> Christ Jesus who died—more than that, who was raised to life—is at the right hand of God and is also interceding for us.
>
> Romans 8:34

But was Christ's agonizing suffering on the cross necessary? At least in part, the purpose of the law of the Old Testament—the old covenant—was to show that we as humans are incapable of the holiness we must possess in order to be in fellowship with our heavenly Father. For the people of Israel, there was an endless stream of sacrifices needed to atone for their sins and restore their fellowship with the Lord. It was impossible for them to become reconciled to God, remain sinless, and never again have to offer a covering or atonement for their failures.

While we may not talk about moral absolutes much anymore, it's hard to deny we've got an internal compass. Think about how little kids are adamant about policing unfairness and enforcing the rules of a game. What about when we have a gut reaction to someone's shady actions in the midst of a business deal? Human beings are built to understand good and evil—right and wrong. And even if we can't articulate it, if we're really paying attention, we can't help but feel like we're falling short and there's no way for us to get ourselves out by our own actions.

One of the toughest things for my late father when his diabetes started to progress was being tethered to dialysis. He never got used to other people telling him what to do, and that's how he viewed that life-saving obligation. His time in the dialysis chair bought him some days of energy and improved function, but it was a commitment that would never go away unless he could get a kidney transplant. He never made peace with spending hours locked into one place, knowing the necessary treatment limited his ability to travel and to live the spontaneous life he had enjoyed to that point. And it only worked temporarily. He would always have to return for more help. Dialysis is a wonderful thing, but it can never be true healing.

That's how the generations who lived under the Old Testament law on sacrifices must have felt. There were all kinds of offerings they were directed to make, each one serving as a reminder that they would never be fully covered for sins they had committed—or may commit in the future. There would always be another requirement just ahead. Scholars have outlined the primary sacrifices as falling into these categories:

1. Burnt offering (*'olah* in Hebrew, Leviticus 1): This is a sacrifice involving a whole animal that is burned as a gift to God, except for its hide, which the Levites are allowed to keep and sell.
2. Grain offering (*minhah*, Leviticus 2): This would be an offering of a common grain mixed with salt—"The salt of the covenant of your God." It would be finely ground and burned, having been doused with oil and incense, and followed by a drink offering of wine.
3. Fellowship offering (*zevah shelamim*, Leviticus 3): Only the fat and some internal organs of an animal were burned, but the rest, having been waved before the altar, would be eaten as a feast.
4. Sin offering (*hattā't*, Leviticus 4:1–5:13): The sin offering consists of an animal or grain offering (selected based on what a person can afford) that is sacrificed and burned to atone for sin and make a person clean after they had become unclean.
5. Guilt offering (*'asham*, Leviticus 5:14–6:17): This sacrifice was only ever a ram, and was often associated with sacrifices offered for sins that required compensatory payments to people wronged.

Under the Jewish Old Testament law, there was no perfect offering, no unblemished sacrifice that could pay the penalties of the people's sins once and for all. Just like my father, who could only hope for a transplant that would give him a chance at a permanent solution, the Jewish people could only hope for and get glimpses from God's prophets of a distant future when something or someone would provide a payment so spotless that it would end the cycle of imperfect sacrifices.

> ... he will swallow up death forever.
> The Sovereign LORD will wipe away the tears
> from all faces;
> he will remove his people's disgrace
> from all the earth.
>
> Isaiah 25:8

The beginning of Hebrews 10 gives us a deep dive into the debt Christ's death finally satisfied.

> The law is only a shadow of the good things that are coming—not the realities themselves. For this reason it can never, by the same sacrifices repeated endlessly year after year, make perfect those who draw near to worship. Otherwise, would they not have stopped being offered? For the worshipers would have been cleansed once and for all, and would no longer have felt guilty for their sins. But those sacrifices are an annual reminder of sins. It is impossible for the blood of bulls and goats to take away sins. . . .
>
> Day after day every priest stands and performs his religious duties; again and again he offers the same sacrifices, which can never take away sins. But when this priest had offered for all time one sacrifice for sins, he sat down at the right hand of God, and since that time he waits for his enemies to be made his footstool. For by one sacrifice he has made perfect forever those who are being made holy.

The Holy Spirit also testifies to us about this. First he says:
"This is the covenant I will make with them
after that time, says the Lord.
I will put my laws in their hearts,
and I will write them on their minds."
Then he adds:
"Their sins and lawless acts
I will remember no more."
And where these have been forgiven, sacrifice for sin is no longer necessary.

Hebrews 10:1–4, 11–18

No longer necessary. Our debt to the holy God has been paid forever! Death and sin have been defeated, never again to hold power over those who have accepted Christ. What joy, what relief, what salvation. Does it mean we'll never sin again? No, but it means when God looks at us, He doesn't see our sin, but the righteousness of Jesus. When God looks at you, He sees Jesus. That means He can have the relationship with us that He always had with His Son. That's why a holy God can pour His presence out into the hearts of His people. No longer is His glory confined to the Holy of Holies!

So in light of Christ's victory over sin and death, what are we called to do with such a glorious gift?

Therefore, brothers and sisters, since we have confidence to enter the Most Holy Place by the blood of Jesus, by a new and living way opened for us through the curtain, that is, his body, and since we have a great priest over the house of God, let us draw near to God with a sincere heart and with the full assurance that faith brings, having our hearts sprinkled to cleanse us from a guilty conscience and having our bodies washed with pure water.

Hebrews 10:19–22

First, we can boldly go to the heavenly throne of God where Jesus Christ continues to intercede for us 24/7/365. Jesus's death on the cross put an end to the separation between people and God:

> With a loud cry, Jesus breathed his last.
> The curtain of the temple was torn in two from top to bottom.

Mark 15:37–38

No more gatekeeping by a Jewish high priest to make a sacrifice on our behalf to pay for our sins every year. By His sacrificial death on the cross, Jesus has torn down every barrier, and He did it willingly.

> . . . I lay down my life. . . . No one takes it from me, but I lay it down of my own accord.

John 10:17–18

This is the reason we can live in hope. We can let that truth fuel our lives as believers.

> Let us hold unswervingly to the hope we profess, for he who promised is faithful. And let us consider how we may spur one another on toward love and good deeds, not giving

up meeting together, as some are in the habit of doing, but encouraging one another—and all the more as you see the Day approaching.

Hebrews 10:23–25

Hope, love, good deeds, encouragement—all of these are part of our fellowship with God and with other believers because of the eternal assurance that has been secured by Christ's death and resurrection.

When Jesus came up out of that grave, eternity changed forever. What a glorious thing we celebrate every Easter! I have such vivid childhood memories of celebrating with my Grandma Nell. She was a stickler for getting to the sunrise service on the beach when I was growing up. I can still hear her voice as she belted out her favorite hymn:

> Up from the grave He arose
> With a mighty triumph o'er His foes
> He arose a Victor from the dark domain
> And He lives forever with His saints to reign
> He arose! (He arose)
> He arose! (He arose)
> Hallelujah! Christ arose!

My grandmother never got over the joy of that truth! Jesus's courageous, selfless decision to go to the cross, the sinless Son of God giving His life as the once-for-all sacrifice for you and me, is something we must never grow indifferent to. It is not a license to sin, living as if we've been given a get-out-of-jail-free card on a game board of life.

You, my brothers and sisters, were called to be free. But do not use your freedom to indulge the flesh; rather, serve one another humbly in love.

Galatians 5:13

What shall we say, then? Shall we go on sinning so that grace may increase? By no means! We are those who have died to sin; how can we live in it any longer? Or don't you know that all of us who were baptized into Christ Jesus were baptized into his death? We were therefore buried with him through baptism into death in order that, just as Christ was raised from the dead through the glory of the Father, we too may live a new life.

Romans 6:1–4

Before we come to Christ, we are spiritually dead in our trespasses and sins (Ephesians 2:1, 5). Through Jesus's sacrifice, the greatest threats we could ever face have been vanquished. Sin can no longer enslave and defeat us. Death can no longer destroy our souls or result in eternal separation from our heavenly Father. For believers in Jesus Christ, there is nothing that can separate us from His love (Romans 8:38–39).

When God says "I am with you," He really can be, because He satisfied the debt that separated us with His own blood. This doesn't mean we'll always be happy, or never face difficulty—Jesus was always in close communion with the Father but still felt sorrow and still suffered. But it does mean that we will never, ever be alone. Jesus is the presence of God. Immanuel. God with us, through His Spirit.

When you and I accept God's free gift of salvation through faith in Jesus Christ, we no longer face condemnation or abandonment. We are not left powerless or hopeless against the enemy. There are no rigid rules or impossible standards for us to try to meet through the power of our own strength.

> For what the law was powerless to do because it was weakened by the flesh, God did by sending his own Son in the likeness of sinful flesh to be a sin offering. And so he condemned sin in the flesh, in order that the righteous requirement of the law might be fully met in us, who do not live according to the flesh but according to the Spirit.
>
> Romans 8:3–4

The best news of all is that our ultimate Overcomer is coming back again. We will be a part of His eternal victory. So, let us now live in the Spirit—unshackled, debt-free—each of us overcomers because of all He conquered on our behalf.

Study Questions

1. What was the purpose of the Old Testament law?
2. What did the sacrifices teach the people about their relationship with God?
3. Why was it necessary for Jesus to suffer?
4. Have you fully accepted that your debt has been paid? How does that impact how you view the decisions you make each day?
5. Who can you share the good news with this week?

ACKNOWLEDGMENTS

There are so many people who made it possible for this book to morph from dream to plan to reality. It takes an army of dedicated support to get the words onto the page and into your hands.

To the reader, I hope this book encourages you with God's endless love and challenges you to go deeper with Jesus. Thank you for letting me into your homes and Bible studies, coffee shops and book clubs. It is a blessing to take this journey with you.

My editor, Hannah Long, you are beyond excellent in all you do.

Jennifer Stair, your research and input are inspired and invaluable.

Our Fox News Books team and the broader Fox family are the secret to success: Jennings Grant, Nicole Cooper, Lauren Petterson, Irena Briganti, Jason Klarman, Ali Coscia, Sophie Watson, and so many more!

The *FOX News Sunday* team, you kicked into high gear when the writing demanded all my extra focus. I'm so grateful for you, Sami, Owen, Jess, Andrea, Lori, Olivia, Matt, Nicole, Madie, Quezia, and Maria.

Sami—the world needs more of you. I couldn't manage the blessings and challenges of life and work without you and your constant testimony to God's goodness.

ACKNOWLEDGMENTS

Lisa Sharkey and Lexie Zedlitz of HarperCollins, thank you for continuing to dream with me!

Olivia Metzger, what a gift to have you in my corner. These books happen because you came into our lives.

I will always be indebted to my faithful prayer warriors: Mom and Jazz, Sami, Magen, Debbie, Angie, Cindy, Penny, Jeff and Lynne, Molly, Tamara, John and Sara, Anna, Scott and Missy, and many, many other kind souls—including those I don't even know personally.

Pastors Robert Jeffress, Gary Hamrick, Greg Laurie, and Max Lucado—your theological guidance and wise counsel are an indescribable blessing to me!

Ze'ev Orenstein, thank you for sharing your historical insights and knowledge of the Torah.

And for my closest friends, you are truly treasurers from the Lord.

The Coraggios—prayer and courage

The Sorority—laughter and perspective

FFFF—you know who you are

My constant safe place and nonstop cheerleader, Sheldon, none of this matters without you. All of it is sweeter because of you.

To My Heavenly Father, Savior Jesus Christ, and Holy Spirit—thank you for allowing me to simply be a messenger for your truth and goodness. You are always working. You are always forgiving, saving, and redeeming. A thousand songs would never be enough to sing your praises, but may the words of this book be a start.

INDEX

Aaron, 41–42, 43, 44, 216, 221
Abednego, 143, 144
Abel Meholah, 23
Abraham, 32, 33, 86, 135, 198, 209, 216
   God's covenant with, 35, 204, 230
   willingness to sacrifice his son, 116, 232
Acts
   1, 72
   2, 73
   2:2-6, 73
   2:36-41, 74
   7:22, 37, 50
   9:40, 75
   12:1-18, 73
   12:5, 75
   12:13-17, 76
   15:7-11, 77
Adam, 189, 194, 196, 253
Adam (town), 228
Ahab, 109, 137, 236–38, 241, 242–46, 251, 257–59, 261
   defers to Elijah, 248–49
   Elijah's challenge to, 244–46
   vineyard stolen by, 257
Ahaz, 18
Ahijah, 258

altars
   built by Gideon, 12–13
   built by Noah, 202, 207
Amalekites, 5, 22, 215, 222
Amittai, 108
Amorites, 6, 215, 230
Andrew, 54, 55, 57
angels
   Elijah's encounter with, 252
   Gideon's encounters with, 8, 12
   Jesus strengthened by, 275–76
   Moses's encounters with, 34
   Peter's encounter with, 76
anger
   of God toward Israelites, 217–20
   of Jonah, 124–27
   of Nehemiah, 173–74, 182–83
anxiety. *See* social anxiety
Aramaic, 179
Arioch, 141
ark, Noah's, 191, 193, 207
ark of the covenant, 222, 228–29, 231, 253, 264
Artaxerxes, 162, 163–65, 168, 176, 177, 182, 183
Asaph, 164

INDEX

ascension
- of Elijah, 235, 259
- of Jesus, 72

'asham, 280
Asher, 23
Asherah, 236, 237, 244, 254
Asherah poles
- of Ahab, 236
- Gideon's destruction of, 11–16

Ashpenaz, 138
Assyrian Empire, 109–10
Augustus, Caesar, 267
Azariah, 134

Baal, 25, 236, 237, 241, 248, 249, 254, 256
- Elijah's challenge to worshipers of, 244–47
- Gideon's destruction of altar, 13, 15, 16

Baal-Berith, 25
Baasha, 258
Babylon
- Daniel's exile in, 133–56 *(see also* Daniel)
- fall of, 151
- Israelite captivity in, 159

Belshazzar, 148–51
Benjamin, 83, 97, 98, 99–102, 103, 104
Berossus, 151
Beth Barah, 23
Bethlehem, 267–68
Bethphage, 269
Beth Shittah, 23
betrayal
- of Jesus, 269–70
- of Joseph, 82, 105

Biblehub.com, 162
Bilhah, 86
Boaz, 232
Book of the Law of Moses, 178–79
bread and fishes multiplication, 57
brook of Cherith, 239. *See also* Kerith Ravine

burning bush, 34–35, 252
burnt offering, 280

Caleb, 214–17, 219, 220, 221, 223, 228, 233
Canaan, 208–9
- first spy mission to, 213–17
- second spy mission to, 224–27

Canaanites, 215, 222, 230
Card, Michael, 92
Center for Online Judaic Studies, 109
Cephas (name for Peter), 54
Christian Standard Bible (CSB), 9, 124, 140, 173, 230
2 Chronicles
- 16:9, 114
- 36:22-23, 168

circumcision, 76, 230
clay jars and trumpets, 22–24
Colossians
- 1:9, 139
- 3:11-14, 129
- 3:23, 165
- 3:23-24, 92

"Come Thou Fount of Every Blessing" (hymn), 4–5
community
- encouragement and support from, 256
- in exile, 134–40
- of faith, 148
- during hard times, 144
- of prayer, 143

1 Corinthians 10:13, 110
2 Corinthians
- 4:7, 24
- 12:10, 47

covenants
- with Abraham, 35, 204, 230
- with Israel, 204, 253
- with Noah, 204–7

INDEX

CSB. *See* Christian Standard Bible
cupbearers, 91–92, 94, 162
Cyrus the Great, 151, 159, 168

Daniel, 79–80, 132–57
   attempted indoctrination of, 134–38
   dream interpretation by, 139, 145–46
   in the fiery furnace, 143–45
   finding community in exile, 134–40
   in the lion's den, 152–55
   wisdom from God, 140–43
   writing on the wall interpreted by, 149–50
Daniel (book)
   1-6, 132–57
   1:8-9, 136
   1:12-16, 138
   1:20, 139
   2:2, 140
   2:5, 140
   2:12, 140
   2:14-16, 141
   2:27-28, 142
   2:46-48, 142
   3:15, 143
   3:28-29, 144
   4:9, 145
   4:19, 145
   4:27, 145
   4:30-31, 146
   4:33, 146
   4:34-35, 37, 147
   4:36, 146
   5:17, 150
   5:21, 150
   5:30-31, 150
   6:3, 151
   6:4-5, 151–52
   6:8, 152
   6:10, 152–53
   6:11, 153
   6:14, 154
   6:16, 154
   6:20-23, 154
   6:26-28, 155
Darius, 150–55
David, 159, 186, 232, 256, 268
Day of Atonement, 265
Dead Sea, 228
Deborah, 4
Deuteronomy
   1:1, 50
   7:5, 13
   12:3, 14
   14:14, 238
   16:21-22, 14
   34:1-4, 224
Devarim (Jewish name for Deuteronomy), 50
discouragement. *See* Elijah
divine absence, 186
dove, sign of, 201
dreams
   Daniel's interpretation of, 139, 145–46
   about Gideon, 22
   of Joseph, 84–85, 97, 100
   Joseph's interpretation of, 85, 91–92, 94–96
droughts, 237–38, 239, 244, 245

Easter, 68, 284
Ecclesiastes 2:26, 139
Egypt, 29–51
   Israelites' bondage in, 29–33
   Israelites' desire to return to, 216
   Israelites freed from bondage in, 6, 26
   Joseph in, 29–30, 86–105 (*see also* Joseph)
   murder of Hebrew babies in, 30–31, 35

INDEX

Egypt (cont.)
    plundering of by Israelites, 37, 39, 45
    ten plagues of, 44-45, 46, 216
Eliashib, 182
Elijah, 60, 186, 220, 235-61
    ascension of, 235, 259
    food supplied by ravens, 237-39
    raising from the dead by, 241
    showdown on Mount Carmel, 244-49
    at the Transfiguration, 59, 256
    the widow of Zarephath and, 239-42
    in the wilderness, 238-39, 249-56
Elisha, 256, 259
Enoch, 189
Ephesians
    2:1, 5, 285
    2:8-9, 190, 232
    2:10, 191
    3:20, 27
Ephraim, 23
Esau, 82
Esther, 155, 162, 163
Esther 2:9, 15, 137
Ethbaal, 236
Euphrates River, diversion of, 151
Eve, 189, 194, 253
Exodus
    1-14, 28-51
    2:7, 31
    2:10, 37
    2:11-12, 31, 36
    2:13-15, 31-32
    2:19, 32
    2:23-25, 33
    3:1-4, 34
    3:5-6, 34-35
    3:8, 35
    3:10, 35
    3:11, 36

3:12, 36, 38
3:13-15, 38-39
3:18, 39
4:1-9, 18
4:10, 50
4:10-13, 40
4:14, 40
5:2-9, 42-43
5:21, 43
5:23, 43
6:6-8, 43-44
6:9, 44
6:12, 44
12:35-36, 45
13:17, 46
13:21, 46
13:21-22, 213
14:13-14, 46, 47-48
14:17-18, 48-49
14:24-25, 27-28, 31, 49
26:31-33, 264-65
34:13, 13
Ezekiel 33:11, 111
Ezra, 178-79
Ezra (book)
    1:1-4, 159
    2:64, 159
    7-8, 159

faith
    community of, 148
    Gideon's steps of, 12-16
    grace through, 190-91, 232
    of Noah, 188-89, 194, 197
    Peter's struggle with, 58-59
    of Rahab, 227-28, 232
    works and, 190, 232

INDEX

fear. *See also* social anxiety
   cast out by love, 46–48, 72
   Jonah's, 124
   Peter's (*see under* Peter)
fellowship offering, 280
Field of Blood, 270
flood, the, 197–200, 207–8
foot washing, by Jesus, 63–64
forgiveness, 128–29
free will, 7

Galatians
   5:13, 285
   5:22-23, 184
   6:7, 223
Genesis
   1:27, 188
   2:5-6, 195
   3, 253
   5:24, 189
   6:5-7, 11-13, 188
   6:8, 188
   6:14a, 190
   6:14-16, 191
   6:17-18, 192
   6:19-22, 193
   7:1, 4-5, 197
   7:11-12, 17-24, 199–200
   8:1, 200
   8:4, 201
   8:10-12, 201
   8:15-22, 202
   8:21, 204
   9:5b-7, 204
   9:9-11, 204–5
   9:12-17, 205–6
   9:20-27, 208–9
   9:28-29, 209
   12:6-7, 209
   16:15, 86
   17:11, 230
   25:1-2, 32
   25:2, 86
   32:28, 83
   35, 86
   37-50, 81–106
   37:2, 85
   37:3-4, 83
   37:5-11, 84
   37:18-20, 86
   37:28, 86
   39:2-6, 87–88
   39:6, 89
   39:8-9, 89–90
   39:12, 90
   39:20, 90
   39:21, 92
   39:21, 23, 137
   39:21-23, 91
   40:4, 91
   40:14, 92
   40:22, 92
   40:23, 92
   41:15-16, 94
   41:38-44, 95–96
   41:46, 95
   41:55-56, 96–97
   41:57, 97
   42:6, 97
   42:21, 98
   42:22, 98
   42:23, 99
   42:28, 99
   43:26, 28, 100
   43:30, 101
   44:30-31, 33-34, 101
   45:3, 102
   45:4-8, 102–3

INDEX

Genesis (*cont.*)
   45:8, 96
   45:14-15, 103
   45:24, 104
   46:29-30, 104
   46:34, 32
   48, 8
   50:20, 81-82
Gentiles, 226. *See also* pagans
   Elijah helped by, 239-42
   Peter's advocacy for, 76-77
Geshem the Arab, 167, 176
Gethsemane, 65-67, 275
Gideon, 2, 3-27, 196, 233, 237
   altar built to the Lord by, 12-13
   army formed by, 16
   asked to serve as king, 24-25
   battle against Midian, 18, 20-25
   blaming of God by, 8-9
   death of, 25
   humble status of, 8
   iconic nickname of, 16
   Israelites' threats against, 15-16
   obedience of, 17-19
   strength of, 9-10
   threshing wheat in a winepress, 8, 17
Gilgal, 230
golden calf, 253
Goshen, 103
grace, 190-91, 232, 260
grain offering, 280
guilt offering, 280

Hagar, 86
Ham, 208
Haman, 155
Hanani, 160
Hananiah, 134
ḥaṭṭā't, 280

Hebrew language, 179
Hebrews
   4:14-16, 117
   4:15, 275
   10:1-4, 11-18, 281-82
   10:19-22, 282-83
   10:23-25, 283-84
   11:1, 7a, 194
   11:5, 189
   11:13, 198-99
   11:31, 233
Herod, 57, 75, 267
Herodotus, 151
hesed, 92, 99, 106
Hezekiah, 18
"hiddenness" of God, 185
Hitler, Adolf, 135
Hittites, 215
Holocaust Memorial Museum, 135
Holy of Holies, 264-65, 282
Holy Spirit, 74, 76, 282
   gifted to disciples, 62, 70
   speaking in tongues and, 73
   working ahead of time, 122
hope, 283-84
Hosea 6:1, 7
human sacrifice, 115
humility, 147-48, 258-59
Hyde, Daniel R., 222

idolatry
   "addictive" quality of, 15
   Daniel's response to, 137-38, 143-45
   by Israelites, 4, 6, 11-16, 25, 26, 223
   Jonah and, 111
   toward people one loves, 120
imposter syndrome, 25. *See also* Gideon
ingratitude, 128-31
integrity. *See* Daniel

INDEX

intermarriage, ban on, 236–37
Isaac, 33, 82, 116, 135, 216, 232
Isaiah
   7, 18
   7:14, 266
   25:8, 281
   40:3-4, 268
   40:14, 93
   53:3, 270
   54:9-10, 205
Ishmael, 86
Ishmaelites, 86
ISIS, Christians executed by, 68
Israel, 3–26. *See also* Jerusalem
   Assyrian attack on, 109
   battle against Midian, 18, 20–25
   changing of Jacob's name to, 83
   covenant with, 204, 253
   division of, 236
   40-year period of peace in, 3–4
   Midianite defeat by, 5
   Midianite oppression of, 5–6, 8–10
   sin-redemption cycle of, 4–7
Israelites
   Babylonian captivity of, 159
   bondage of in Egypt, 29–33
   cloud and pillar of fire to guide, 46, 213, 216
   demand for a king, 24–25
   failed coup of, 222
   forced to make bricks without straw, 42–43
   generation of denied entrance to promised land, 219–20, 221
   God's anger at, 217–20
   in the wilderness, 32, 212–14, 220–24

Jacob, 33, 98, 135, 216
   changing of name to Israel, 83
   death and burial of, 105

   love for Benjamin, 97, 99–100, 101–2
   love for Joseph, 82–85, 87
   reunion with Joseph, 104–5
James, 59, 65, 232–33, 275
James (epistle)
   1:5, 139
   2:25, 233
   4:6, 259
   5:16b, 241
   5:16-18, 235–36
Japeth, 208–9
Jebusites, 215
Jefferson, Thomas, 56
Jeremiah, 60, 270
Jeremiah 17:7-8, 220–21
Jericho, 227–31
Jeroboam, 236, 257
Jerub-Baal, 25
Jerusalem, 164–84. *See also* Israel
   backsliding in, 182–83
   destruction of, 159, 160
   Jesus's entrance to, 62
   Jesus's entrance to predicted, 268–69
   Nehemiah appointed governor of, 176
   rebuilding of, 164–78
   return of Jews to, 159
   spiritual homecoming in, 178–84
Jerusalem Council, 76
Jesse, 232
Jesus, 33, 186, 195, 199, 259, 262–86
   arrest of, 53, 66–67
   ascension of, 72
   on asking for signs, 18, 272–73
   betrayal of, 269–70
   birth in Bethlehem, 267–68
   bread and fish blessed by, 57
   confusion about teachings of, 272–74
   continuing advocacy for humanity, 278
   disciples deputized and equipped by, 70

296 INDEX

Jesus (*cont.*)
   on entering the kingdom of heaven, 219–20
   entrance to Jerusalem, 62
   entrance to Jerusalem predicted, 268–69
   explanation for suffering and death of, 278–86
   forerunnrer of predicted, 268
   Gethsemane, 65–67, 275
   at the Last Supper, 62–65
   ministry to the least liked, 10
   Moses referenced by, 50–51
   Noah referenced by, 207–8
   Noah's foreshadowing of, 203
   pain of being misunderstood, 274–76
   parables of, 271–72
   parallels with Jonah, 112, 116–17, 128–29
   parallels with Joseph, 105
   Peter and, 52–78 (*see also* Peter)
   praying by, 276–78
   prediction of His own death, 60, 62
   Rahab in lineage of, 231–32
   raising of the dead by, 59
   rejection by those he came to save, 270
   resurrection of, 60, 68–70, 273–74, 284
   as a sacrificial lamb, 45
   sweating of blood, 276
   Transfiguration, 59–60, 256
   unconventionality of, 271
   utilizing the glorious gift of, 282–86
   virgin birth of, 266–67
   walking on water, 56, 58
   washing of disciples' feet, 63–64
   the way of the cross, 68–70
   words on the cross, 270–71
Jethro, 32, 34, 42
Jezebel, 236, 237, 239, 241, 242, 243, 244, 257, 261
   devoured by dogs, 258
   Elijah's fear of, 249–50, 251, 253–54
Jezreel, 249
Joash, 15–16
Job 36:22-23, 93
Jochebed, 30–31, 37, 197
Joel 2:25, 94
John, 59, 65, 68, 275
John (gospel)
   1:11, 270
   1:14, 51
   1:17, 50
   1:23, 268
   1:35-42, 54
   1:36, 54
   1:37-39, 54
   1:40-42, 54
   2:18-21, 272–73
   3:16, 265
   5:46-47, 51
   10:11, 273
   10:11-13, 72
   10:17-18, 283
   13:1, 63
   13:1-17, 62
   13:5-9, 63
   13:13-17, 64
   14:21, 199
   17:1-3, 277
   17:11, 277
   17:14-16, 220
   17:15, 278
   17:20, 278
   18:10, 66
   20:3-9, 69
   20:22-23, 70
   20:29, 18
   21:1-17, 70–72
   21:6, 70
   21:7, 70
   21:11, 71

21:15-17, 71
21:25, 263
1 John 2:1, 278
John the Baptist, 54, 56-57, 60, 268
Jonah, 79, 107-31, 237
  anger of, 124-27
  in the belly of the great fish, 116-21, 128, 272
  lament of, 124-27
  parallels with Jesus, 112, 116-17, 128-29
  plant given to, 126-27
  as a reluctant prophet, 121-24
  running from God, 107-11, 113, 114
  sacrifice of averted, 115-17
  in the storm, 111-16
Jonah (book)
  1-4, 107-31
  1:1-2, 108
  1:1-3, 108
  1:3, 113
  1:4-6, 111
  1:7-10, 113
  1:11-16, 115
  1:17, 116
  2:1-9, 118-19
  2:8, 120, 121
  2:10, 121
  3:1-5, 121-22
  3:6-10, 123
  3:10, 123
  4:1-4, 124
  4:5, 125
  4:6-9, 126
  4:10-11, 127
Jordan River, 23, 225, 228-29
Joseph, 29-30, 32, 79, 81-106, 162
  brothers' plot to kill, 85-86
  death and burial of, 105
  dream interpretation by, 85, 91-92, 94-96
  dream of, 84-85, 97, 100
  dysfunctional family of, 82-85
  false accusations against, 89-90
  good from evil intended for, 87-88, 89, 103, 105-6
  imprisonment of, 90-94
  ornate robe of, 83-84, 87
  parallels with Daniel, 136-37
  parallels with Jesus, 105
  parallels with Moses, 30
  reunification with brothers, 97-104
  rise of in status, 94-96
  sibling rivalry and, 83-87
  sold into slavery, 86-87
Joseph (foster father of Jesus), 267
Joshua, 185, 211-34
  approach to Jericho, 228-29
  change of name from Hoshea, 214
  designated as Moses's successor, 223
  faithfulness in the wilderness, 220-24
  marching around Jericho, 230-31
  takes charge of Israelites, 224-27
  understanding of God's character, 214-17
Joshua (book)
  1-6, 211
  1:3, 5-7, 9, 224-25
  1:14-15, 225
  1:16, 18, 226
  2:3-6, 226
  2:24, 228
  3:5, 228
  3:15-17, 228-29
  4:18, 230
  4:24, 229
  5:1, 230
  5:9, 230
  6:2, 231
  6:10-14, 231
  6:15-16, 20, 231

Judah (Joseph's brother), 87, 100–102
Judah (region), 236
Judah (tribe), 215
Judas, 66
Judges
  4:1, 4
  5, 3
  6, 5, 21
  6-8, 3–27
  6:2-6, 6
  6:8-10, 6
  6:12, 8
  6:13, 8–9
  6:14, 9
  6:15, 10
  6:16, 10
  6:17-19, 11
  6:20-21, 12
  6:22-23, 12
  6:25-26, 13
  6:27-30, 15
  6:31b, 16
  6:36-40, 17
  7:2, 20
  7:3-8, 20–21
  7:9-11a, 21
  7:16-24, 22–23
  8:22-23, 25
  8:28, 25
  8:32, 25
  8:33-35, 25

Kerith Ravine, 237–38, 239
Keturah, 32, 86
1 Kings
  14:23, 11
  16-19, 21, 235
  16:30-33, 236
  17:1-6, 237–38

  17:8-16, 240
  17:21, 241
  17:24, 242
  18:3, 242
  18:7-14, 243
  18:17-19, 244
  18:21, 245
  18:23-24, 245
  18:25-29, 246
  18:30-32, 247
  18:33-35, 247
  18:36b-39, 248
  18:41-46, 248–49
  19:1-5a, 249–50
  19:5b-9a, 252
  19:9b-10, 253
  19:11-13a, 254
  19:13b-14, 255
  19:18, 256
  21:4, 257
  21:17-26, 257–58
  21:27-29, 258
  22:1-28, 245
2 Kings
  1, 259
  1-2, 235
  2:9, 259
  2:11, 235, 259
  20:8-11, 18
kintsugi, 74–75

Lake of Gennesaret, 58
Last Supper, 62–65
Leah, 83
Levites, 280
Leviticus
  1, 280
  2, 280
  3, 280

INDEX

4:1-5:13, 280
5:14-6:17, 280
16:34, 265
Lewis, C. S., 185, 196
loneliness, 235, 251–52
Lot, 209
love
  fear cast out by, 46–48, 72
  obedience bound with, 199
Love Stories of the Bible (Bream), 143, 232
Luke
  2:4, 268
  4:1-13, 18
  5:1-11, 54
  5:6-7, 55
  5:16, 276
  6:12, 276
  9:22, 273
  11:30, 117
  18:1, 277
  22:31-32, 62
  22:32, 65
  22:42-44, 276
  22:51, 66
  22:54, 67
  22:61, 68
  23:8, 18
  23:46, 271
  24:12, 69
  24:52-53, 72

Madoff, Bernie, 125–26
Malchus, 66
Manasseh (clan), 10
Manasseh (patriarch), 8
Manasseh (region), 23
Mark
  1:16-20, 54
  1:17, 55
  1:35, 276
  5:37-42, 59
  9:2-10, 59, 60
  10:45, 272
  14:54, 67
  14:66-72, 65, 67
  15:37-38, 283
Mary, mother of Jesus, 267
Matthew
  1:5-6, 232
  1:18, 22-23, 267
  2:1, 267
  4:1-11, 18
  4:18-22, 54
  4:19, 55
  7:13-14, 220
  8, 112
  12:40, 272
  12:40-41, 116–17
  13:13-15, 271–72
  14:13, 57
  14:13-31, 56–59
  14:14, 57
  14:16, 57
  14:25, 58
  14:26-32, 58
  14:28-29, 56
  16:1-4, 18
  16:3, 195
  16:13-17, 60
  16:13-23, 59
  16:16, 54
  16:18, 55
  16:21-23, 61
  16:24, 66–67
  17:22-23, 273
  19:13, 276
  20:17-19, 274
  20:19, 62, 274

INDEX

Matthew (*cont.*)
  21:1-4, 6-7, 269
  21:1-11, 62
  21:9, 62
  23:12, 148
  24:37-39, 207-8
  26:31-35, 62
  26:33-35, 64
  26:36-46, 65
  26:37-39, 275
  26:38, 65
  26:39, 129
  26:40-41, 66
  26:58, 67
  27:6-10, 270
  27:46, 271
Medes, 151, 152
Meshach, 143, 144
Messiah, Jesus as, 54, 60-61, 74
Micah 5:2, 267
Midian (son of Abraham), 86
Midianites, 86
  Gideon's battle against, 18, 20-25
  Israel oppressed by, 5-6, 8-10
  Israel's defeat of, 5
  Moses settles among, 32
minhah, 280
miracles. *See also* specific miracles
  Israelites' skepticism in spite of, 212
  performed by Elijah, 235, 259
  performed by Jesus, 259
  performed by Peter, 75
Miriam, 31, 37
Mishael, 134
Miss America pageant, author in, 158
Mordecai, 155
Moses, 2, 18, 28-51, 162, 196, 197, 213, 214, 216, 217-19, 221, 222, 225, 252-53
  attempts to avoid God's commands, 38-40
  banned from entering the promised land, 223
  burning bush encounter, 34-35, 252
  Elijah compared with, 254
  fear cast out by love, 46-48
  from fugitive to prophet, 37-42
  God's instructions for the Holy of Holies, 264-65
  intercedes on behalf of the Israelites, 218
  killing of Egyptian by, 31, 41
  naming of, 37
  obedience of, 42-45
  people's trust in, 49-50
  permitted to view promised land, 224
  from prince to fugitive, 32-33
  from slave to prince, 29-32
  social anxiety of, 29, 40-42, 47
  Ten Commandments given to, 253
  at Transfiguration, 59
  understanding of God's character, 218
  women saved from rival shepherds by, 32
Mothers and Daughters of the Bible Speak, The (Bream), 241
Mount Carmel, 244-49, 251
Mount Horeb. *See* Mount Sinai
Mount of Olives, 207-8, 269
Mount Sinai, 36, 252-53
My Modern Met (Richman-Abdou), 75

Nabonidus, 148
Naboth, 257
Nahum 3:1-5, 19, 129-30
Naphtali, 23
Nazism, 135
Nebat, 236, 257
Nebuchadnezzar, 137-38, 140-48, 150
  Daniel thrown in furnace by, 143-45
  death of, 148
  dream of, 145-46

INDEX

exile of, 146
sanity restored to, 146-48
Negev, 215
Nehemiah, 79, 80, 137, 158-84
   anger of, 173-74, 182-83
   birth in captivity, 160
   as a cupbearer, 162
   enemies of, 165-72
   friends of, 172-75
   as governor of Jerusalem, 176
   peace from prayer, 159-62
   power rejected by, 176-78
   preparation and prayer, 162-65
   spiritual homecoming prepared by, 178-84
Nehemiah (book)
   1-13, 158-84
   1:1-4, 160
   1:5-11, 160-61
   1:11, 161
   2:1-4, 163
   2:5-9, 164
   2:10, 165
   2:11-12, 166
   2:17-18, 166-67
   2:19-20, 167
   3, 168
   4:1-3, 168-69
   4:4-5, 169
   4:6, 169
   4:9, 170
   4:10, 170
   4:12, 170
   4:14-15, 170
   4:17, 171
   4:18-20, 171
   4:23, 171
   5, 172
   5:1-6, 173
   5:7-12, 174-75
   5:12, 175
   5:13, 175
   5:15-16, 176
   5:19, 176
   6:5-9, 176-77
   6:14-15, 177
   6:16, 178
   7:66, 159
   8:2-4, 5-6, 178-79
   8:10, 179
   8:17, 180
   9:2, 180
   9:33-38, 180-81
   10:30-39, 181
   12:43, 181
   13:7, 182
   13:25, 182
Nephilim, 215
Nile River
   Moses placed in, 31, 37
   water of turned to blood, 40
Nineveh, 108, 109, 121-31, 259
   judgment and destruction of, 129-31
   mourning and repentance in, 122-23
Noadia, 177
Noah, 185, 187-210
   ark of, 191, 193, 207
   daring to be different, 189-94
   drunkenness of, 208-9
   the flood and, 197-200
   life span of, 209
   a new promise and covenant with, 201-7
   novelty of rain in time of, 194-95
   obedience of, 194-200
   sacrifice to God, 202-3, 207
Numbers
   13-14, 211
   13:1-2, 213
   13:16, 214

Numbers (*cont.*)
  13:27, 214
  13:28-29, 215
  13:30, 215
  13:31-33, 215
  14:1-4, 216
  14:6-9, 217
  14:8, 223
  14:11, 217
  14:17-19, 218
  14:20-23, 218-19
  14:25, 221
  14:29, 221
  14:32-25, 221
  14:40, 222
  20:12, 223
  27:18-23, 223
  33:52-53, 223

Obadiah, 137, 162, 242-45
Obed, 232
obedience
  of Gideon, 17-19
  Jonah's rejection of, 107-11, 113, 114
  of Joshua (*see* Joshua)
  love bound with, 199
  of Moses, 42-45
  of Noah, 194-200
offerings. *See* sacrifices/offerings
Og, 227
'*olah,* 280
Omri, 236
optimism. *See* Joshua

pagans, 112, 114, 115, 116. *See also* Gentiles
pandemic, 192-93
parables, 271-72
Passover, 45

patience. *See* Noah
Paul, 24, 77, 88, 115, 129, 171, 260
Pentecost, 73
Persian Empire, 159, 173, 179
Persians, 151, 152
Peter, 2, 52-78, 275
  absolutes used by, 61, 64
  action taken by, 52, 59, 70-71
  calling of, 55
  death of predicted by Jesus, 72
  denial of Jesus by, 67-68, 71, 72, 74
  ear of servant sliced off by, 53, 66
  fear cast out by love, 72
  fear of, 53, 58-59, 60
  as a good shepherd, 72, 73-77
  Jesus's prediction of denial by, 64-65
  lesson of, 74-75
  liberation from prison, 75-76
  miracles performed by, 75
  misunderstanding of Jesus, 56-59, 61
  as rock of the church, 54-55
  second calling of, 70-72
  sermon delivered by, 73-74
  at Transfiguration, 59-60
  visit to the empty tomb of Jesus, 68-69
1 Peter
  2:11, 220
  5:8-10, 172
2 Peter
  2:5, 190, 195
  2:7, 209
  2:9, 190
Pharaoh(s)
  Joseph and, 94-96, 104
  Moses and, 29, 30-31, 32, 35-36, 37, 39, 40, 42-43, 44, 45, 46
Philippians
  2:14-16, 88
  3:13-14, 77

Philistines, 46
Potiphar, 87–88, 89–90
potter's field, 270
power, temptation of, 176–78
prayer
  community of, 143
  by Jesus, 276–78
  peace from, 159–62
  preparation and, 162–65
presence of God, 264–65, 277, 278
pride, 147–48, 150
Proverbs
  3:34, 147
  12:18, 53
Psalms
  22:1, 270
  31:5, 271
  78:18-22, 19
  95:8-11, 219
  106:23, 218
  118:6, 48
  127:1, 183
  139:7-10, 114
  145:8-9, 110
public speaking, fear of, 28–29, 40–42
Purah, 21, 22

Rachel, 83, 97
Rahab, 226–28, 231–33
rainbow sign, 205–6
raising from the dead. *See also* resurrection of Jesus
  by Elijah, 241
  by Jesus, 59
  by Peter, 75
ram, sacrifice of, 280
ravens, food brought to Elijah by, 237–39
red cord in Jericho, 228
Red Sea parting, 48–49, 212, 213, 216, 227

repentance
  in Jerusalem, 180
  in Nineveh, 122–23
resurrection of Jesus, 60, 68–70, 273–74, 284
Reuben, 86–87, 90, 98, 100
Rhoda, 76
Richman-Abdou, Kelly, 75
Romans
  2:12-14, 115
  6:1-4, 285
  8, 19
  8:3-4, 286
  8:28, 30, 106
  8:31, 48, 171
  8:32, 265
  8:34, 278
  8:38-39, 285
  11:2b-5, 260
  11:34, 93
  12:2, 220
Ruth, 232

sacrifices/offerings
  of Gideon, 11–12, 13, 15
  historical need for endless stream of, 279–82
  human, 115
  of Jesus, 203, 207, 265–66
  of Jonah, averted, 115–17
  of Noah, 202–3, 207
  types of, 280
sacrificial lamb
  of Israelites fleeing Egypt, 45–46, 228
  Jesus as, 45
Salmon, 232
Sanballat the Horonite, 165–66, 167, 168–69, 170, 176–77, 182
Sarah, 32, 198

Sea of Galilee, 58
Sea of the Arabah, 228
Seth, 189
sexual immorality, 223
Shadrach, 143, 144
Shem, 208–9
shepherds
  Moses as, 32–33, 34
  Peter as, 72, 73–77
shofars, 23
Sidon, 237
signs
  given to Gideon, 11–12, 17–19
  Jesus's disapproval of asking for, 18, 272–73
Sihon, 227
Simeon, 98, 99–100, 104
sin
  allure of, 6
  consequences for, 7
  historical need for endless atonement for, 279–82
  intimacy with God prevented by, 264
  Jesus's taking on burden of, 263, 284–86
sin offering, 280
sin-redemption cycle, 4–7
social anxiety, of Moses, 29, 40–42, 47
solar eclipse, 122
speaking in tongues, 73
Spurgeon, Charles, 239
Stephen, 37
Susa, 162, 183
sword(s)
  of Gideon, 22, 23
  God's Word as, 48–51, 218
  Peter's casting off of, 72
  words as, 53

Tabbath, 23
Tabernacle, 253, 264
Tarshish, 108–9, 113
temple of Jerusalem, 159, 264
Ten Boom, Corrie, 2
Ten Commandments, 253
ten plagues of Egypt, 44–45, 46, 216
Tobiah the Ammonite official, 165–66, 167, 169, 170, 177, 181, 182
tongues, speaking in, 73
Transfiguration, 59–60, 256
trumpets
  of Gideon, 22–24
  of Joshua, 231

virgin birth, 266–67

way of the cross, 68–70
widow of Zarephath, 239–42
wisdom
  of Daniel, 140–43
  of Nehemiah (*see* Nehemiah)
Women of the Bible Speak (Bream), 226
wool fleece sign, 17–19
writing on the wall, 149–50

Xenophon, 151
Xerxes, 163

Zarephath, 239–42
Zarethan, 228
Zechariah
  9:9, 268–69
  11:12-13, 269
Zererah, 23
Zerubbabel, 159
zevah shelamim, 280
Ziegler, Geoff, 24

ABOUT THE AUTHOR

Shannon Bream currently serves as anchor of *FOX News Sunday*. She is author of the number-one *New York Times* bestseller *Women of the Bible Speak*. Shannon also serves as Chief Legal Correspondent for the network and host of the *Livin' the Bream* podcast. She's anchored a wide variety of coverage for high-profile stories including landmark Supreme Court decisions, history-making storms, Capitol Hill scandals, and endless presidential campaigns.

She graduated magna cum laude from Liberty University and earned a Juris Doctorate with honors from Florida State University College of Law. Before beginning her journalism career, Shannon worked as an attorney specializing in sex harassment and race discrimination cases. She's grateful to be a messenger of the greatest story ever told: God loves you and wants a relationship with you. Shannon is happiest at home with her husband, Sheldon, their dog, Biscuit, and a good book!